TASCHEN's LONDON

Hotels, Restaurants & Shops

Photos David Crookes
Texts Christine Samuelian

TASCHEN's LONDON
Hotels, Restaurants & Shops

Angelika Taschen

TASCHEN

Hotels

Price categories without VAT:
£   up to £150
££   up to £250
£££   up to £450
££££   over £450

Preiskategorien ohne Steuern:
£   bis 150 £
££   bis 250 £
£££   bis 450 £
££££   über 450 £

Catégories de prix, sans taxes :
£   jusqu'à 150 £
££   jusqu'à 250 £
£££   jusqu'à 450 £
££££   plus de 450 £

Restaurants

Shops

Preface | Vorwort | Préface

7.4 million residents and 32 boroughs over 610 square miles: London is so confusingly huge that it has taken me many years even to begin to find my way around this truly cosmopolitan city. The aim of this book is to assist the visitor in finding the most attractive and interesting places and hotels quickly and reliably. I recommend hotels primarily when they provide the guest with some inkling of the history and individuality of London.

The right choice of district for accommodation is extremely important for the visitor. Soho is the best place for those who love night life with clubs and fashionable pubs. Those who prefer a little more peace and quiet should choose South Kensington. Solid, traditional England is to be found in Mayfair (also the best place for shopping), the creative live in East Central, and the trendy in Notting Hill. The cultural range in London is so enormously varied and exciting that this book has deliberately decided against presenting the classic sites like Buckingham Palace, Big Ben, the Houses of Parliament, the National Gallery, Trafalgar Square, Portobello Road and Carnaby Street.

If Paris is defined by fashion, perfume and luxury, it's the pubs, parks and picnics of London that spring to my mind. Again and again the bad air and the din of traffic drive me into the wonderful, rambling parks to relax on a bench or a hired deckchair and to read. It can even be a pleasure to walk in the drizzle – if you have previously bought a stylish umbrella at James Smith & Sons. In summer it's a good idea to enjoy a picnic in the park with

7,4 Millionen Menschen und 32 Stadtbezirke auf 1579 Quadratkilometern: London ist so verwirrend groß, dass ich viele Jahre gebraucht habe, um mich in dieser wahrhaften Weltstadt einigermaßen zurechtzufinden. Dieses Buch soll dem Besucher helfen, schnell und zuverlässig die schönsten und interessantesten Plätze und Hotels zu finden. Hotels empfehle ich vor allem dann, wenn sie dem Gast etwas über die Geschichte und die Eigenheiten Londons erzählen.

Extrem wichtig für den Besucher ist die Wahl des Viertels, in dem er übernachten möchte. Liebt man das Nachtleben mit Klubs und Szene-Kneipen, ist man in Soho gut aufgehoben. Hat man es gern etwas beschaulicher, ist South Kensington die richtige Wahl. In Mayfair erlebt man das traditionsreiche, gediegene England (und die beste Shoppinggegend), in East Central leben die Kreativen, in Notting Hill die Hippen. Das Kulturangebot in London ist so immens vielfältig und aufregend, dass dieses Buch bewusst darauf verzichtet, Klassiker vorzustellen, wie Buckingham Palace, Big Ben, Houses of Parliament, National Gallery, Trafalgar Square, Portobello Road und Carnaby Street.

Wenn Paris durch Mode, Parfüm und Luxus geprägt wird, fallen mir für London Pubs, Parks und Picknicks ein. Der Verkehrslärm und die oft schlechte Luft treiben mich immer wieder in die wunderbar großzügigen Parks, um dort auf einer Bank oder in einem gemieteten Liegestuhl zu lesen. Sogar ein Spaziergang im Nieselregen kann ein Genuss sein – wenn man vorher stilvoll bei James Smith & Sons einen Re-

7,4 millions de personnes et 32 arrondissements sur 1579 kilomètres carrés : Londres est si vaste que l'on si perd, et il m'a fallu de nombreuses années pour apprendre à m'y orienter. Le présent ouvrage est conçu pour aider le visiteur à trouver rapidement et facilement les sites et les hôtels les plus beaux et les plus intéressants. Je mentionne surtout des hôtels qui peuvent transmettre à leurs clients un peu de l'histoire et de l'originalité de la métropole.

Le choix du quartier où l'on désire séjourner est capital. Ceux qui aiment la vie nocturne, les clubs et les bars apprécieront Soho, alors que South Kensington est le bon choix pour les amateurs de calme et de méditation. À Mayfair, la bonne vieille Angleterre riche en traditions est au rendez-vous (et c'est aussi le meilleur endroit pour faire des achats). Les créatifs vivent à East Central, les trendys à Notting Hill. L'offre culturelle est si vaste, si variée et si excitante à Londres, que ce livre renonce à présenter des classiques tels le Buckingham Palace, Big Ben, le Parlement, la National Gallery, Trafalgar Square, Portobello Road et Carnaby Street.

Si Paris est la ville de la mode, des parfums et du luxe, Londres est pour moi celle des pubs, des parcs et des piqueniques. Voulant fuir la circulation bruyante et l'air souvent vicié, je me réfugie dans les parcs merveilleusement vastes, où je lis sur un banc ou une chaise-longue de location. Même une promenade sous la bruine peut être un délice – lorsqu'on a acheté auparavant un splendide parapluie chez James Smith & Sons. L'été, c'est

sandwiches – two English inventions. England was considered a culinary wasteland for many years (rightly so, in my opinion), but today there are countless excellent restaurants in London. I mainly recommend places which offer good, classic English cuisine. Best of all are the pubs, I find, and there are more than five thousand of them in London. The "gastropubs" also serve hearty meals, such as fish 'n' chips, and stews, and there is serious competition as to who makes the best batter and the best home-made salad cream.

Sincerely

genschirm gekauft hat. Im Sommer empfiehlt es sich, im Park ein Picknick mit Sandwiches zu zelebrieren – beides englische Erfindungen.
Nachdem England lange als kulinarische Wüste galt (zu Recht, wie ich meine), gibt es in London heute unzählige exzellente Restaurants. Ich empfehle vor allem Lokale mit guter klassisch-englischer Küche. Am tollsten finde ich die Pubs, von denen es in London mehr als fünftausend gibt. Die „Gastropubs" servieren dazu noch herzhaftes Essen wie Fish 'n' Chips und Stews, und es herrscht ein regelrechter Wettbewerb, wer die beste Panade (Batter) und die beste hausgemachte Remoulade macht.

Ihre

Angelika Taschen

Angelika Taschen

le temps de pique-niquer, et les sandwiches, autre invention anglaise, s'imposent.
L'Angleterre a été longtemps considérée – non sans raison – comme un désert culinaire, mais aujourd'hui les bons restaurants sont légion à Londres. Je recommande surtout ceux qui proposent la cuisine britannique classique. À mon avis les meilleurs sont les pubs, et ils sont plus de 5000 à Londres. Les gastropubs servent en plus des plats simples et savoureux, fish 'n' chips et stews par exemple, et c'est à celui qui réussira la meilleure pâte à frire et la meilleure rémoulade maison.

Votre

Hotels

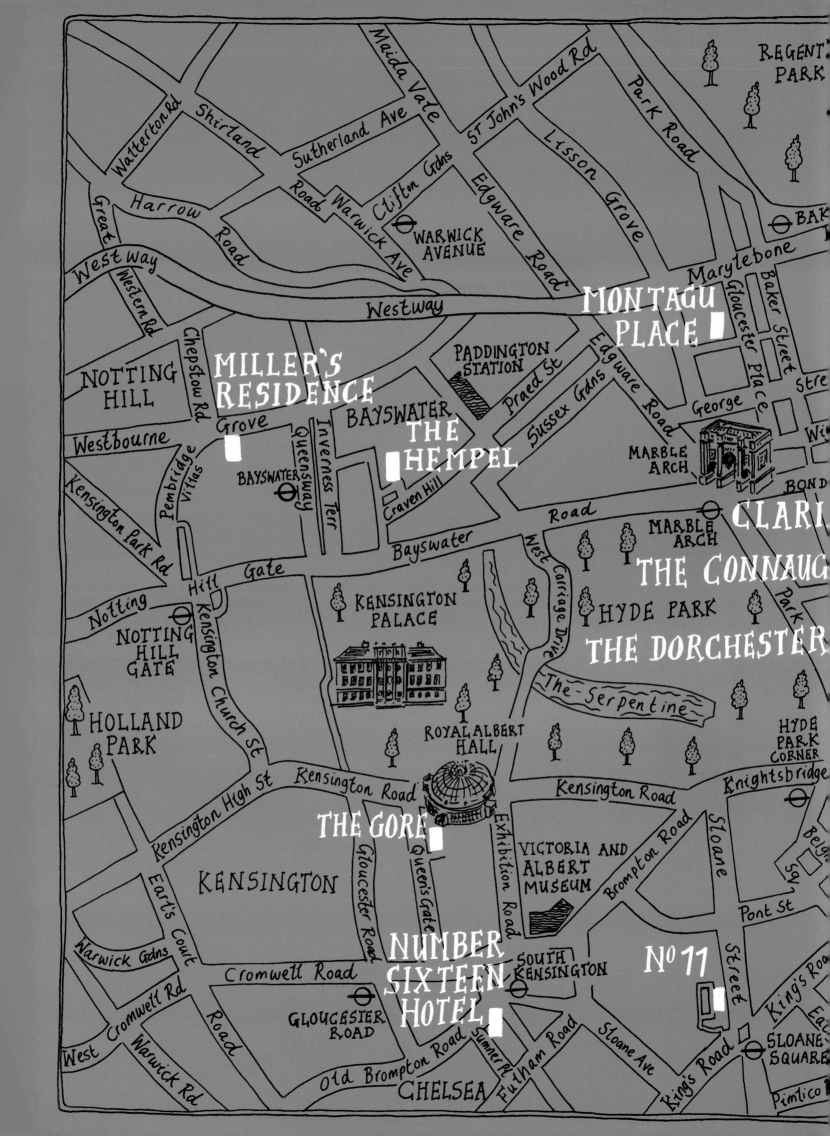

The Dorchester

_____

Park Lane, London W1K 1QA
☎ +44 20 7629 8888   📄 +44 20 7629 8080
info@thedorchester.com
www.thedorchester.com
Tube: Hyde Park Corner

The Dorchester dominates London's Park Lane with its yellow and white awnings blinking like giant eye-lids. If you can navigate your way through the Bentleys parked out front and make it through the door, then be braced: the décor at The Dorchester is seriously over the top. Sit on one of the plump sofas at The Promenade lobby restaurant, sip tea accompanied by a plate of macaroons and spy on the weird and wonderful mix of big-haired American belles; English families nibbling finger sandwiches; cigar-smoking men and their veiled wives; and the sugar daddies accompanied by women tottering around in vertiginous heels. Pick a deluxe English-style room with views of Hyde Park and enjoy the space: many rooms come with walk-in wardrobes, and the bathtubs are some of the deepest in London. If hunger strikes, head down to The Grill Room: the Scottish-themed tartan décor will either destroy your appetite or whet it for the traditional roasts.

Price category: £££.
Rooms: 250 (53 suites).
Restaurants: The Grill Room, The Promenade, China Tang and Alain Ducasse at The Dorchester.
History: The Dorchester opened its doors in 1931 and such luminaries as Alfred Hitchcock, Elizabeth Taylor, Barbra Streisand and General Eisenhower have all stayed here.
X-Factor: The gorgeous Floris products in the bathrooms.
Internet: Broadband access at £18.50 per day.

Mit seinen gelb-weißen Markisen ist das Dorchester der Blickfang der Park Lane. Wer durch die unzähligen Bentleys den Weg ins Innere findet, dem stockt zunächst der Atem: Das Dekor ist fast zu viel des Guten. Die Szenerie eignet sich allerdings bestens für Feldstudien: Man lässt sich dazu auf einem der üppigen Sofas im Lobby-Restaurant Promenade nieder, nippt am Tee, nascht „Macaroons". Und schon flanieren sie an einem vorbei, die Amerikanerinnen mit Superfrisur, die britischen Familien, die an Finger-Sandwiches knabbern, die Zigarren schmauchenden Herren und die Sugar Daddys in Begleitung von Damen auf schwindelerregenden Absätzen. Nicht zu vergessen: Die Deluxe-Zimmer in englischem Dekor sind geräumig, die meisten verfügen über einen begehbaren Schrank und supertiefe Badewannen. Ein Kuriosum ist das Restaurant The Grill Room mit schottischem Karomusterdekor: Hier bekommt man unsägliche Lust auf einen traditionellen „Roast".

Le Dorchester domine Park Lane avec ses dais à rayures jaunes et blanches qui claquent au vent. Si vous parvenez à vous glisser jusqu'à la porte entre les cheiks arabes et leurs Bentley, préparez-vous à un choc : le décor est chargé. Installez-vous sur les canapés douillets du restaurant Promenade et, devant un thé accompagné de macarons, savourez l'étrange mélange de belles Américaines aux crinières de lionne, de familles british grignotant des mini sandwichs, de fumeurs de cigare suivis de leurs épouses voilées et de vieux messieurs offrant le bras à de jeunes femmes perchées sur des talons vertigineux. Choisissez une spacieuse chambre « de luxe » décorée à l'anglaise avec vue sur Hyde Park ; la plupart sont équipées de grands dressings et les baignoires sont réputées les plus profondes de Londres. Un petit creux ? Descendez à la rôtisserie : si le décor tout en tartans écossais ne vous coupe pas l'appétit, vous vous régalerez avec les grillades traditionnelles.

Preiskategorie: £££.
Zimmer: 250 (53 Suiten).
Restaurants: The Grill Room, The Promenade, China Tang und Alain Ducasse at The Dorchester.
Geschichte: The Dorchester eröffnete 1931 und beherbergte so illustre Gäste wie Alfred Hitchcock, Elizabeth Taylor, Barbra Streisand und General Eisenhower.
X-Faktor: In den Badezimmern stehen Beauty-Produkte von Floris.
Internet: Breitbandanschluss für 18,50 £ pro Tag.

Catégorie de prix : £££.
Chambres : 250 (53 suites).
Restauration : The Grill Room, The Promenade, China Tang et Alain Ducasse at The Dorchester.
Histoire : Le Dorchester a ouvert ses portes en 1931 et a accueilli des célébrités telles qu'Alfred Hitchcock, Elizabeth Taylor, Barbra Streisand et le général Eisenhower.
Le « petit plus » : Les fabuleux produits Floris dans les salles de bains.
Internet : Accès haut débit à 18,50 £ par jour.

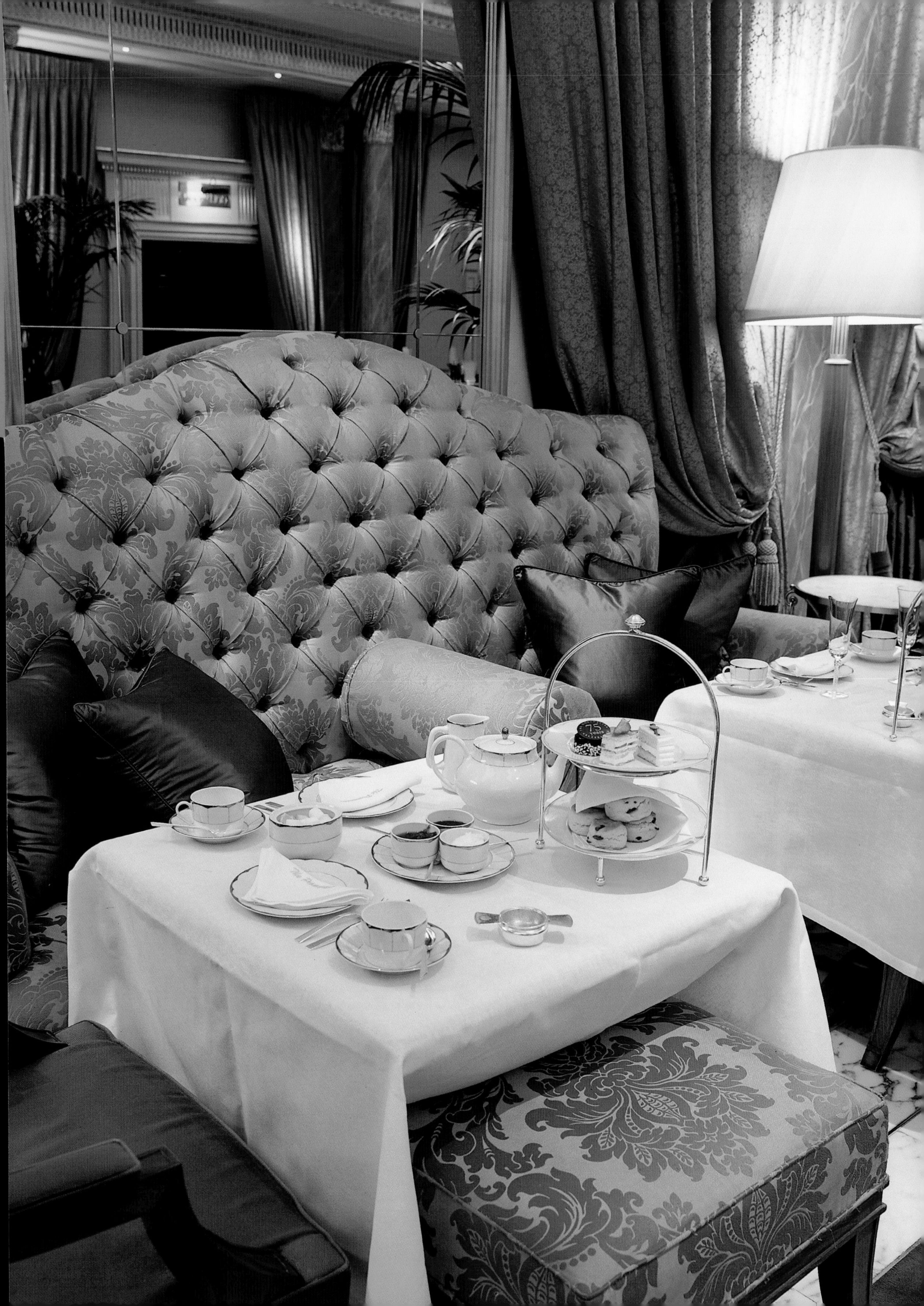

The Connaught

Carlos Place, London W1K 2AL
☎ +44 20 7499 7070   📠 +44 20 7495 3262
info@the-connaught.co.uk
www.the-connaught.co.uk
Tube: Bond Street

One of the grand old ladies of the London hotel scene has treated herself to a makeover of the very finest quality: at a cost of £70 million, international designers have put a modern face on The Connaught, a house with a long tradition. Peppermint, silver-grey and champagne tones freshen up the classical furnishings of the elegant rooms, and the bars and restaurants combine British atmosphere with contemporary colours and forms. David Collins has given the Connaught Bar a wonderfully glamorous look, and the more intimate Coburg Bar, which India Mahdavi has fitted out in black lacquer with lilac and caramel fabrics, has been voted the best bar in the city. Do not fail to book a table for dinner at Hélène Darroze at The Connaught, where since summer 2008 the Michelin-starred chef has been serving menus from her home area Les Landes in the southwest of France. For all the renewal, one thing that the hotel has retained is its perfect service: the butlers at The Connaught are masters of their trade.

Price category: ££££.
Rooms: 122 (42 suites).
Restaurants: Hélène Darroze at The Connaught, Espelette (bistro style), Connaught Bar, Coburg Bar.
History: The Connaught opened in 1897 as The Coburg Hotel. In 1917, during the First World War, it was renamed after Queen Victoria's third son, Prince Arthur, Duke of Connaught.
X-Factor: Toiletries by the exclusive British brand Asprey in the marble bathrooms.
Internet: Free of charge in all rooms (broadband and WiFi).

Es war eine Schönheitskur vom Feinsten, die sich eine der Grand Old Ladies der Londoner Hotellerie gegönnt hat: Unter den Händen von internationalen Designern und für 70 Millionen Pfund erhielt die Traditionsadresse The Connaught ein modernes Gesicht. Mit eleganten Zimmern, in denen Pfefferminz-, Silbergrau- oder Champagnertöne das klassische Mobiliar auffrischen, sowie mit Bars und Restaurants, die britisches Flair mit zeitgenössischen Farben und Formen verbinden. David Collins hat die Connaught Bar wunderbar glamourös gestaltet, und die intimere Coburg Bar, die India Mahdavi mit schwarzem Lack sowie Stoffen in Lila und Karamell ausgestattet hat, wurde bereits zur besten Bar der Stadt gekürt. Ein Tisch für ein Dinner sollte man unbedingt im Hélène Darroze at The Connaught reservieren – die Sterneköchin serviert hier seit Sommer 2008 Menüs aus ihrer Heimat Les Landes im Südwesten Frankreichs. Was das Hotel bei allen Neuerungen behalten hat, ist sein perfekter Service – die Butler des Connaught sind Meister ihres Fachs.

Une des Grand Old Ladies de l'hôtellerie londonienne s'est accordé une cure de beauté des plus raffinées : après être passée entre les mains de designers internationaux et avoir dépensé 70 millions de livres, la maison traditionnelle The Connaught offre maintenant un visage moderne. Avec des chambres élégantes dans lesquelles des tons menthe, gris argent et champagne rafraîchissent le mobilier classique et des bars et des restaurants qui marient la classe britannique aux formes et aux couleurs contemporaines. David Collins a fait du Connaught Bar un endroit merveilleusement glamour et le Coburg Bar plus intime qu'India Mahdavi a décoré à l'aide de laque noire et de tissus couleur mauve et caramel a déjà été élu meilleur bar de la ville. Il faut absolument réserver une table pour dîner au Hélène Darroze at The Connaught – la grande cuisinière (deux étoiles au Michelin) propose ici depuis l'été 2008 une carte inspirée de la cuisine des Landes dont elle est originaire. Un élément est resté inchangé : le service parfait – les majordomes du Connaught sont des maîtres en la matière.

Preiskategorie: £££££.
Zimmer: 122 (42 suites).
Restaurants: Hélène Darroze at The Connaught, Espelette (Bistrostil), Connaught Bar, Coburg Bar.
Geschichte: Das Connaught wurde 1897 als The Coburg Hotel eröffnet. 1917, während des Ersten Weltkrieges, wurde es nach Königin Victorias drittem Sohn, Prinz Arthur, Duke of Connaught, umbenannt.
X-Faktor: In den Marmorbädern stehen Pflegeprodukte der edlen britischen Marke Asprey.
Internet: Kostenfrei in allen Räumen (Breitband und WiFi).

Catégorie de prix : £££££.
Chambres : 122 (42 suites).
Restauration : Hélène Darroze at The Connaught, Espelette (style bistrot), Connaught Bar, Coburg Bar.
Histoire : Le Connaught a été ouvert en 1897 sous le nom de The Coburg Hotel. En 1917, pendant la guerre, il a pris le nom du troisième fils de la reine Victoria, le prince Arthur, Duke of Connaught.
Le « petit plus » : Dans les salles de bains habillées de marbre, on trouve des produits de soin de la noble marque britannique Asprey.
Internet : Gratuit dans toutes les pièces (haut débit et WiFi).

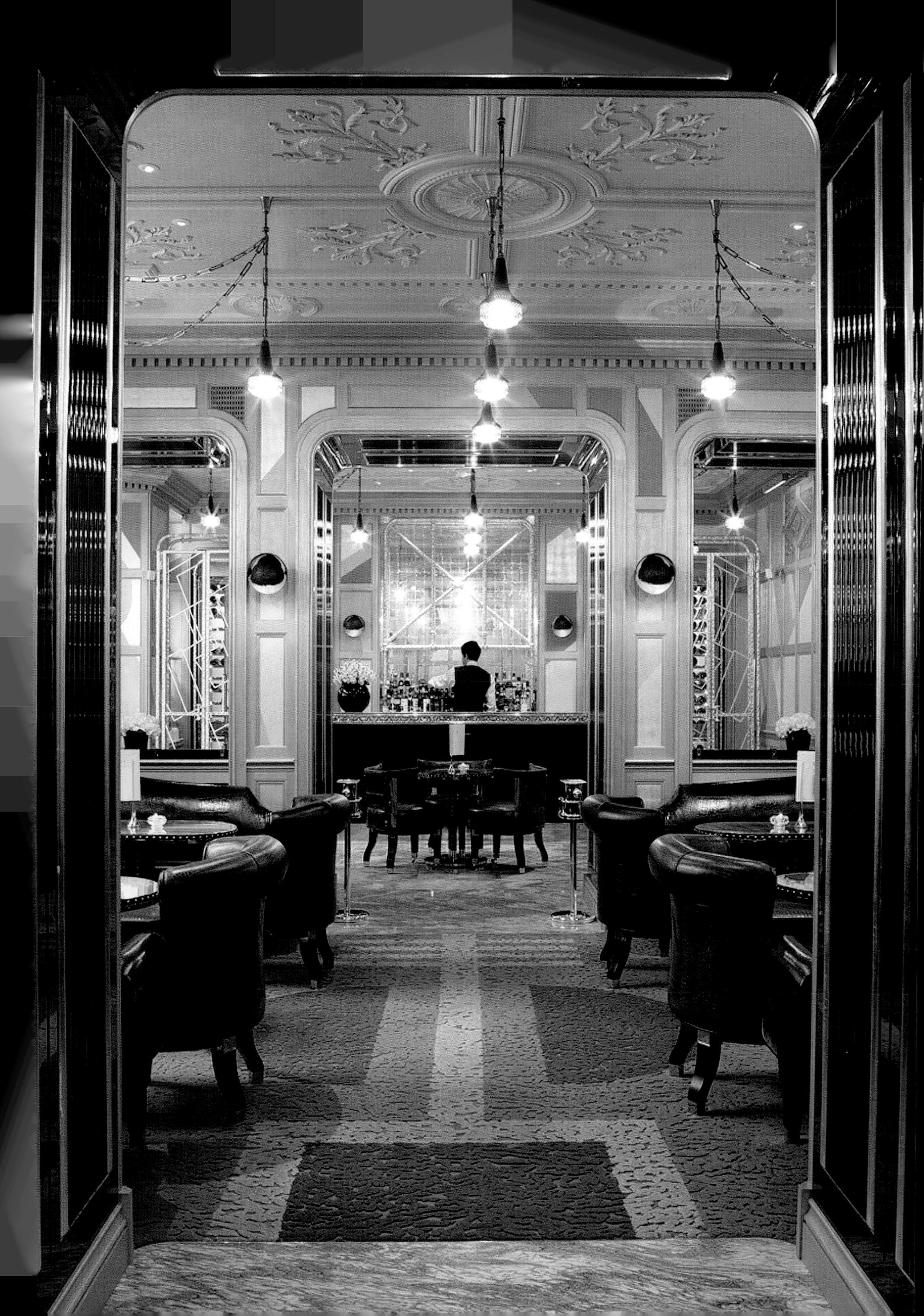

Claridge's

Brook Street, London W1K 4HR
☏ +44 20 7629 8860   ☐ +44 20 7499 2210
info@claridges.co.uk
www.claridges.co.uk
Tube: Bond Street

If there is a hotel in London that embodies English gentility and glamour, it is Claridge's, right in the heart of Mayfair. The lobby has a rich golden glow, gleaming black-and-white floors, swooping chandeliers and a dramatic winding staircase. In The Foyer and Reading Room at high tea, you may see the handsome Tom Ford sipping his tipple while a gaggle of Saudi wives and children take tea (one of 30 different kinds) at another table, munching cucumber sandwiches. Claridge's Bar is also a hive of activity, with London's suited financiers and intellectuals gathered for drinks and fashionable gossip. Claridge's draw, of course, is that it is slightly stuffy and a bit old-fashioned, as all very charming British things are. Rooms are decorated either in a Victorian fashion or with authentic 1930s detailing. Don't leave without visiting the original Art Deco public bathroom, and say hello to the nice lady who turns on the taps so you can wash your hands.

Price category: ££££.
Rooms: 203 (67 suites).
Restaurants: Gordon Ramsay at Claridge's, The Foyer, Reading Room.
History: James Mivart first opened a hotel in a house on the current site in 1812, but Claridge's as it is today was built in 1898. Many areas and rooms were redesigned in Art Deco style in the early 1930s.
X-Factor: The Claridge's "C" monogrammed towels.
Internet: Broadband in all rooms at £20 per day.

Kein Hotel verkörpert den Stil und Glamour der britischen Upper Class besser als das Claridge's mitten in Mayfair. In der golden schimmernden Lobby glänzen die schwarzweißen Böden wie Lack. Dazu sorgen imposante Leuchter und eine dramatisch geschwungene Treppe für standesgemäßen Prunk. In den Zimmern bestimmt der viktorianische Stil den Look, manchmal sind auch Dekors aus den 1930ern zu finden. Es ist diese leicht verstaubte, typisch englische Atmosphäre, die den Charme des Hotels ausmacht. Es kann gut sein, dass man beim High Tea im Foyer oder Lesezimmer auf Tom Ford trifft. Am Nebentisch sitzen dann ziemlich sicher saudische Ehefrauen mit ihrem Nachwuchs, trinken Tee (30 verschiedene Sorten) und vertilgen dazu Gurken-Sandwiches. Die Bar des Claridge's hingegen ist Treffpunkt für Londons Financiers und Intellektuelle. Nicht verpassen: die öffentlichen Art-déco-Toiletten. Hier muss man zum Händewaschen nicht einmal den Wasserhahn aufdrehen. Dafür sorgt eine freundliche Angestellte.

Aucun hôtel à Londres ne personnifie mieux la distinction et le chic anglais que le Claridge's, au cœur de Mayfair, avec son hall aux tons dorés, ses sols en damier noir et blanc étincelants, ses grands lustres et son escalier spectaculaire. L'après-midi, vous pourrez voir Tom Ford dans le Foyer ou la Reading Room sirotant un verre pendant que quelques épouses saoudiennes et leurs enfants goûtent une des quelque trente variétés de thé accompagnée de sandwiches au concombre. Le bar est une vraie ruche, les banquiers de la City et les intellectuels s'y retrouvant pour boire un verre et échanger des potins mondains. Le principal attrait du Claridge's, c'est son atmosphère légèrement désuète et guindée, tout ce qui fait le charme anglais. Le décor des chambres est victorien ou années 1930. N'oubliez pas de faire une visite aux toilettes publiques Art Déco et de saluer la dame charmante qui vous ouvre le robinet pour que vous vous laviez les mains.

Preiskategorie: ₤₤₤₤.
Zimmer: 203 (67 Suiten).
Restaurants: Gordon Ramsay at Claridge's, The Foyer, Reading Room.
Geschichte: James Mivart eröffnete 1812 auf diesem Grundstück ein Hotel. Das heutige Claridge's wurde allerdings erst 1898 gebaut. In den frühen 1930ern wurde ein Teil des Hotels im Art-déco-Stil umgebaut.
X-Faktor: Die Badetücher sind mit dem „C" für Claridge's bestickt.
Internet: Breitbandanschluss in allen Zimmern für 20 ₤ pro Tag.

Catégorie de prix : ₤₤₤₤.
Chambres : 203 (67 suites).
Restauration : Gordon Ramsay at Claridge's, The Foyer, Reading Room.
Histoire : James Mivart a ouvert un hôtel en 1812 mais le Claridge's actuel a été construit en 1898. De nombreux espaces et chambres ont été redécorés dans le style Art Déco au début des années 1930.
Le « petit plus » : Les serviettes de bain ornées du monogramme « C ».
Internet : Accès haut débit dans toutes les chambres pour 20 ₤ par jour.

Brown's Hotel

Albemarle Street, London W1S 4BP
☎ +44 20 7493 6020   📠 +44 20 7493 9381
reservations.browns@roccofortecollection.com
www.roccofortecollection.com
Tube: Green Park

Designed by Olga Polizzi, Brown's Hotel is a blend of contemporary and luxurious touches, such as wood floors in some rooms and one-off pieces of original Art Deco furniture, all punctuated with spacious rooms that have super-modern amenities. What's more, each room has a selection of books, such as *The Oxford Book of English Verse* or works by Charles Dickens, D. H. Lawrence and William Shakespeare for guests to read. If finances allow, book into one of the Royal Suites and pretend you are staying in your own Mayfair apartment. Or go for a more urban experience in one of the loft rooms with Mary Poppins-style views over London rooftops. From 3pm on the dot (not a minute earlier) join the pencil-thin, Russian blondes for High Tea in the English Tea Room, where they seek respite from a hard day's shopping. Latch on to this English philosophy: any care in the world can be erased with a scone, clotted cream and a cup of tea in fine china.

Price category: £££.
Rooms: 117 (29 suites).
Restaurants: The Albemarle, The English Tea Room, The Donovan Bar.
History: The hotel opened in 1837 and has a rich history. Alexander Graham Bell made the UK's first telephone call from the hotel in 1876; Rudyard Kipling penned *The Jungle Book* and Agatha Christie wrote *At Bertram's Hotel* here.
X-Factor: The spa is wonderful for de-stressing.
Internet: WiFi in public areas at £6 per hour; £10 per day. Broadband in all rooms at £15 per day.

Designerin Olga Polizzi hat es verstanden, das Brown's Hotel genauso zeitgemäß wie luxuriös zu gestalten. Die meisten der großzügigen Gästezimmer sind modern eingerichtet und einige mit Holzböden und originalen Art-déco-Möbeln ausgestattet. In jedem Zimmer liegt eine interessante Auswahl an Büchern aus, etwa das „Oxford Book of English Verse" oder Werke von Charles Dickens, D. H. Lawrence und William Shakespeare. Wer es sich leisten kann, sollte eine der Royal-Suiten buchen und sich so wie ein Besitzer eines eleganten Mayfair-Apartments fühlen. Für ein urbaneres Feeling wählt man eines der Loft-Zimmer mit Blick über die Dächer Londons. Punkt 15 Uhr (keine Minute früher) wird der High Tea im English Tea Room serviert. Unter den Gästen: spargeldünne, blonde Russinnen, die hier nach einem harten Shoppingtag eine englische Weisheit auf die Probe stellen: Kleine und große Sorgen, so sagt man, lösen sich bei Scone-Gebäck, etwas Clotted Cream und Tee in edler Porzellantasse in Luft auf.

Décoré par Olga Polizzi, le Brown's Hotel associe les touches contemporaines et luxueuses tels que parquets et meubles Art Déco dans de spacieuses chambres au confort ultramoderne. Petite note attentionnée : dans chacune d'elle, on trouve des anthologies de poésie anglaise et des œuvres de Charles Dickens, D. H. Lawrence ou William Shakespeare. Si vos finances vous le permettent, réservez une des suites royales où vous vous croirez dans votre propre appartement de Mayfair. Ou optez pour une expérience plus urbaine dans un des lofts avec ses vues à la Mary Poppins sur les toits de Londres. À quinze heures pile, un troupeau de poupées russes blondes platine à taille de guêpe débarque dans le salon de thé pour souffler un peu après une rude journée de shopping. Accrochez-vous à cette devise philosophique toute britannique : tous les soucis du monde s'évaporent avec un scone, un peu de crème et un thé dans une tasse en porcelaine.

Preiskategorie: £££.
Zimmer: 117 (29 Suiten).
Restaurants: The Albemarle, The English Tea Room, The Donovan Bar.
Geschichte: Das Hotel wurde 1837 eröffnet, 1876 tätigte Alexander Graham Bell von hier aus den ersten Telefonanruf in Großbritannien, Rudyard Kipling schrieb im Brown's das „Dschungelbuch" und Agatha Christie „Bertrams Hotel".
X-Faktor: Das Spa ist Entspannung pur.
Internet: WiFi in allen öffentlichen Räumlichkeiten für 6 £ pro Stunde und 10 £ pro Tag. Breitbandanschluss in allen Gästezimmern für 15 £ pro Tag.

Catégorie de prix : £££.
Chambres : 117 (29 suites).
Restauration : The Albemarle, The English Tea Room, The Donovan Bar.
Histoire : Alexander Graham Bell y a passé le premier coup de téléphone en 1876. Rudyard Kipling y a rédigé « Le Livre de la jungle » et Agatha Christie y a écrit « À l'Hôtel Bertram ».
Le « petit plus » : Le spa est idéal pour destresser.
Internet : WiFi dans les zones publiques pour 6 £ l'heure ; 10 £ par jour. Haut débit dans toutes les chambres pour 15 £ par jour.

Dukes

35 St James's Place, London SW1A 1NY
☎ +44 20 7491 4840   ☐ +44 20 7493 1264
bookings@dukeshotel.com
www.dukeshotel.com
Tube: Green Park

Tucked away in a quiet courtyard between Mayfair and
Green Park, Dukes is an oasis in one of the busiest parts
of town. The rooms are comfortable and in clear, bright
colours. However, the common areas far overshadow the
rooms here. Dukes Bar – decorated like a private gentlemen's club with a collection of framed political cartoons
on the walls and cosy leather chairs – is a secret little hideaway and famous in London for its dry Martinis. Winston
Churchill and Ian Fleming have both been patrons. These
days, high-powered judges might confer here after an
afternoon's shopping for tailored shirts and hand-made
shoes; or a politician might conduct an affair away from
the public eye. If it's the wagon you're on, then head to the
drawing room, flop on one of the comfortable armchairs,
order tea and enjoy pouring it from fine silverware and
drinking it from dainty porcelain while chewing on a lovely
biscuit. A visit to London does not get much more English
than that.

Price category: £££.
Rooms: 90 (6 suites).
Restaurants: The Dining Room at Dukes and Dukes Bar.
History: The historical courtyard at Dukes has been traced back
to 1532. The building was erected in 1885 and has functioned as
Dukes since 1908.
X-Factor: The Martinis. Don't leave this hotel without trying one.
Internet: WiFi at £18 per day.

Das Dukes ist eine Oase mitten im Stadtchaos zwischen Mayfair und Green Park und liegt versteckt an einem ruhigen Hinterhof. Die Zimmer, behaglich und in klaren, hellen Farben, überlassen den großen Auftritt den anderen Räumlichkeiten. Die Dukes Bar etwa, mit bequemen Sesseln und Polit-Karikaturen an den Wänden, erinnert an einen Gentlemen's Club. Bekannt wurde sie als diskretes Refugium für Gäste wie Winston Churchill und Ian Fleming – und nicht zuletzt für die Dry Martinis. Auch heute tummeln sich in der Dukes Bar wichtige Persönlichkeiten: Richter, die sich hier nach dem Einkauf von maßgeschneiderten Hemden und maßgefertigten Schuhen treffen, Politiker, die von der Öffentlichkeit abgeschirmt, ihren Geschäften nachgehen. Wer aufs Naschen aus ist, nimmt auf einem der bequemen Sessel im Salon Platz, bestellt Tee, der aus feinstem Tafelsilber in zierliche Tassen gegossen wird, und genießt dazu ein köstliches Biskuit. Viel englischer kann es nicht werden.

Niché dans une cour tranquille entre Mayfair et Green Park, le Dukes est une oasis dans un des quartiers les plus animés de la ville. Les chambres claires sont confortables, de style traditionnel anglais avec des imprimés fleuris. Mais ce sont surtout les parties communes qui épatent. Le bar, douillet et décoré comme un club privé pour gentlemen avec des dessins satiriques politiques aux murs et d'épais fauteuils en cuir, est célèbre pour ses Martinis dry. Winston Churchill et Ian Fleming en raffolaient. Aujourd'hui, de hauts magistrats s'y réfugient pour souffler un peu en sortant de chez leur tailleur ou leur bottier, ou des hommes politiques y amènent leurs maîtresses loin des regards indiscrets. Vautrez-vous dans un des fauteuils confortables du salon et commandez du thé qui vous sera servi dans de l'argenterie et de la porcelaine délicate, accompagné de délicieux petits biscuits. On ne peut pas faire plus british.

Preiskategorie: ££££.
Zimmer: 90 (6 Suiten).
Restaurants: The Dining Room at Dukes und Dukes Bar.
Geschichte: Der historische Hinterhof des Dukes wurde 1532 erstmals erwähnt. Erst 1885 wurde auf dem Gelände ein Haus gebaut. Seit 1908 ist es als Hotel Dukes in Betrieb.
X-Faktor: Die köstlichen Martinis. Das Hotel kann man nicht verlassen, ohne vorher einen probiert zu haben.
Internet: WiFi für 18 £ pro Tag.

Catégorie de prix : ££££.
Chambres : 90 (6 suites).
Restauration : The Dining Room at Dukes et Dukes Bar.
Histoire : La cour historique du Dukes remonte à 1532. Le bâtiment a été construit en 1885 et transformé en hôtel en 1908.
Le « petit plus » : Les Martinis. Ne quittez pas l'hôtel sans y avoir goûté.
Internet : WiFi pour 18 £ par jour.

The Trafalgar

2 Spring Gardens, Trafalgar Square, London SW1A 2TS
☎ +44 20 7870 2900   📠 +44 20 7870 2911
www.thetrafalgar.com
Tube: Charing Cross

The Trafalgar sits right on London's famous and hectic Trafalgar Square and, although it is a Hilton hotel, it is far from faceless. Decorated in dark woods and simple Scandinavian colour schemes, its bustling Rockwell bar and lobby area are a testament to the kind of young and energetic crowd it attracts. The hotel's location is super central: close to the Thames, to the Mall and St James's Park, to Covent Garden and its numerous galleries, theatres and restaurants. Also, shopping is very close by with a jaunt to Jermyn Street or Regent Street. The Trafalgar's rooms are modern and comfortable but the best thing about this hotel is the views. Some rooms overlook the heaving crowds, thousands of pigeons and Nelson's Column in Trafalgar Square, but take the lift to the bar on the roof garden. On a good summer's day there will be a light warm breeze, you will have a glass of champagne in your hand and you can gaze down at this beautiful city working its magic beneath your feet.

Price category: £.
Rooms: 129 (2 rooftop studios).
Restaurant: Rockwell (bar and restaurant).
History: The Trafalgar's building was originally the headquarters of the Cunard Shipping Line, the company that built and ran the Titanic.
X-Factor: The rooftop views.
Internet: WiFi in the rooms at £15 per day.

Das Trafalgar, direkt am genauso bekannten wie hektischen Trafalgar Square gelegen, gehört zur Hilton-Gruppe. Gesichtslos ist es trotzdem nicht. Die Rockwell Bar (dunkles Holz, skandinavische Farbtöne) ist ebenso angesagt und energiegeladen wie seine Gäste. Das Hotel ist sehr zentral gelegen: gleich in der Nähe der Themse, der Mall, des St James's Park und ein Katzensprung von Covent Garden mit seinen unzähligen Galerien, Theatern und Restaurants. Auch die Shoppingnirvanas Jermyn Street oder Regent Street liegen ganz in der Nähe. Die Gästezimmer sind modern-schick und komfortabel, dennoch ist das Schönste die Aussicht. Zum Beispiel auf den Trafalgar Square mit einer emsig herumschwirrenden Menge, Tausenden von Tauben und der Nelson-Säule. Doch es wird noch besser: im Fahrstuhl auf den Dachgarten hochfahren, ein Glas Champagner bestellen und die Magie dieser tollen Stadt auf sich wirken lassen. Am schönsten ist das an lauen Sommerabenden.

Bien qu'appartenant à la chaîne Hilton, l'hôtel Trafalgar situé directement sur la célèbre et trépidante place du même nom n'a rien d'anonyme. Décoré de boiseries sombres dans des tons scandinaves simples, son bar Rockwell et son hall très animés rendent hommage à sa clientèle jeune et énergique. L'emplacement ne peut être plus central : à deux pas de la Tamise, du Mall, de St James's Park, des galeries, théâtres et restaurants de Covent Garden, des boutiques de Jermyn et Regent Street. Les chambres sont modernes et confortables mais la cerise sur le gâteau, ce sont les vues. Certaines chambres donnent sur la foule bigarrée, les pigeons frénétiques et la colonne de Nelson. Prenez l'ascenseur jusqu'au bar en terrasse sur le toit. Par une belle journée d'été, dans une légère brise chaude, une coupe de champagne à la main, vous verrez la ville déployer sa beauté magique à vos pieds.

Preiskategorie: £.
Zimmer: 129 (2 Dachterrassen-Studios).
Restaurant: Rockwell (Bar und Restaurant).
Geschichte: Das Trafalgar war ursprünglich der Hauptsitz der Schifffahrtgesellschaft Cunard, der Besitzerin der legendären Titanic.
X-Faktor: Die Aussicht von der Dachterrasse.
Internet: WiFi in allen Zimmern für 15 £ pro Tag.

Catégorie de prix : £.
Chambres : 129 (2 studios sur le toit).
Restauration : Rockwell (bar et restaurant).
Histoire : Le bâtiment était autrefois le siège de la compagnie de navigation Cunard, qui a construit le Titanic.
Le « petit plus » : Les vues depuis la terrasse sur le toit.
Internet : WiFi dans les chambres pour 15 £ par jour.

The Soho Hotel

4 Richmond Mews (off Dean Street), London W1D 3DH
☎ +44 20 7559 3000   📠 +44 20 7559 3003
soho@firmdale.com
www.sohohotel.com
Tube: Tottenham Court Road

The Soho Hotel is the embodiment of all that is cool and colourful about London's Soho district. It is the Firmdale group's largest and most striking property yet retains the cosy refinement for which its hotels are so well known. Just off busy Dean Street, the building used to function as a multi-storey car park and was completely knocked down to create the hotel's spacious rooms and suites. The enormous Fernando Botero cat statue in the lobby is the first clue that this is not like any other hotel. Designer Kit Kemp has gone all out with the use of colourful, graphic fabrics, oversized paintings and flower arrangements as well as larger-than-life furniture to fill this cavernous space. Luxury doubles are very roomy but, if you possibly can, opt for the Terrace Suite. It has a kitchenette, a butler, an enormous bathroom with freestanding bath and a balcony that wraps around the building.

Price category: £££.
Rooms: 91 (29 suites, 6 apartments).
Restaurant: Refuel.
History: The car park that used to occupy the hotel's land was knocked down and the Soho Hotel erected by architect Peter French.
X-Factor: The staff uniforms – charcoal-grey suits – are by Soho-based bespoke tailor Mark Powell, ties by Paul Smith and hot pink knits by John Smedley.
Internet: WiFi in all rooms for £20 per day.

Das Soho Hotel verkörpert die coole und farbige Seite Sohos. Es ist das größte und ausgefallenste Objekt von Firmdale – allerdings mit derselben komfortablen Eleganz, für die die Hotelgruppe bekannt ist. Das Hotel liegt in der Nähe der belebten Dean Street. Ursprünglich stand hier ein mehrstöckiges Parkhaus, das für den Hotelbau mit seinen großzügigen Gästezimmern und Suiten weichen musste. Einen ersten Hinweis darauf, dass dies kein gewöhnliches Hotel ist, gibt die riesige Katzenplastik von Fernando Botero in der Lobby. Designerin Kit Kemp hat hier mit bunten, grafischen Stoffen, übergroßen Bildern, Möbeln und Blumenarrangements ihre Akzente gesetzt. Obschon die Luxury-Doppelzimmer sehr geräumig sind, empfiehlt es sich (sofern es das Budget erlaubt), die Terrace Suite zu buchen. Neben einer kleinen Küche steht ein Butler zu Diensten. Das riesige Badezimmer verfügt zudem über eine frei stehende Badewanne und einen rund ums Gebäude gehenden Balkon.

Le Soho est à l'image de son quartier coloré et nonchalant. Hôtel le plus branché et le plus grand du groupe Firmdale, il n'a rien sacrifié au raffinement cosy qui fait la réputation de la chaîne. À deux pas de la grouillante Dean Street, le bâtiment abritait autrefois un parking sur plusieurs étages entièrement démoli pour créer des chambres et des suites spacieuses. Dès le chat monumental de Fernando Botero qui orne le lobby, on sait qu'on ne se trouve pas dans un hôtel ordinaire. Pour décorer cet espace immense, Kit Kemp n'a pas lésiné sur les couleurs, les tissus graphiques, les tableaux démesurés, les arrangements floraux et le mobilier plus grand que nature. Les chambres doubles de luxe sont agréables mais, tant qu'à faire, optez pour la suite avec terrasse. Elle possède une kitchenette, un majordome, une immense salle de bains avec baignoire sur pied et un balcon panoramique.

Preiskategorie: £££.
Zimmer: 91 (29 Suiten, 6 Apartments).
Restaurant: Refuel.
Geschichte: Das Soho Hotel wurde vom Architekten Peter French entworfen – dafür musste ein Parkhaus abgerissen werden.
X-Faktor: Die anthrazitgrauen Anzüge der Angestellten wurden von Mark Powell maßgeschneidert, die Krawatten sind von Paul Smith und der rosa Strick von John Smedley.
Internet: WiFi in allen Zimmern für 20 £ pro Tag.

Catégorie de prix : £££.
Chambres : 91 (29 suites, 6 appartements).
Restauration : Refuel.
Histoire : L'hôtel a été construit par l'architecte Peter French à la place d'un ancien parking.
Le « petit plus » : Les uniformes du personnel – costumes gris anthracite faits sur mesure par le tailleur Mark Powell, basé à Soho, cravates de Paul Smith et petits pulls roses de John Smedley.
Internet : WiFi dans toutes les chambres pour 20 £ par jour.

Our desires do not age. The sudden leaping up of feeling, as a flame leaps up, or the sea rises, mounts

Hazlitt's

6 Frith Street, London W1D 3JA
☎ +44 20 7434 1771   📠 +44 20 7439 1524
reservations@hazlittshotel.co.uk
www.hazlittshotel.com
Tube: Tottenham Court Road/Leicester Square

Hazlitt's is a magical little nook in Soho where you can imagine yourself hiding away to write that novel you've been putting off, or a secret place in which to conduct les liaisons dangereuses. It is in the centre of the action – innocent or naughty (your choice) – that this part of town offers. Hazlitt's occupies three historic houses that date back to 1718 and, because the building is listed, crooked stairs and leaning walls are all part of the deal. The rooms are decorated with a mixture of English and French antiques; walls are painted rich, dark colours, such as raspberry and charcoal grey, and four-poster beds are so plush and high that it's a wonder guests don't fall off in the middle of the night. Instead of room numbers, each chamber is named after 18th- or 19th-century residents or visitors to the house. The Jonathan Swift Room is the most luxurious, all mysterious and dark woods with an elegant chandelier making it look more like a salon than a bedroom.

Price category: ££.
Rooms: 30 (1 suite, 2 junior suites).
Restaurants: None although there is 24-hour room service and breakfast is served in your room.
History: Author William Hazlitt, after whom the hotel is named, was the son of a clergyman who had founded the Unitarian Church in Boston.
X-Factor: Writers who stay here (notable names include J.K. Rowling and Terry Pratchett) leave signed copies of their latest books for others to read.
Internet: Complimentary WiFi access.

Das Hazlitt's ist ein magischer kleiner Ort in Soho. Man kann sich gut vorstellen, hier den Roman zu schreiben, den man schon immer schreiben wollte. Oder unbemerkt irgendwelchen „Liaisons Dangereuses" nachzugehen. Was immer man tut, und sei's noch so harmlos, das Hotel bleibt das Zentrum des Geschehens. Das Hazlitt's liegt in drei historischen Häusern, die auf das Jahr 1718 zurückgehen. Weil das Gebäude unter Denkmalschutz steht, gehören schräge Treppen und Wände zum Erlebnis. Die Gästezimmer sind mit französischen und englischen Antiquitäten eingerichtet, die Wände in kräftigen, dunklen Farben gehalten – etwa Himbeerrot oder Anthrazit. Ein Wunder, dass noch niemand aus einem der Himmelbetten gefallen ist – sie sind riesig und sehr hoch! Die Zimmer haben keine Nummern, sie tragen die Namen von Bewohnern aus dem 18. und 19. Jahrhundert. Das Jonathan-Swift-Zimmer ist das luxuriöseste von allen. Mit dunklem Holz und elegantem Leuchter sieht es mehr aus wie ein Salon als ein Schlafzimmer.

Le Hazlitt's est le petit nid magique au cœur de Soho où écrire ce roman que vous repoussez depuis si longtemps ou ourdir en secret vos Liaisons Dangereuses. Dans ce quartier, c'est ici que tout se passe, innocent ou coquin (à vous de choisir). Occupant trois maisons classées datant de 1718, les escaliers sont tordus et les murs penchent. Les chambres peintes de couleurs riches et sombres comme framboise ou gris anthracite sont meublées avec des antiquités anglaises et françaises, et les somptueux lits à baldaquins sont si hauts que c'est un miracle que les clients n'en tombent pas au milieu de la nuit. À la place de numéros, les chambres portent le nom d'anciens visiteurs célèbres du XVIIIe et du XIXe siècles. La Jonathan Swift est la plus luxueuse. Mystérieuse avec ses boiseries sombres et son lustre élégant, on se croirait dans un salon.

Preiskategorie: ££.
Zimmer: 30 (1 Suite, 2 Junior-Suiten).
Restaurants: Keines. 24-Stunden-Zimmerservice, das Frühstück wird aufs Zimmer gebracht.
Geschichte: Das Hotel ist nach dem Autor William Hazlitt benannt, dem Sohn des Gründers der Unitarian Church in Boston.
X-Faktor: Schriftsteller wie J. K. Rowling und Terry Pratchett, die hier abgestiegen sind, haben für andere Gäste signierte Bücher hinterlassen.
Internet: Kostenloser WiFi-Zugang.

Catégorie de prix : ££.
Chambres : 30 (1 suite, 2 junior suites).
Restauration : Service assuré 24h/24 et petit-déjeuner servi dans les chambres.
Histoire : L'auteur William Hazlitt était le fils du fondateur de l'église protestante unitaire de Boston.
Le « petit plus » : Les écrivains qui y ont séjourné (notamment J. K. Rowling et Terry Pratchett) ont laissé des exemplaires dédicacés de leurs œuvres pour les autres clients.
Internet : Accès WiFi gratuit.

Covent Garden Hotel

10 Monmouth Street, London WC2H 9HB
☎ +44 20 7806 1000   📠 +44 20 7806 1100
covent@firmdale.com
www.coventgardenhotel.co.uk
Tube: Covent Garden

Covent Garden is one of the most wonderful and diverse neighbourhoods in London. It's a mix of flats, cool shops, fabulous restaurants and theatres. It goes without saying, then, that one expects a bit of drama from the Covent Garden Hotel. The lobby resembles a stage set; the marvellous stone staircase swoops to one side and leads up to the drawing room and bedrooms, where the drama continues. Designed by owner Kit Kemp, the hotel is a modern update of traditional English design. Florals are done with flair and in abundance, and her signature is a mannequin in each chamber covered in the dominant fabric used in the room's decoration. The hotel's Brasserie Max is a brilliant little restaurant in which to spy on the theatre actors, Hollywood producers and local media pros gathered over drinks and dinner. Try the chips (French fries): they are delicious with a glass of red wine after a hard day's stomping around the greatest city in the world.

Price category: ££.
Rooms: 58 (8 suites).
Restaurant: Brasserie Max.
History: The building that the hotel now occupies was once a French hospital.
X-Factor: The bathroom products by London perfumer Miller Harris.
Internet: Broadband access at £20 per day.

Covent Garden gehört zu den interessantesten Stadtteilen Londons – ein Mix aus Wohnungen, coolen Shops, ausgezeichneten Restaurants und Theatern. Das Covent Garden Hotel reflektiert diese außergewöhnliche Melange perfekt. Bereits die Lobby überrascht mit einer bühnenreifen Szenerie und prächtiger Steintreppe, die sich auf einer Seite hochschwingt und nach oben in den Salon und zu den Gästezimmern führt. Das Interieur wurde von der Besitzerin Kit Kemp entworfen: traditionell englisches Design neu interpretiert – natürlich mit vielen üppigen, floralen Mustern. Sogar die stummen Diener, die als Dekorelement in jedem der Gästezimmer stehen, sind mit dem Blümchenstoff des jeweiligen Zimmers bezogen. Hervorragend ist die Brasserie Max. Hier verkehren Theaterschauspieler, Hollywood-Produzenten und die Medienprominenz. Besonders gut schmecken die Pommes frites. Zusammen mit einem guten Glas Rotwein sind sie eine Wohltat nach einem langen Tag in einer der aufregendsten Städte der Welt.

Covent Garden est l'un des quartiers les plus fascinants et variés de Londres, mélange d'appartements, de boutiques branchées, d'excellents restaurants et de théâtres. Le Covent Garden Hotel se devait donc d'être à la hauteur. Son hall rappelle un décor de théâtre avec son merveilleux escalier en pierre qui mène au salon et aux chambres où le spectacle continue. Sa propriétaire Kit Kemp l'a décoré dans une version moderne du style traditionnel anglais, agrémenté de merveilleux et nombreux bouquets de bon goût. Chaque chambre contient un mannequin de couture tapissé du même tissu que les murs. Max, la brasserie de l'hôtel, est un délicieux petit restaurant où espionner les acteurs, les producteurs hollywoodiens et les professionnels des médias. Essayez les frites, délicieuses avec un verre de vin rouge après avoir arpenté toute la journée la ville la plus excitante du monde.

Preiskategorie: ££.
Zimmer: 58 (8 Suiten).
Restaurant: Brasserie Max.
Geschichte: Das Hotelgebäude war früher ein französisches Krankenhaus.
X-Faktor: Im Badezimmer stehen Produkte des Londoner Parfümeurs Miller Harris.
Internet: Breitbandanschluss für 20 £ pro Tag.

Catégorie de prix : ££.
Chambres : 58 (8 suites).
Restauration : Brasserie Max.
Histoire : Le bâtiment abritait autrefois un hôpital français.
Le « petit plus » : Les salles de bains sont équipées de produits du parfumeur londonien Miller Harris.
Internet : Accès haut débit pour 20 £ par jour.

Charlotte Street Hotel

15 Charlotte Street, London W1T 1RJ
☎ +44 20 7806 2000   📠 +44 20 7806 2002
charlotte@firmdale.com
www.charlottestreethotel.com
Tube: Goodge Street

The Charlotte Street Hotel is a perfect reflection of the neighbourhood in which it is located. Fitzrovia, just north of groovy Soho and west of intellectual Bloomsbury, is a healthy mix of the cool and the clever. The hotel holds court on buzzing Charlotte Street among the small galleries, cute shops and eclectic restaurants frequented by advertising executives, film makers, students and artists. The hotel was inspired by the Bloomsbury Group, which included the writer Virginia Woolf. There is a sense of calm that pervades this hotel, much like entering a fancy library. It's a beautiful mix of oak-panelled walls with a cat statue by Botero guarding the premises. Oscar, the restaurant and bar, has an air of low-key glamour and has been so popular that it has been expanded. Whether it's for a business breakfast or the cocktail hour, it's a venue that is particularly great in summer, when the big windows can be opened to the street and patrons can spill out onto the sidewalk.

Price category: ££.
Rooms: 52 (13 suites).
Restaurant: Oscar.
History: The building the hotel now occupies used to be a dental warehouse.
X-Factor: The artworks by Vanessa Bell, Duncan Grant, Roger Fry and Henry Lamb, as well as Roger Cecil.
Internet: WiFi in all rooms at £20 per day.

Das Charlotte Street Hotel passt bestens in seine Umgebung. Fitzrovia, das nördlich an das unternehmungslustige Soho und westlich an das eher intellektuelle Bloomsbury grenzt, ist die perfekte Mischung aus beidem. Das Hotel liegt an der lebendigen Charlotte Street mit kleinen Galerien, entzückenden Läden und eklektischen Restaurants, die Werber, Filmemacher, Studenten und Künstler zu ihren Gästen zählen. Inspiriert wurde das Hotel von der Bloomsbury Group, der unter anderem die Schriftstellerin Virginia Woolf angehörte. So wie in einer ehrwürdigen Bibliothek herrscht hier eine wunderbare Ruhe. Eichenpaneele zieren die Wände, der Eingang wird von einer Katzenplastik von Botero bewacht, und Oscar, das Restaurant mit Bar, ist von schlichtem Glamour. Das Oscar ist so beliebt, dass es vergrößert werden musste. Hier ist es besonders schön im Sommer, wenn die großen Fenster geöffnet werden und die Gäste draußen auf dem Gehsteig sitzen.

Le Charlotte Street Hotel reflète parfaitement son quartier, Fitzrovia, situé entre le Soho branché au nord et Bloomsbury l'intellectuel à l'ouest. La rue animée accueille des petites galeries, des boutiques charmantes et des restaurants éclectiques fréquentés par des gens de la pub, du cinéma, des étudiants et des artistes. L'hôtel, décontracté et raffiné, a été inspiré par le groupe de Bloomsbury, dont Virginia Woolf faisait partie. Il y règne un calme serein, un peu comme dans une élégante bibliothèque. Ses belles boiseries en chêne sont gardées par un chat sculpté par Botero. Le chic discret d'Oscar, le restaurant-bar, a rencontré un tel succès que les lieux ont dû être agrandis. Pour un petit-déjeuner d'affaires ou un cocktail, c'est un endroit idéal en été quand les grandes fenêtres s'ouvrent pour faire terrasse sur le trottoir.

Preiskategorie: ££.
Zimmer: 52 (13 Suiten).
Restaurant: Oscar.
Geschichte: Das Hotelgebäude diente früher als Lager für Dentalprodukte.
X-Faktor: Kunstwerke von Vanessa Bell, Duncan Grant, Roger Fry, Henry Lamb und Roger Cecil.
Internet: WiFi in allen Zimmern für 20 £ pro Tag.

Catégorie de prix : ££.
Chambres : 52 (13 suites).
Restauration : Oscar.
Histoire : Le bâtiment abritait autrefois un entrepôt de dentisterie.
Le « petit plus » : Les œuvres originales de Vanessa Bell, Duncan Grant, Roger Fry, Henry Lamb et Roger Cecil.
Internet : WiFi dans toutes les chambres pour 20 £ par jour.

Montagu Place

2 Montagu Place, London W1H 2ER
☎ +44 20 7467 2777   📠 +44 20 7467 2778
stay@montagu-place.co.uk
www.montagu-place.co.uk
Tube: Baker Street

If less really is more, then Montagu Place has it right. Opened in 2006, this small, simple hotel has three types of rooms: Comfy, Fancy and Swanky, with Fancy being larger than Comfy and Swanky being the largest of all. The hotel occupies a Grade II listed Georgian townhouse that was once gutted in a fire. It has been refurbished and fitted with super modern bathrooms, and decorated with contemporary furniture with warm browns and whites on the walls and floors. The prices are as accessible as the décor and the hotel is right in Marylebone, one of the best residential neighbourhoods in the city. The restaurant serves a delicious breakfast, with organic and fair trade options, all of which can also be brought up to guest bedrooms. The lobby bar is also great for a cocktail. If you possibly can, plump for a spacious Swanky room with views of Montagu Place.

Price category: £.
Rooms: 16 (10 Comfy, 3 Fancy, 3 Swanky).
Restaurant: The restaurant provides a buffet breakfast; there is room service and the bar is open 24 hours a day.
History: The hotel is housed in a Grade II listed Georgian townhouse.
X-Factor: It is lovely to see that the building's original features have been so painstakingly restored.
Internet: WiFi is available in the lounge and wired broadband access is available in the bedrooms.

Im Montagu Place gilt die Maxime „weniger ist mehr". Das kleine, schlichte Hotel liegt in einem denkmalgeschützten georgianischen Stadthaus, das während eines Feuers fast abbrannte. Nachdem es instand gesetzt worden war, konnte es 2006 eröffnet werden. Die Zimmertypen Comfy (klein), Fancy (mittelgroß) und Swanky (groß) sind mit ultramodernen Badezimmern und zeitgemäßen Möbeln ausgestattet. Als Farbthema wurde ein warmes Braun und Weiß gewählt. Obschon das Hotel in einem der besten Wohnquartiere der Stadt, Marylebone, liegt, sind die Preise durchaus vernünftig. Im Restaurant wird ein deliziöses Bio-Frühstück (mit Fair-Trade-Produkten) serviert, das man auch mit aufs Zimmer nehmen kann, und in der Lobby lädt die Bar zum Cocktail ein. Die beste Wahl sind die luftigen Zimmer der Kategorie Swanky: Sie haben einen schönen Blick auf den Montagu Place.

Le Montagu Place a tout compris du minimalisme. Inauguré en 2006, ce petit hôtel simple est situé dans un ancien hôtel particulier classé du XVIIIe siècle autrefois détruit par un incendie. Entièrement restauré et équipé de salles de bains ultramodernes, il propose à des prix accessibles trois types de chambres, par ordre de taille : Comfy, Fancy et Swanky. Le décor, avec un mobilier contemporain aux tons bruns chauds, des murs et des sols blancs, cadre parfaitement avec Marylebone, un des meilleurs quartiers résidentiels de la ville. Le restaurant vous propose un délicieux petit-déjeuner bio (avec des produits du commerce équitable), que vous pourrez prendre aussi dans votre chambre. Le bar du lobby est idéal pour prendre l'apéritif. Si vous le pouvez, optez pour une spacieuse Swanky avec vue sur Montagu Place.

Preiskategorie: £.
Zimmer: 16 (10 Comfy, 3 Fancy, 3 Swanky).
Restaurant: Im Restaurant wird ein Frühstücksbüfett serviert. Es gibt einen Zimmerservice; die Bar ist 24 Stunden geöffnet.
Geschichte: Das Hotel befindet sich in einem denkmalgeschützten georgianischen Stadthaus.
X-Faktor: Das Haus wurde originalgetreu mit viel Liebe zum Detail restauriert.
Internet: WiFi in der Lounge und Breitbandanschluss in den Zimmern.

Catégorie de prix : £.
Chambres : 16 (10 Comfy, 3 Fancy, 3 Swanky).
Restauration : Le restaurant sert un buffet petit-déjeuner ; le service dans les chambres est assuré ; le bar est ouvert 24h/24.
Histoire : L'hôtel est situé dans un hôtel particulier du XVIIIe siècle classé.
Le « petit plus » : Le soin avec lequel les détails du bâtiment original ont été restaurés.
Internet : WiFi disponible dans le grand salon et accès haut débit dans les chambres.

The Gore

190 Queen's Gate, London SW7 5EX
☎ +44 20 7584 6601   📱 +44 20 7589 8127
reservations@gorehotel.com
www.gorehotel.com
Tube: South Kensington/Gloucester Road

Walking into The Gore is like visiting a loopy uncle's house. The walls of the chandeliered reception are covered in gilt-framed artwork. There are pictures of Queen Victoria and Prince Albert, of children in buckled shoes and paintings of farm animals. It would all be overkill if it wasn't so very whimsical and delightful. The hotel's busy restaurant, 190 Queen's Gate, serves food sourced from UK farms. The Gore's clientele are as eclectic as the décor. Supermodels and their rock star boyfriends hide out here when press intrusion gets too much. At the same time, you'll find businessmen tapping away at their laptops; or you could come across an elegant woman, lashed in diamonds, mysteriously accompanied by a three-tonne bodyguard. The rooms at The Gore are quirky, eccentric and furnished with an amazing collection of English and French antiques. The deluxe Judy Garland Room has a huge antique bed, topped with raw silk swag and tails, which apparently belonged to Judy Garland.

Price category: £.
Rooms: 50 (1 suite).
Restaurants: 190 Queen's Gate, Bar 190.
History: The Gore has two rooms dedicated to Miss Fanny and Miss Ada, who once lived in the hotel and ran it as a lodging house when all the family's men were lost to war.
X-Factor: The Green Room, which is actually pink, is a lovely place to have a drink and relax.
Internet: Complimentary WiFi access.

Im Gore ist es wie zu Besuch bei einem exzentrischen Onkel. Die Rezeption ist vollgestopft mit Leuchtern und goldgerahmten Porträts von Königin Victoria, Prinz Albert, Kindern in Schnallenschuhen und Gemälden von Tieren auf dem Bauernhof. Zum Glück spürt man hier ein Augenzwinkern, sonst wäre das ganze Dekor etwas zu viel des Guten. Die buntgemischte Klientel passt perfekt in die Szenerie: Supermodels in Begleitung von Rockstar-Boyfriends suchen hier Zuflucht vor der neugierigen Journaille, diamantenübersäte Damen stolzieren vor ihren drei Tonnen schweren Bodyguards, dazwischen sieht man auch ein paar mit Laptops ausgerüstete Geschäftsleute. Die Gästezimmer mit englischen und französischen Antiquitäten sind so eigenwillig wie der Rest. So protzt im luxuriösen Judy Garland Room ein riesiges antikes Bett (es soll Judy Garland gehört haben) mit rohseidenen Vorhängen und Girlanden. 190 Queen's Gate, das Hotelrestaurant, allerdings setzt auf natürliche Zutaten und verwendet lokale Landwirtschaftsprodukte.

En entrant au Gore, on se croirait chez un vieil oncle un peu fou. Le hall, orné d'un lustre, est tapissé de tableaux dans des cadres dorés. On y trouve des portraits de la reine Victoria et du prince Albert, d'enfants aux souliers à boucle et d'animaux de ferme. Cela paraîtrait trop chargé si ce n'était aussi fantasque et plein d'humour. Le restaurant très prisé de l'hôtel, le 190 Queens Gate, s'approvisionne directement dans des fermes du pays. La clientèle est aussi éclectique que le décor. On y croise des top-modèles avec leurs fiancés rock stars fuyant les paparazzis, des hommes d'affaires pianotant sur leur ordinateur ou des élégantes couvertes de diamants flanquées d'un garde du corps pesant trois tonnes. Les chambres merveilleusement excentriques sont meublées d'antiquités françaises et anglaises. La luxueuse Judy Garland Room possède un immense lit ancien surmonté d'un drapé en soie sauvage qui aurait appartenu à Judy Garland.

Preiskategorie: £.
Zimmer: 50 (1 Suite).
Restaurants: 190 Queen's Gate, Bar 190.
Geschichte: The Gore hat zwei seiner Zimmer Miss Fanny und Miss Ada gewidmet. Die beiden Frauen betrieben das Haus als Pension, nachdem sie ihre Ehemänner im Krieg verloren hatten.
X-Faktor: The Green Room ist ein wunderbarer Ort zum Entspannen. Übrigens ist der Raum ganz in Rot – trotz des Namens.
Internet: Kostenloser WiFi-Zugang.

Catégorie de prix : £.
Chambres : 50 (1 suite).
Restauration : 190 Queen's Gate, Bar 190.
Histoire : Le Gore conserve deux chambres consacrées à Miss Fanny et Miss Ada, qui vivaient autrefois dans la maison et la transformèrent en pension après que tous les hommes de la famille furent morts à la guerre.
Le « petit plus » : La Green Room, qui en fait est rose, est un endroit charmant où prendre un verre et se détendre.
Internet : Accès WiFi gratuit.

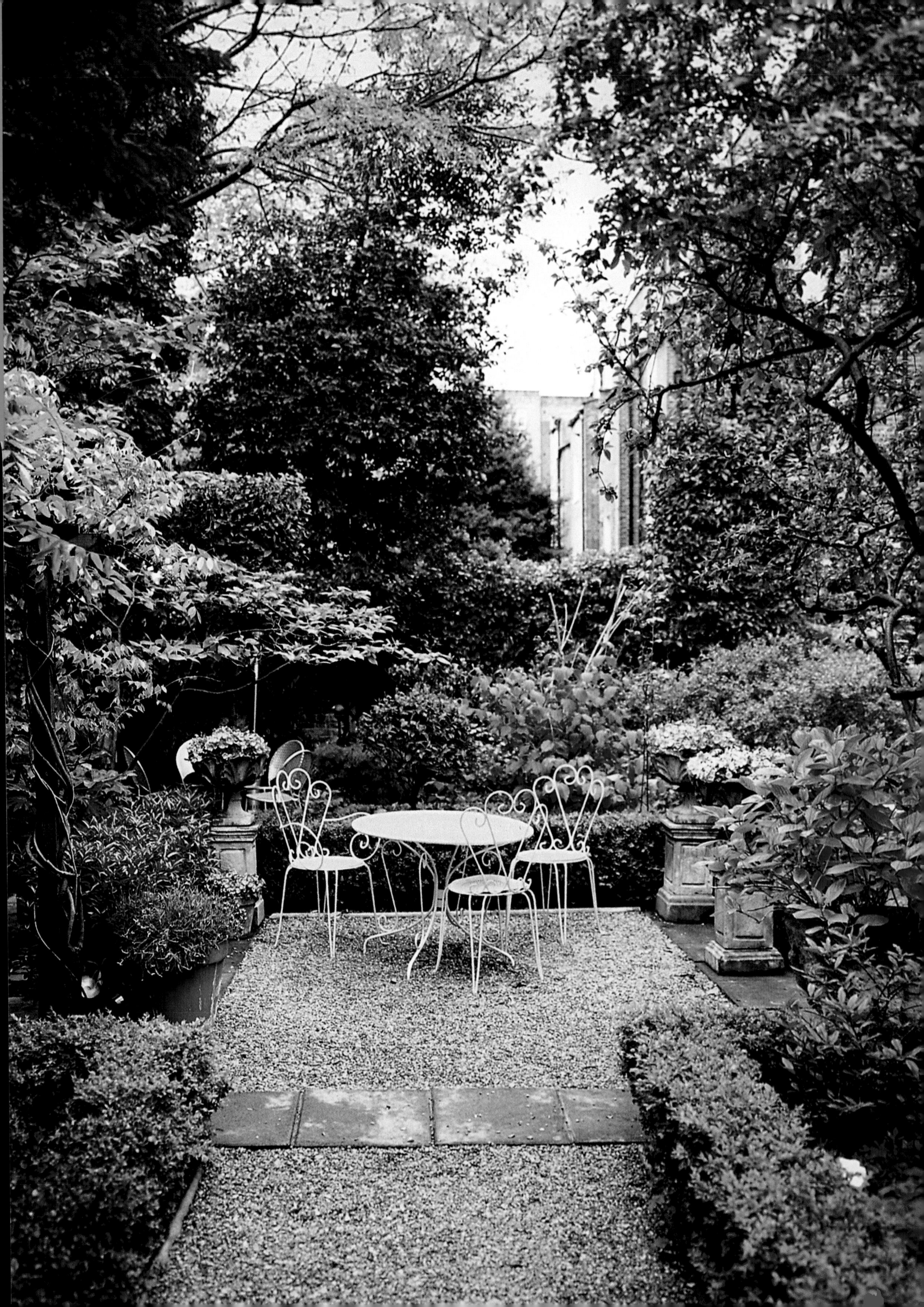

Number Sixteen Hotel

16 Sumner Place, London SW7 3EG
☎ +44 20 7589 5232   📠 +44 20 7584 8615
reservations@numbersixteenhotel.co.uk
www.numbersixteenhotel.co.uk
Tube: South Kensington

The sparkling white row of Victorian townhouses that make up Number Sixteen give away little about how fantastic this hotel really is. Compact but perfectly formed, this little jewel of an inn in South Kensington boasts a near-perfect London location, close to the V&A and great shopping. Decorated by owner Kit Kemp in what is best described as South Kensington chic – a bit flowery, a bit contemporary, very London – Number Sixteen is bright, modern and very fresh. The two drawing rooms have fluffy sofas and sun streaming in through the windows. Then there is the conservatory, decorated with African and Asian prints collected by Kemp on her travels around the world; it is light, airy and leads out to the pièce de résistance at Number Sixteen: the lush garden replete with fountain and perky carp swimming around. Whatever you do, don't leave London before you have sat out here with a full afternoon tea (the delicious scones are home-made) and a good English newspaper.

Price category: £.
Rooms: 42.
Restaurants: None but there is 24-hour room service.
History: The property was a hotel before the Firmdale group purchased it and redecorated it in its own style.
X-Factor: The tranquil garden is simply amazing and the beds are very comfortable.
Internet: Broadband access at £20 per day.

Das Number Sixteen Hotel besteht aus einer Reihe zucker-gussweißer viktorianischer Stadthäuser. Wie fantastisch das Hotel tatsächlich ist, lässt sich von außen kaum erahnen. Hinter der Fassade verbirgt sich ein kleines Juwel in bester Lage in South Kensington: der nahezu perfekte Aufenthalts-ort in London. Gleich in der Nähe befindet sich das V&A-Museum, die Shoppinggelegenheiten sind erstklassig. Be-sitzerin Kit Kemp hat die Inneneinrichtung (ein Stil, den man mit „South Kensington Chic" bezeichnen könnte) selbst entworfen – ein bisschen floral, ein bisschen zeitge-mäß, sehr frisch und vor allem typisch London. Das Haus verfügt über zwei helle Salons mit superbequemen Sofas und einen Wintergarten, dekoriert mit afrikanischen und asiatischen Prints, die Kemp von ihren Reisen mitgebracht hat. Das Prachtstück ist der lauschige Garten mit Karpfen-brunnen. Die Stadt kann man unmöglich verlassen, ohne hier einen Afternoon Tea mit den deliziösen hausgemachten Scones genossen zu haben.

La rangée de maisons victoriennes d'un blanc étincelant qui constituent le Number Sixteen ne laisse pas deviner à quel point cet hôtel est magique. Compact mais parfaite-ment aménagé, ce petit bijou jouit d'un emplacement qua-si parfait : à deux pas du V&A et des meilleures boutiques. Décoré par sa propriétaire Kit Kemp dans ce qu'on pourrait appeler le style « South Kensington chic » (un peu floral, un peu contemporain, très londonien), il est lumineux, moderne et très frais. Les deux salons inondés de lumière possèdent des canapés douillets ; le jardin d'hiver est décoré d'imprimés africains et asiatiques glanés par Kemp au fil de ses voyages. Mais la pièce de résistance, c'est le jardin luxuriant avec sa fontaine et son bassin où nagent des carpes. Ne quittez pas Londres avant d'y avoir pris le thé (les délicieux scones sont faits maison) devant un bon journal anglais.

Preiskategorie: £.
Zimmer: 42.
Restaurants: Keines. 24-Stunden-Zimmerservice.
Geschichte: Das Haus war bereits ein Hotel, bevor es die Firmdale-Gruppe übernommen und renoviert hat.
X-Faktor: Die Stille im Garten ist wunderbar, und die Betten in den Zimmern sind unglaublich bequem.
Internet: Breitbandanschluss für 20 £ pro Tag.

Catégorie de prix : £.
Chambres : 42.
Restauration : Aucune, mais service assuré dans les chambres 24h/24.
Histoire : L'établissement était déjà un hôtel avant d'être racheté et réaménagé par le groupe Firmdale dans son propre style.
Le « petit plus » : Le jardin tranquille est magnifique et les lits sont d'un confort indécent.
Internet : Accès haut débit pour 20 £ par jour.

N° 11 London

11 Cadogan Gardens, London SW3 2RJ
☎ +44 20 7730 7000   📠 +44 20 7730 5217
reservations@no11london.com
www.no11london.com
Tube: Sloane Square

When designer Paul Davies bought this hotel early in 2007, it was still called Eleven Cadogan Gardens and, thanks to its upper-class British understatement, was an address of choice for European country-house owners staying in London. Davies changed not only the name but also the design: as N° 11 London it has taken on a more glamorous and dramatic appearance, and visitors might almost feel they are entering a theatre set of dark wood with brocade fabrics in dark red and purple, Murano glass and gold-framed mirrors. However, there is still an emphasis on privacy and discretion here: the rooms, also opulent but decorated in quieter colours, keep out the noise of London – those who wish to stay longer can rent an apartment – and the limousines available for shopping tours include a Rolls Royce and a Bentley Town Car. Evening guests in the Dining Room, stylish with light-coloured furniture and black-and-white portrait photographs, almost feel they have come to an elegant private house.

Price category: £££.
Rooms: 60 (11 suites, 4 apartments).
Restaurant: Breakfast, lunch and dinner, as well as high tea, are served in the Dining Room.
History: Lord Chelsea had this Victorian mansion built on his cricket ground near Buckingham Palace. In 1949 it was converted into a hotel.
X-Factor: The ayurveda treatments in the spa and the superbly equipped gym.
Internet: Free of charge in all rooms (WiFi).

Als der Designer Paul Davies dieses Hotel im Frühjahr 2007 kaufte, hieß es noch „Eleven Cadogan Gardens" und war dank seines britischen Upper-Class-Understatements eine bevorzugte Adresse europäischer Landhausbesitzer, wenn sie nach London kamen. Davies änderte nicht nur den Namen, sondern auch das Design: Als N° 11 London gibt sich das Haus glamouröser und dramatischer – man glaubt beinahe, eine Theaterkulisse aus dunklem Holz mit dunkelroten und purpurfarbenen Brokatstoffen und Muranoglas sowie goldumrahmten Spiegeln zu betreten. Privatsphäre und Diskretion werden hier aber immer noch großgeschrieben: Die ebenfalls opulenten, jedoch in ruhigeren Tönen gehaltenen Zimmer schirmen vom lauten London ab – wer die Ruhe länger genießen möchte, kann auch ein Apartment mieten – und für Shoppingtouren stehen unter anderem ein Rolls Royce sowie ein Bentley Town Car zur Verfügung. Fast wie in einem eleganten Privathaus fühlt man sich abends im Dining Room, der mit hellen Möbeln und Porträtfotografien in Schwarz-Weiß Stil beweist.

Preiskategorie: £££.
Zimmer: 60 (11 Suiten, 4 Apartments).
Restaurant: Im Diningroom werden Frühstück, Mittag- und Abendessen sowie High Tea serviert.
Geschichte: Lord Chelsea hatte die viktorianischen Mansions nahe des Buckingham Palace auf seinem Cricketplatz bauen lassen. 1949 wurde daraus ein Hotel.
X-Faktor: Die Ayurveda-Behandlungen im Spa sowie der perfekt ausgestattete Fitnessraum.
Internet: Kostenfrei in allen Räumen (WiFi).

Cet hôtel s'appelait « Eleven Cadogan Gardens » lorsque le designer Paul Davies l'a acheté au printemps 2007, et l'understatement très upper-class qui y régnait faisait de lui l'adresse privilégiée des propriétaires de maisons de campagne européens en visite à Londres. Mais Davies ne s'est pas contenté de le rebaptiser : le N° 11 London est plus glamoureux, plus dramatique – ses bois sombres, ses brocarts pourpres et bordeaux, ses verreries de Murano et ses miroirs encadrés de dorures donnent l'impression de pénétrer dans des décors de théâtre. Ici la vie privée et la discrétion sont encore au centre des préoccupations : les chambres meublées avec opulence mais montrant des teintes claires tiennent éloignés les bruits de la rue – celui qui veut profiter plus longtemps du calme peut aussi louer un appartement – et les amateurs de shopping ont une Rolls Royce et un Bentley Town Car à leur disposition. Le soir, dans la salle à manger élégante avec son mobilier clair et ses portraits photographiés en noir et blanc, on se sent presque comme dans une habitation privée.

Catégorie de prix : £££.
Chambres : 60 (11 suites, 4 appartements).
Restauration : Le petit-déjeuner, le déjeuner et le dîner ainsi que le high tea sont servis au Dining Room.
Histoire : Lord Chelsea avait fait construire les Mansions victoriens sur son terrain de cricket, à côté du palais de Buckingham. Les bâtiments ont été transformés en hôtel en 1949.
Le « petit plus » : Les traitements ayurvédiques au spa et la salle de remise en forme parfaitement équipée.
Internet : Gratuit dans toutes les pièces (WiFi).

Miller's Residence

111a Westbourne Grove, London W2 4UW
☎ +44 20 7243 1024   📠 +44 20 7243 1064
enquiries@millershotel.com
www.millershotel.com
Tube: Bayswater/Notting Hill Gate

Miller's Residence in Notting Hill is for the unashamed
maximalist in all of us. Just about every inch of the walls,
ceilings and floors is covered by something: antique furniture, dried flowers, gilt-framed paintings, more antique
furniture… you get the picture. Its location is excellent –
it is right off Westbourne Grove above a row of shops and
it is, without a doubt, the most bohemian hotel in town.
Owned by Martin Miller, a renowned antiques dealer,
Miller's Residence is very much a work-in-progress and
furniture is constantly being moved around and rearranged.
The lounge, where guests take their breakfast, is as busy as
the rest of the house and yet as cosy as your own living
room. Rooms at Miller's Residence are comfortable, clean
and come with a small bathroom. If you want a trip to
London with a good dose of English eccentricity thrown
in, it doesn't get better than this.

Price category: ££.
Rooms: 8.
Restaurants: None.
History: The hotel opened in 1995. Before that the location was
derelict.
X-Factor: The abundant wrapped sweets available at every turn.
Internet: Complimentary WiFi and broadband access.

„Nur nichts übertreiben" ist man versucht, beim Anblick der Miller's Residence in Notting Hill auszurufen: Wände, Decken und Böden – jeder Millimeter ist vollgestopft mit Antiquitäten, getrockneten Blumen, goldgerahmten Bildern und noch mehr Antiquitäten. Mit Sicherheit ist dies das verrückteste Hotel der Stadt. In ausgezeichneter Lage, gleich beim Westbourne Grove, besetzt es den zweiten Stock über einer ganzen Reihe von Läden. Vom Besitzer Martin Miller, einem bekannten Antiquitätenhändler, veranlasst, werden hier ständig Möbel verschoben und Bilder umgehängt. Die Lounge, in der die Gäste ihr Frühstück einnehmen, ist so opulent wie der Rest des Hauses und so gemütlich wie ein Wohnzimmer. Die Gästezimmer sind behaglich, blitzblank und verfügen über ein eigenes Badezimmer. Liebhaber englischer Exzentrik sind hier genau richtig. Besser als hier wird's garantiert nirgends.

Miller's Residence à Notting Hill s'adresse au maximaliste éhonté qui sommeille en chacun de nous. Du sol au plafond, il n'y pas un centimètre carré qui ne soit occupé par des tableaux, des antiquités, des bouquets séchés… et encore des antiquités. L'emplacement est idéal, sur Westbourne Grove au-dessus d'une rangée de boutiques. C'est sans conteste l'hôtel le plus bohème de Londres. Martin Miller, son propriétaire, est un célèbre antiquaire. Il entretient son établissement en évolution constante, déplaçant sans cesse les meubles. Le salon cosy, où l'on prend ses petits-déjeuners, est aussi chargé que le reste de la maison mais vous vous y sentirez chez vous. Les chambres sont confortables, propres et équipées d'une petite salle de bains. Si vous souhaitez insuffler une bonne dose d'excentricité britannique dans votre séjour à Londres, il n'y a pas mieux.

Preiskategorie: ££.
Zimmer: 8.
Restaurants: Keines.
Geschichte: Das Hotel wurde 1995 eröffnet. Zuvor war das Gebäude vom Zerfall bedroht.
X-Faktor: Überall im Haus findet man zum Naschen hübsch verpackte Süßigkeiten.
Internet: Kostenloser WiFi-Zugang und Breitbandanschluss.

Catégorie de prix : ££.
Chambres : 8.
Restauration : Aucune.
Histoire : Inauguré en 1995. Avant cela, le bâtiment n'était qu'une ruine.
Le « petit plus » : L'abondance de bonbons mis à disposition dans tous les coins.
Internet : Accès WiFi et haut débit gratuit.

The Hempel

31–35 Craven Hill Gardens, London W2 3EA
☎ +44 20 7298 9000   📱 +44 20 7402 4666
hotel@the-hempel.co.uk
www.the-hempel.co.uk
Tube: Bayswater

White, white and more white, The Hempel is an exercise in 1990s minimalism, but somehow retains a currency despite its homage to neutrals. Anouska Hempel knocked together five houses to create the hotel and her design is, without a doubt, the strongest statement here, but one must not overlook its amazing location mere minutes from Hyde Park. Service can be patchy but the rooms are peaceful, particularly those that look onto the square, and the Eastern influence in the interior lends it a Zen quality. The lobby is particularly impressive, created entirely from white Portland stone with elegant fireplaces and sunken seating areas. The Hempel's perfectly manicured garden square is one of its big selling points, especially during warm summer evenings, when it is filled with candles and guests are invited to sit out there for dinner or to knock back a cocktail or two.

Price category: ££.
Rooms: 35 rooms (6 suites, 6 private apartments).
Restaurant: From end of 2009 The Hempel Restaurant.
History: Five Georgian houses were knocked together in 1998 to create the hotel.
X-Factor: The garden square is, without a doubt, the best thing about this hotel.
Internet: Complimentary WiFi in all rooms.

Überall wo man hinblickt, sieht man nur Weiß. Das Hempel ist der Inbegriff des Minimalismus der 1990er. Trotz monochromen Dekors ist das Hotel ein klares Statement, für das die Designerin Anouska Hempel fünf nebeneinanderstehende Häuser zusammenlegen ließ. Natürlich ist ihr Design der wichtigste Grund, hier abzusteigen. Doch auch die Lage, ein paar Minuten vom Hyde Park entfernt, ist ein großes Plus. Die Gästezimmer sind alle sehr ruhig, besonders diejenigen auf der Hofseite. Mit fernöstlich inspiriertem Dekor vermitteln sie zudem ein zenbuddhistisches Ambiente. Die Lobby aus weißem Portlandstein mit eleganten Kaminen und Sitzecken wirkt besonders beeindruckend. Toll ist auch der perfekt gestaltete Garten: Besonders schön ist es, an einem lauen Sommerabend bei Kerzenlicht draußen zu dinieren oder an einem Cocktail zu nippen. Einziger Minuspunkt im Haus: Der Service ist mal so, mal so.

Du blanc, encore du blanc, rien que du blanc. Le Hempel est un exercice en minimalisme des années 1990 avec quelques concessions aux tons neutres. Anouska Hempel a rassemblé cinq maisons pour créer son hôtel et apposé son style inimitable à la décoration, ce qui en fait son attrait outre son emplacement idéal à quelques minutes de Hyde Park. Le service n'est pas toujours à la hauteur mais les chambres sont tranquilles, notamment celles donnant sur le jardin, et l'influence orientale crée une ambiance zen. Le hall est particulièrement impressionnant, tout en pierre blanche de Portland avec d'élégantes cheminée et des banquettes encastrées. Le square/jardin carré parfaitement manucuré est l'un de ses principaux atouts, notamment les soirs chauds d'été quand il est illuminé de bougies et que l'on peut y dîner ou y prendre un verre.

Preiskategorie: ££.
Zimmer: 35 (6 Suiten, 6 Privatapartments).
Restaurant: Ab Ende 2009 The Hempel Restaurant.
Geschichte: Fünf georgianische Häuser wurden 1998 zu diesem Hotel zusammengefügt.
X-Faktor: Der rechteckig angelegte Garten ist zweifellos die größte Attraktion des Hotels.
Internet: Kostenloser WiFi-Zugang in allen Zimmern.

Catégorie de prix : ££.
Chambres : 35 (6 suites, 6 appartements privés).
Restauration : Nouveauté fin 2009, The Hempel Restaurant.
Histoire : Cinq maisons datant du XVIIIe siècle ont été reliées en 1998 pour créer cet hôtel.
Le « petit plus » : Le jardin carré est sans aucun doute le point fort de cet hôtel.
Internet : Accès WiFi gratuit dans toutes les chambres.

Malmaison

18–21 Charterhouse Square, London EC1M 6AH
☎ +44 20 7012 3700   ☐ +44 20 7012 3702
london@malmaison.com
www.malmaison.com
Tube: Barbican/Farringdon

The clever folk behind the Malmaison chain, which started in the north of England, have stayed true to their philosophy of "real places for real people" with a hotel that provides comfortable, modern rooms at reasonable prices. Malmaison London is in busy Clerkenwell, right in quiet Charterhouse Square, nestled among the enormous trees and next to the Chapel of Sutton's Hospital, which dates back to the 17th century. The lobby looks serious at first glance, with its dark velvet chairs, the low lighting and the Veuve Cliquot Champagne bar. But the bust of Napoleon leading to the lifts hints at something a bit more playful. There are also photographs of London scenes peppered on the walls, so there is plenty to admire. During the week Malmaison hosts business people but the weekends are when lovestruck couples set up base for gallery-hopping and sampling the wine bars around the area. Make sure to try one of the Malmaison's own Bellinis and don't miss the Sunday brunch.

Price category: £.
Rooms: 97 (2 suites).
Restaurant: Brasserie.
History: Malmaison is named after the chateau that Napoleon built for Josephine. The Malmaison's red brick building was once home to the nurses of nearby St Bartholomew's Hospital.
X-Factor: Own-brand Malmaison bathroom products are great and can be taken along when you leave.
Internet: Complimentary broadband connections in rooms; WiFi in the lobby and Brasserie.

Die Malmaison-Gruppe aus dem Norden Englands ist glücklicherweise ihrer Philosophie „kein Firlefanz" treu geblieben. Das fängt bei den Preisen an: Die elegant-modernen Zimmer kosten nicht die Welt. In London liegt das Malmaison zwischen riesigen Bäumen am ruhigen Charterhouse Square gleich neben der Kapelle des Sutton's Hospital aus dem 17. Jahrhundert. Ein Privileg im sonst so belebten Clerkenwell. Die Lobby wirkt auf den ersten Blick etwas förmlich: Die Stühle sind mit dunklem Samt bezogen, und das Licht an der Veuve Cliquot Bar wirkt gedämpft. Doch eine Napoleon-Büste beim Fahrstuhl und Fotografien von London verraten, dass das Hotel durchaus eine spielerische Seite hat. Unter der Woche steigen im Malmaison vor allem Geschäftsleute ab. An den Wochenenden dient es als Basisstation für Paare, die die Galerien der Gegend besuchen oder die umliegenden Weinbars entdecken wollen. Im Malmaison unbedingt ausprobieren: die ausgezeichneten Bellinis und den Sonntagsbrunch.

Les petits malins derrière la chaîne Malmaison, qui a vu le jour dans le nord de l'Angleterre, sont restés fidèles à leur devise « des lieux authentiques pour des gens authentiques ». Leur hôtel londonien offre des chambres confortables et modernes à des prix raisonnables. Il est situé dans le quartier animé de Clerkenwell mais sur le square paisible de Charterhouse à l'ombre d'arbres géants près de la chapelle de l'hôpital Sutton, qui date du XVIIe siècle. Avec ses fauteuils en velours sombre, son éclairage tamisé et son bar à champagne Veuve Cliquot, le hall paraît sérieux mais le buste de Napoléon menant aux ascenseurs est un clin d'œil. Les murs sont tapissés de vues de Londres. En semaine, le Malmaison accueille surtout des hommes d'affaires mais, le week-end, des couples d'amoureux viennent s'y poser pour faire le tour des galeries et essayer les bars à vin du quartier. Goûtez les Bellini faits maison et ne ratez pas le brunch du dimanche.

Preiskategorie: £.
Zimmer: 97 (2 Suiten).
Restaurant: Brasserie.
Geschichte: Das Hotel wurde nach Schloss Malmaison benannt – ein Geschenk Napoleons an Joséphine. Einst diente es als Unterkunft für die Schwestern des nahe gelegenen Krankenhauses St Bartholomew's.
X-Faktor: Die feinen, eigens für Malmaison hergestellten Badeprodukte kann man mit nach Hause nehmen.
Internet: Kostenloser Breitbandanschluss in allen Zimmern; WiFi in der Lobby und der Brasserie.

Catégorie de prix : £.
Chambres : 97 (2 suites).
Restauration : La Brasserie.
Histoire : Le Malmaison doit son nom au château construit par Napoléon pour Joséphine. Le bâtiment abritait autrefois les infirmières de l'hôpital St Bartholomew.
Le « petit plus » : Le Malmaison a sa propre marque de produits de salle de bains que vous pouvez emporter avec vous en partant.
Internet : Accès haut débit gratuit dans les chambres ; WiFi dans le lobby et la Brasserie.

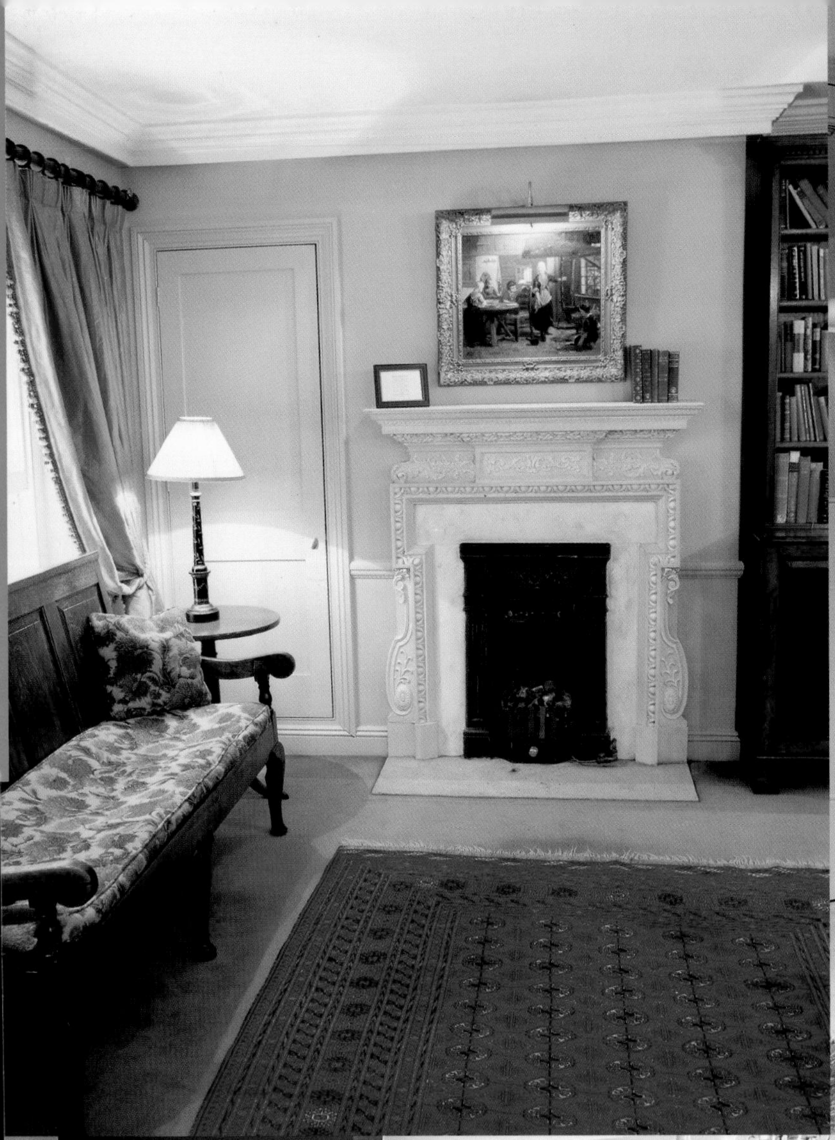

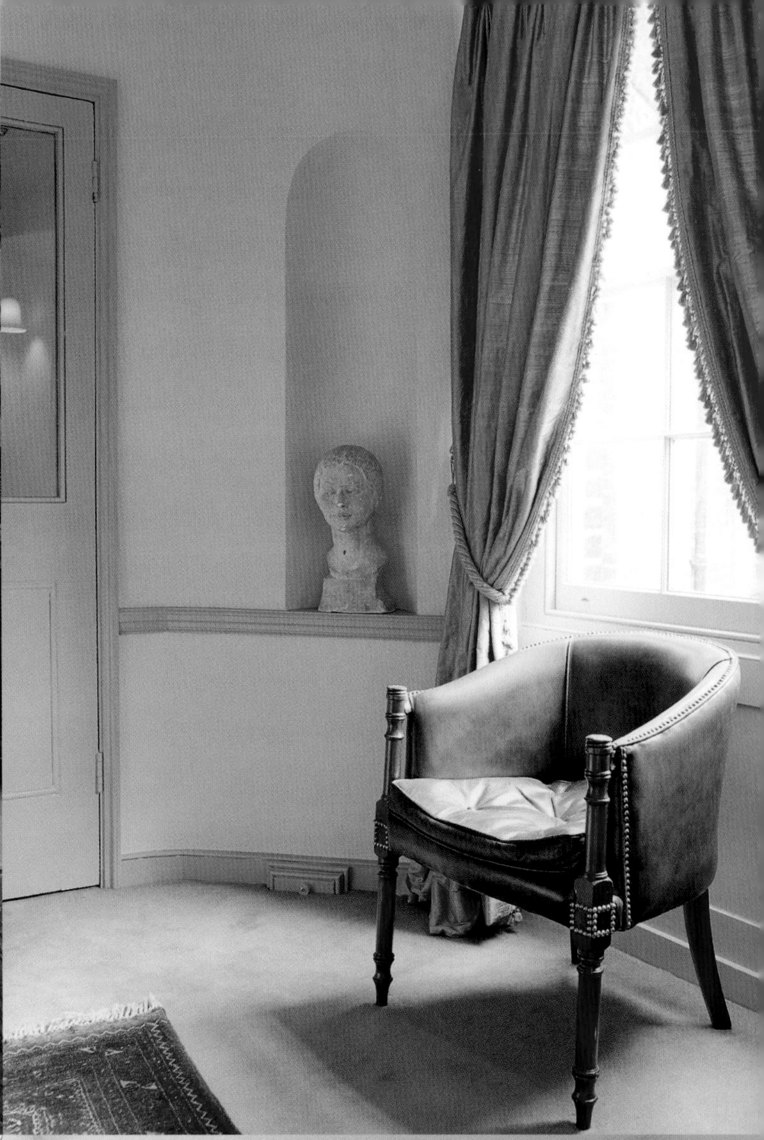

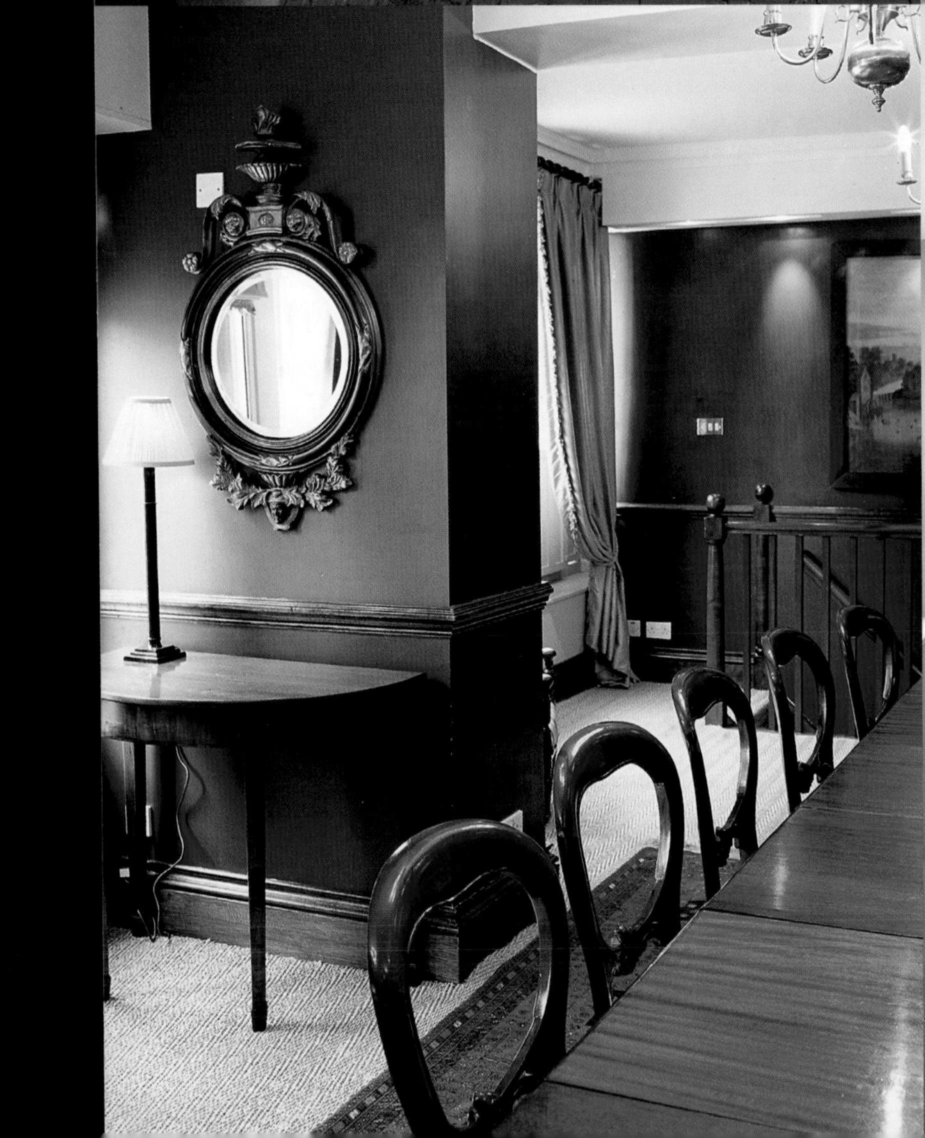

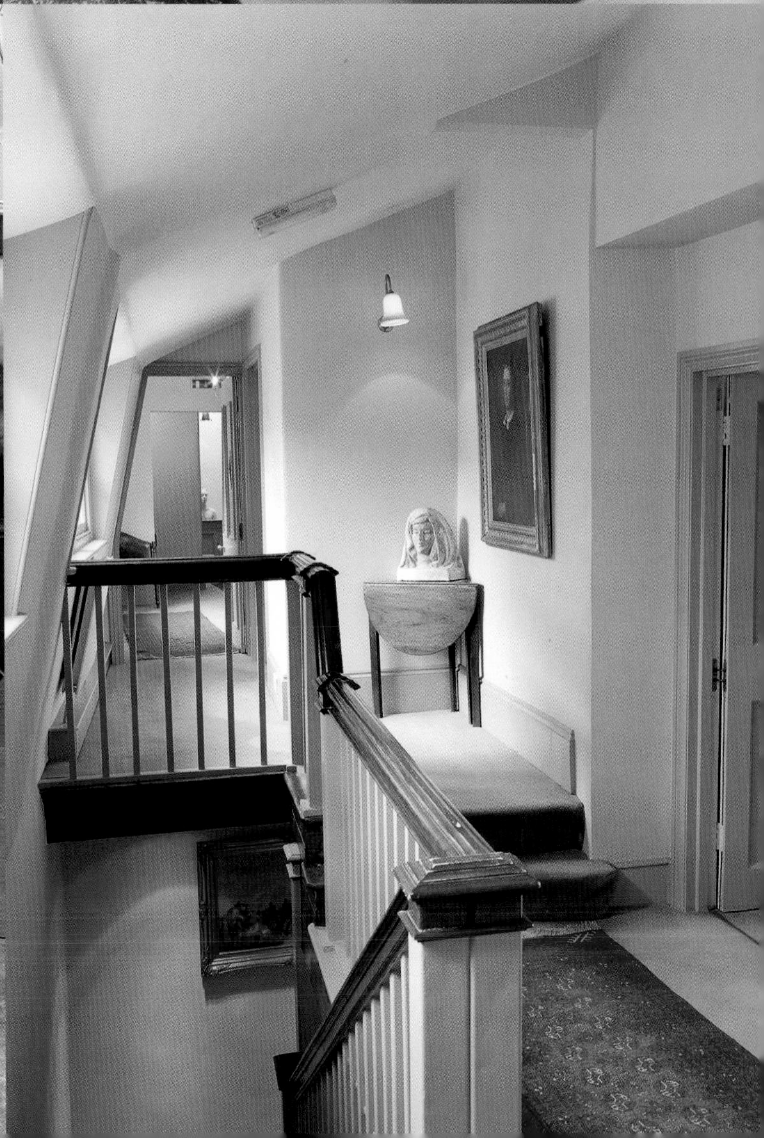

The Rookery

Cowcross Street, London EC1M 6DS
☎ +44 20 7336 0931   📄 +44 20 7336 0932
reservations@rookery.co.uk
www.rookeryhotel.com
Tube: Farringdon

In the mid-18th century the word "rookery" was used to describe a notorious neighbourhood known for criminal activity. Clerkenwell, where The Rookery hotel is located, is a very different place than it once was, though it is no less colourful. It is a one-minute walk from Smithfield Market, one of Europe's largest meat markets, and it's an area full of lively wine bars, pubs, restaurants and cafés. During the week, it hosts creatives in town for business; at weekends, a more fun and indulgent crowd, including Hollywood royalty, checks in. Rooms are spacious and lush, with antiques, dark walls, rich fabrics, beds with four posters or giant wooden headboards. The suite called The Rook's Nest is the cherry on top of the sundae: it is a loft room, replete with Victorian roll-top bathtub-cum-shower in the middle of the room, kinky mirrored headboard and, best of all, a ceiling that electronically slides open to reveal a living room/office balcony up above.

Price category: ££.
Rooms: 33 (1 suite).
Restaurants: None but there is 24-hour room service and many restaurants in the area. Breakfast is served in your room.
History: The three houses date back to the mid-18th century and were once three shops: a baker's, a butcher's and a chemist's. Each of the 33 rooms is named after locals of the time: knights, prostitutes etc.
X-Factor: Delicious-smelling Aveda products in all the bathrooms.
Internet: Complimentary WiFi access for all guests.

Mitte des 18. Jahrhunderts nannte man in London berüchtigte Stadtteile „Rookery". Obschon in Clerkenwell immer noch ein buntes Treiben herrscht, ist von diesem rauen Geist nicht mehr viel übrig geblieben. Das Hotel liegt eine Gehminute vom Smithfield Market, einem der größten Fleischmärkte Europas, und in einer belebten Gegend mit Weinbars, Pubs, Restaurants und Cafés. Unter der Woche steigen im Rookery vor allem Reisende aus dem Kreativbusiness ab, und an den Wochenenden nistet sich hier eine unternehmungslustige Gästeschar ein, darunter auch Hollywood-Prominenz. Die Zimmer bieten viel Platz und sind opulent luxuriös: dunkle Wände, üppige Stoffe, Antiquitäten und Himmelbetten. Die Perle ist die Suite „The Rook's Nest". Sie ist vollgestopft mit Möbeln, Stoffen und Objekten, darunter eine viktorianische Badewanne und ein verspiegeltes Kopfteil am Bett. Damit nicht genug: Wie bei „Sesam öffne dich" schiebt sich die Decke auf Knopfdruck zur Seite und gibt den Blick frei nach oben ins Arbeitszimmer.

Au milieu du XVIIIe siècle, le terme « rookery » désignait un coin malfamé. Clerkenwell a bien changé depuis tout en restant toujours aussi pittoresque. À une minute à pied de Smithfield Market, un des marchés de viande les plus grands d'Europe, ce quartier animé abonde en bars à vin, pubs, restaurant et cafés. Pendant la semaine, l'hôtel accueille surtout des créatifs en ville pour affaires. Le week-end, il voit débarquer une clique plus festive et indulgente, dont des stars de Hollywood. Les chambres sont spacieuses et luxueuses, meublées d'antiquités, décorées de murs sombres, d'étoffes précieuses, de baldaquins ou de têtes de lit monumentales. La suite Rook's Nest est la cerise sur le gâteau : un loft avec une grande baignoire/douche à cylindre au milieu de la chambre, une tête de lit coquine en miroir et, surtout, un plafond qui s'ouvre électroniquement pour révéler un salon/bureau en mezzanine.

Preiskategorie: ££.
Zimmer: 33 (1 Suite).
Restaurants: Keines. Jedoch viele Restaurants in der Umgebung und 24-Stunden-Zimmerservice. Das Frühstück wird aufs Zimmer gebracht.
Geschichte: Die drei Häuser stammen aus dem 18. Jahrhundert: eine Bäckerei, eine Metzgerei und eine Apotheke. Jedes der 33 Zimmer wurde nach den Bewohnern der damaligen Zeit benannt: Ritter, Kurtisanen usw.
X-Faktor: In den Badezimmern stehen fein riechende Produkte von Aveda.
Internet: Kostenloser WiFi-Zugang.

Catégorie de prix : ££.
Chambres : 33 (1 suite).
Restauration : Service dans les chambres 24h/24. Le quartier abonde en restaurants. Petit-déjeuner servi dans les chambres.
Histoire : Les trois maisons datent du milieu du XVIIIe siècle et abritaient autrefois un boulanger, un boucher et une pharmacie. Chacune des 33 chambres porte le nom d'occupants d'antan : chevalier, prostituée, etc.
Le « petit plus » : Les produits Aveda, sentant délicieusement bon dans les salles de bains.
Internet : Accès WiFi gratuit.

William Pettit Griffith

Bar Menu

BRUSCHETTA WITH PROSCIUTTO DI
PARMA & FRESH PEAR

BUFFALO MOZZARELLA WITH
ROAST BEETROOT, ROCKET &
BALSAMIC VINEGAR

SMOKED SALMON WITH ROCKET,
WATERCRESS & FRESH HORSERADISH

GRANSEOLA ROLLE WITH PICKLED
FIG & SARDINIAN FLATBREAD

SMALL PIZZA WITH SCAMORZA,
TAGGIASCHE NICOISE OLIVES
ROCKET & ROSEMARY

SMALL PIZZA WITH SPECK,
OYSTER MUSHROOMS & FIOR
LATTE

ALL AT £6.50

MARINATED OLIVES

ROAST ALMONDS

ROAST PISTACHIOS

ALL AT £3.50

PLEASE ORDER
AT THE HATCH

The Zetter

86–88 Clerkenwell Road, London EC1M 5RJ
☎ +44 20 7324 4444   🖷 +44 20 7324 4445
reservations@thezetter.com
www.thezetter.com
Tube: Farringdon

Original and affordable, contemporary but not minimalist, The Zetter Restaurant & Rooms is a modern-day inn with a light-hearted attitude. The Zetter is located in a former 19th-century warehouse and attracts those who want to stay well away from the tourist trail. Its quirky, cosy rooms and rooftop studios, which come with terraces looking over the city and St John's Square (St John's Gate, now called the Priory Gate, was built in 1504 and its gateway is still in the square), set it apart from traditional hotels. Furthermore, rooms are decorated with colourful textiles, unique furniture and Penguin Classics on bedside tables. Each bed is decorated with a cute Zetter throw but please avoid putting these in your bag when you leave. Don't miss out on chef Diego Jacquet's seasonal, light modern Mediterranean menu. Also, sample the delicious Zetter water, collected from the hotel's well, 1,500 ft underground.

Price category: ££.
Rooms: 59 (7 rooftop studios).
Restaurant: The Zetter Restaurant.
History: The Zetter is housed in a Victorian Grade II listed building. It used to be the Zetter Football Pools Hall headquarters.
X-Factor: Each room has a bright, wool-knit hot-water bottle but, sadly, these must stay in the room.
Internet: Broadband £10 per day/WiFi £15 per day.

The Zetter Restaurant & Rooms ist die zeitgemäße – aber nicht übertrieben minimalistische – Version des guten alten Gasthauses. Es liegt in einem ehemaligen Lagerhaus aus dem 19. Jahrhundert und zieht Leute an, die das Außergewöhnliche suchen, ohne dabei allzu tief in die Tasche greifen zu müssen, und vor allem die üblichen Touristenpfade meiden. Von den kuschligen Zimmern und Dachterrassen-Studios mit ungewöhnlichem Möbelmix kann man über die City und den St John's Square blicken. (Das Tor des St John's Gate, heute Priory Gate, wurde übrigens 1504 gebaut und befindet sich heute noch auf dem St John's Square.) Besonders schön: die farbigen Textilien, die Literaturklassiker auf dem Nachttisch und die bunten Bettdecken mit Zetter-Logos. Auf jeden Fall im Restaurant Diego Jacquets leichte saisonale Mittelmeerküche ausprobieren. Dazu Zetter-Wasser bestellen: Es stammt aus der hoteleigenen Quelle – sie liegt 457 Meter unter der Erde.

Original et abordable, contemporain sans être minimaliste, le Zetter est une auberge décontractée des temps modernes. Située dans un ancien entrepôt du XIXᵉ siècle, elle accueille ceux qui préfèrent éviter les sentiers battus touristiques. Elle se distingue des hôtels traditionnels par ses chambres douillettes décorées de tissus colorés, de meubles uniques, de classiques en livre de poche sur les tables de chevet, ainsi que par ses studios sur le toit agrémentés de terrasses dominant St Johns Square (bâti en 1504, la porte de St John, aujourd'hui The Priory Gate, se dresse toujours au milieu du square). Chaque lit est orné d'un charmant plaid Zetter que l'on évitera de glisser dans ses bagages. Ne manquez pas la cuisine méditerranéenne légère et moderne à base de produits de saison du chef Diego Jacquet, ainsi que la délicieuse eau Zetter, puisée dans le puits de l'hôtel, profond de 457 mètres.

Preiskategorie: ££.
Zimmer: 59 (7 Dachterrassen-Studios).
Restaurant: The Zetter Restaurant.
Geschichte: Das viktorianische Zetter, einst der Hauptsitz der Zetter Football Pools Hall, steht unter Denkmalschutz.
X-Faktor: Jedes Zimmer ist mit einer bunt bestrickten Wärmflasche ausgestattet – leider darf man diese nicht mit nach Hause nehmen.
Internet: Breitbandanschluss für 10 £ pro Tag; WiFi-Zugang für 15 £ pro Tag.

Catégorie de prix : ££.
Chambres : 59 (7 studios sur le toit).
Restauration : The Zetter Restaurant.
Histoire : Le Zetter se trouve dans un bâtiment victorien classé, autrefois le siège du Zetter Football Pools Hall.
Le « petit plus » : Des bouillottes en tricot dans les chambres que, hélas, on ne peut pas emporter.
Internet : Accès haut débit pour 10 £ par jour ; WiFi 15 £ par jour.

Restaurants

Fish of the day
Oysters
Savoy Cab

Rules

NAKED CHEF

THE COACH & HORSES

Golden Hind

St. John

Grenadier

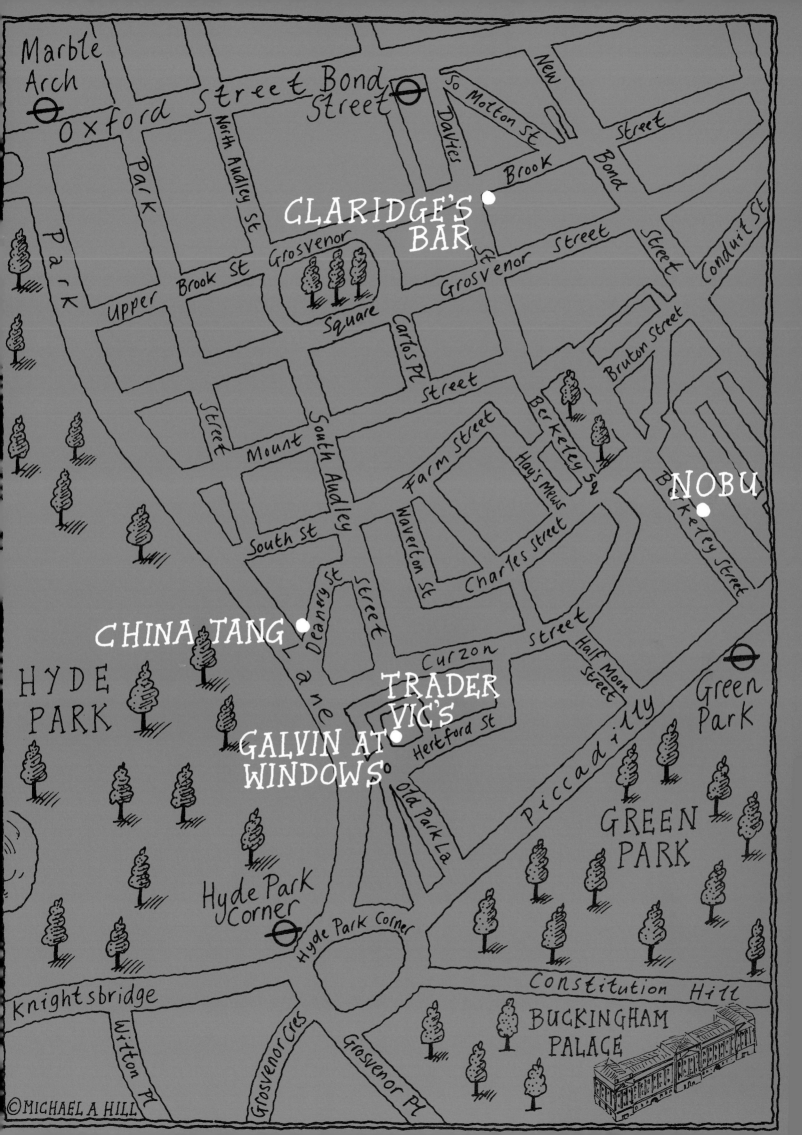

© MICHAEL A HILL

Nobu Berkeley St

15 Berkeley Street
London W1J 8DY
☎ +44 20 7290 9222
www.noburestaurants.com
Tube: Green Park

Nobu Matsuhisa's second restaurant in London is a bit cooler and more glamorous than his first at the Metropolitan Hotel. In addition to the Nobu classics, the menu includes dishes prepared in a Japanese wood oven – anyone who has tasted the Wagyu Tataki will understand why the cuisine was awarded a Michelin star after just five months. After dinner the guests enjoy themselves in the glamorous Lounge Bar – along with socialites like Jade Jagger.

Das zweite Londoner Restaurant von Nobu Matsuhisa ist noch ein bisschen cooler und glamouröser als sein erstes Lokal im Metropolitan Hotel. Neben den Nobu-Klassikern stehen hier auch im japanischen Holzofen zubereitete Gerichte auf der Karte – wer das Wagyu Tataki gekostet hat, versteht, warum über die Küche nur fünf Monate nach Eröffnung bereits ein Michelin-Stern leuchtete. Nach dem Dinner feiern die Gäste in der glamourösen Lounge Bar – gemeinsam mit Socialites wie Jade Jagger.

Le deuxième restaurant londonien de Nobu Matsuhisa est encore un peu plus cool et glamoureux que son premier établissement au Metropolitan Hotel. Outre les classiques de Nobu, la carte propose aussi des plats préparés dans un four à bois japonais. Celui qui a déjà goûté au Wagyu Tataki comprend pourquoi le restaurant a décroché une étoile au Guide Michelin cinq mois seulement après son ouverture. Après le dîner les clients font la fête au Lounge Bar glamoureux, en compagnie de socialites comme Jade Jagger.

Interior: Very sophisticated: David Collins has combined Japanese minimalism with romantic elements.
Open: Mon–Fri midday–2.15pm, Mon–Wed 6–11pm, Thu–Sat 6–midnight, Sun 6–9.15pm.
Prices: Menu from £50 (lunch) and £70 (dinner).
X-Factor: If you don't want to have to wait for a table, the sushi bar is ideal for a delicious meal.

Interieur: Sehr sophisticated: David Collins kombinierte japanischen Minimalismus mit romantischen Elementen.
Öffnungszeiten: Mo–Fr 12–14.15, Mo–Mi 18–23, Do–Sa 18–24, So 18–21.15 Uhr.
Preise: Menü ab 50 £ (Lunch) und 70 £ (Dinner).
X-Faktor: Wenn man nicht auf einen Tisch warten möchte, ist die Sushi-Bar ideal für ein köstliches Essen.

Intérieur : Très sophistiqué : David Collins combine le minimalisme japonais et les éléments romantiques.
Horaires d'ouverture : Lun-Ven 12h–14h15, Lun-Mer 18h– 23h, Jeu-Sam 18h–24h, Dim 18h–21h15.
Prix : Menu à partir de 50 £ (déjeuner) et 70 £ (dîner).
Le « petit plus » : Pour ceux qui ne désirent pas attendre qu'une table soit libre, le bar aux sushis propose des plats succulents.

Claridge's Bar

Davies Street/Brook Street, London W1K 2JQ
☎ +44 20 7629 8860
www.claridges.co.uk
Tube: Bond Street

Claridge's Bar hosts the most stylish and interesting people in the media, business and art world. It was designed by David Collins, which means that it is glamorous and has beautiful details such as a silver-leafed ceiling and rich red banquettes. Languish in the gorgeous Art Deco surroundings and sip champagne: it is the drink of choice with a great list of special and rare ones for the chic clientele.

Die Claridge's Bar ist Treffpunkt gestylter und interessanter Leute aus der Medien- und Kunstszene. Interior-Designer David Collins hat der Bar mit glamourösen, wunderschönen Details, wie der versilberten Decke und den sattroten Sitzbänken, seinen Stempel aufgesetzt. Hier kann man in traumhaftem Art-déco-Dekor schwelgen und dabei an einer der außergewöhnlichen Champagner-Raritäten nippen.

Le Claridge's Bar est l'antre des personnalités les plus chics et intéressantes des médias et du monde de l'art. L'élégant décor Art Déco signé David Collins inclut de superbes détails tels que le plafond à la feuille d'argent et les banquettes en cuir rouge. Prélassez-vous devant une coupe de champagne, la carte propose à sa clientèle sélecte une magnifique liste de cuvées rares et spéciales.

Interior: The Art Deco bar by David Collins not only has comfortable leather seats, it is also bathed in a delightfully flattering light.
Open: Mon–Sat midday–1am, Sun 4pm–midnight.
Prices: Cocktails from £11.50.
X-Factor: The excellent barfood, such as the Bento Boxes or hummus sandwiches.

Interieur: Die Bar im Art-déco-Stil von David Collins hat nicht nur bequeme Ledersessel, sondern auch erfreulich schmeichelndes Licht.
Öffnungszeiten: Mo–Sa 12–1, So 16–24 Uhr.
Preise: Cocktails ab 11,50 £.
X-Faktor: Die exzellenten Bar-Snacks wie die Bento Boxes oder Hummus-Sandwiches.

Intérieur : Le bar Art Déco de David Collins a non seulement des fauteuils en cuir confortables, mais aussi un éclairage particulièrement flatteur.
Horaires d'ouverture : Lun–Sam 12h–1h, Dim 16h–24h.
Prix : Cocktails à partir de 11,50 £.
Le « petit plus » : Les snacks chics comme les Bento Boxes ou les sandwichs-houmus.

China Tang

The Dorchester on Park Lane
London W1K 1QA
☎ +44 20 7629 9988
www.thedorchester.com
Tube: Hyde Park Corner

China Tang (a David Tang creation) is altogether charming and as glamorous as The Dorchester is flashy. Opt for one of the low banquettes, order a Cosmopolitan (avoid the wine list, which is sadly lacking) and watch the wonderfully mixed crowd. Rupert Everett is as likely to be there with a gaggle of beautiful men as is a grand American dame with her facelift and appropriately suave husband.

China Tang, ein Projekt des Lifestyle-Unternehmers David Tang, ist so glamourös, dass selbst das Dorchester erblasst. Von einem der Sitzbänke lässt sich die bunt gemischte Szenerie schön beobachten. Gut möglich, Rupert Everett mit seiner Entourage anzutreffen oder aber eine der eleganten, gelifteten Amerikanerinnen mit entsprechend gepflegtem Gatten an der Seite. Da die Weinliste nicht beeindruckt, besser einen Cosmopolitan bestellen.

Le China Tang (créé par David Tang) est aussi charmant et chic que le Dorchester est clinquant. Préférez les banquettes basses, commandez un Cosmopolitan (la carte des vins n'est pas à la hauteur) et observez la clientèle bigarrée. Vous y croiserez peut-être Rupert Everett entouré de jolis garçons ainsi que des grandes dames américaines liftées accompagnées de leurs maris dociles.

Interior: The ambience, inspired by the Art Deco style of the 1920s China Clubs, has been created with works of traditional and contemporary Chinese art personally selected by David Tang.
Open: Mon–Fri 11am–3.30pm (Sat/Sun till 4pm); Mon–Sun 5.30pm–midnight.
Prices: Dishes £6–60.
X-Factor: The Peking Duck with prune sauce served rolled in a thin pancake.

Interieur: Das vom Art-déco-Stil der China Clubs in den 1920er-Jahren inspirierte Ambiente hat David Tang persönlich mit ausgesuchten Werken traditioneller und zeitgenössischer chinesischer Kunst geschmückt.
Öffnungszeiten: Mo–Fr 11–15.30 (Sa/So bis 16); Mo–So 17.30–24 Uhr.
Preise: Gerichte 6–60 £.
X-Faktor: Die Peking-Ente mit Pflaumensauce, eingerollt in dünne Pfannkuchen.

Intérieur : En sélectionnant des œuvres d'art chinoises traditionnelles et contemporaines, David Tang a recréé en personne l'ambiance inspirée du style Art déco des clubs chinois dans les années 1920.
Horaires d'ouverture : Lun–Ven 11h–15h30 (Sam/Dim jusqu'à 16h) ; Lun–Dim 17h30–24h.
Prix : Plats 6–60 £.
Le « petit plus » : Le canard à la sauce aux pruneaux, roulé dans de fines crêpes.

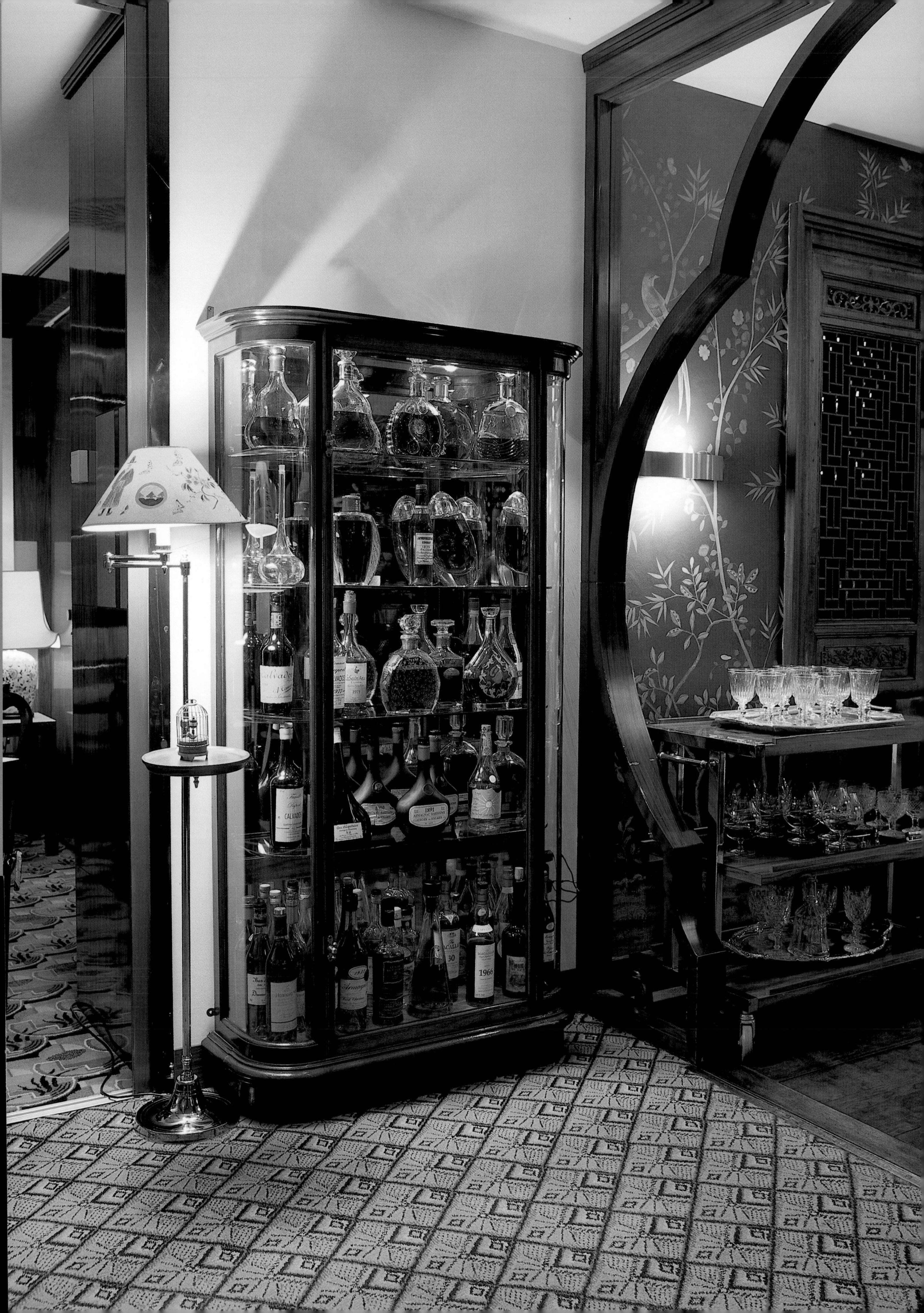

Trader Vic's

The London Hilton on Park Lane
22 Park Lane, London W1Y 4BE
☎ +44 20 7208 4113
www.tradervics.com
Tube: Hyde Park Corner

There are some restaurants and bars you dare not enter for fear you are not cool enough. Before venturing into Trader Vic's in the basement of the London Hilton on Park Lane, you will check your attitude in at the door and walk in with the knowledge that tacky Tiki can sometimes be far more fun than trendy. Don't let the faux South Pacific style put you off: go with good friends, order a Mai Tai and relax.

Manchmal steht man vor einem Restaurant oder einer Bar und traut sich kaum hinein, so cool sind sie. Bei Trader Vic's im London Hilton on Park Lane ist es genau umgekehrt. Kaum drinnen, wird man jedoch feststellen, dass kitschiger Tiki-Stil viel mehr Spaß machen kann als eine supercoole Attitüde. Man lasse sich also vom südpazifischen Imitationsdekor nicht abschrecken. Ein Mai Tai zusammen mit ein paar guten Freunden ist hier ein toller Spaß.

Il y a des restaurants et des bars où l'on n'ose à peine entrer de peur de faire tache. Avant de descendre au sous-sol du London Hilton on Park Lane, où se trouve Trader Vic's, laissez vos appréhensions à la porte et plongez-vous sans vergogne dans l'atmosphère Tiki pur toc. Allez-y avec des amis, commandez un Mai Tai et détendez-vous.

Interior: French-Polynesian décor in Tiki style with plenty of raffia and bamboo.
Open: Mon–Thur midday–1am, Fri midday–3am, Sat 6pm–3am, Sun 6–11.30pm.
Prices: Mai Tai £8, dishes from £8.50.
X-Factor: The dishes prepared in Chinese wood ovens from the time of the Han Dynasty.

Interieur: Südseedekor im Tiki-Stil mit viel Bast und Bambus.
Öffnungszeiten: Mo–Do 12–1, Fr 12–3, Sa 18–3, So 18–23.30 Uhr.
Preise: Mai Tai 8 £, Gerichte ab 8,50 £.
X-Faktor: Die Gerichte, die in chinesischen Holzfeueröfen aus der Zeit der Han-Dynastie zubereitet werden.

Intérieur : Décor des mers du Sud dans le style tiki avec raphia et bambou à profusion.
Horaires d'ouverture : Lun–Jeu 12h–1h, Ven 12h–3h, Sam 18h–3h, Dim 18h–23h30.
Prix : Mai Tai 8 £, plats à partir de 8,50 £.
Le « petit plus » : Les plats préparés dans les fours à bois datant de la dynastie Han.

Galvin at Windows

The London Hilton on Park Lane,
22 Park Lane, London W1K 1BE
☎ +44 20 7208 4021
www.hilton.co.uk/londonparklane
Tube: Hyde Park Corner

Galvin at Windows closely follows brothers Chris and Jeff Galvin's successful launch of Galvin Bistrot de Luxe on Baker Street earlier in 2006. Go for the views from the 28th floor of the London Hilton on Park Lane, they are unbeatable at night. Drink a cocktail while you gaze out the window towards Hyde Park and Buckingham Palace. You may even catch a glimpse of the Queen.

Die Brüder Chris und Jeff Galvin haben mit dem Galvin Bistrot de Luxe an der Baker Street bereits eine Erfolgsformel gefunden. Das Galvin at Windows wurde Anfang 2006 im 28. Stockwerk des London Hilton auf der Park Lane eröffnet. Die Aussicht hier ist spektakulär, vor allem nachts. Tipp: An einem Cocktail nuckeln, dabei Richtung Hyde Park und Buckingham Palace gucken und vielleicht einen Blick auf die Queen erhaschen.

Galvin at Windows a ouvert peu après l'inauguration en 2006 du très branché Galvin Bistrot de Luxe des frères Chris et Jeff Galvin sur Baker Street. Les vues depuis le 28e étage du London Hilton de Park Lane sont imprenables. Prenez un cocktail en contemplant Hyde Park et le palais de Buckingham. Vous apercevrez peut-être la reine.

Interior: The elegant interior by Keith Hobbs draws on a subdued range of colours, from cream, to gentle pastel green, to black and silver.
Open: Mon–Thur 10–1am, Fri 10–3am, Sat 5.30pm–3am, Sun 10am–10.30pm.
Prices: Drinks and dishes from £10.
X-Factor: The exquisitely modern French cuisine has already earned the restaurant several prizes.

Interieur: Das elegante Interior von Keith Hobbs beruht auf einer gedämpften Farbpalette in Crème, zartem Lindgrün, Schwarz und Silber.
Öffnungszeiten: Mo–Do 10–1, Fr 10–3, Sa 17.30–3, So 10–22.30 Uhr.
Preise: Drinks und Gerichte ab 10 £.
X-Faktor: Die exquisite moderne französische Küche brachte dem Lokal bereits mehrere Preise ein.

Intérieur : L'élégant intérieur de Keith Hobbs est décoré dans une palette de tons assourdis : crème, vert tendre, noir et argent.
Horaires d'ouverture : Lun–Jeu 10h–1h, Ven 10h– 3h, Sam 17h30–3h, Dim 10h– 22h30.
Prix : Boissons et plats à partir de 10 £.
Le « petit plus » : L'excellente cuisine française moderne a valu de nombreux prix à l'établissement.

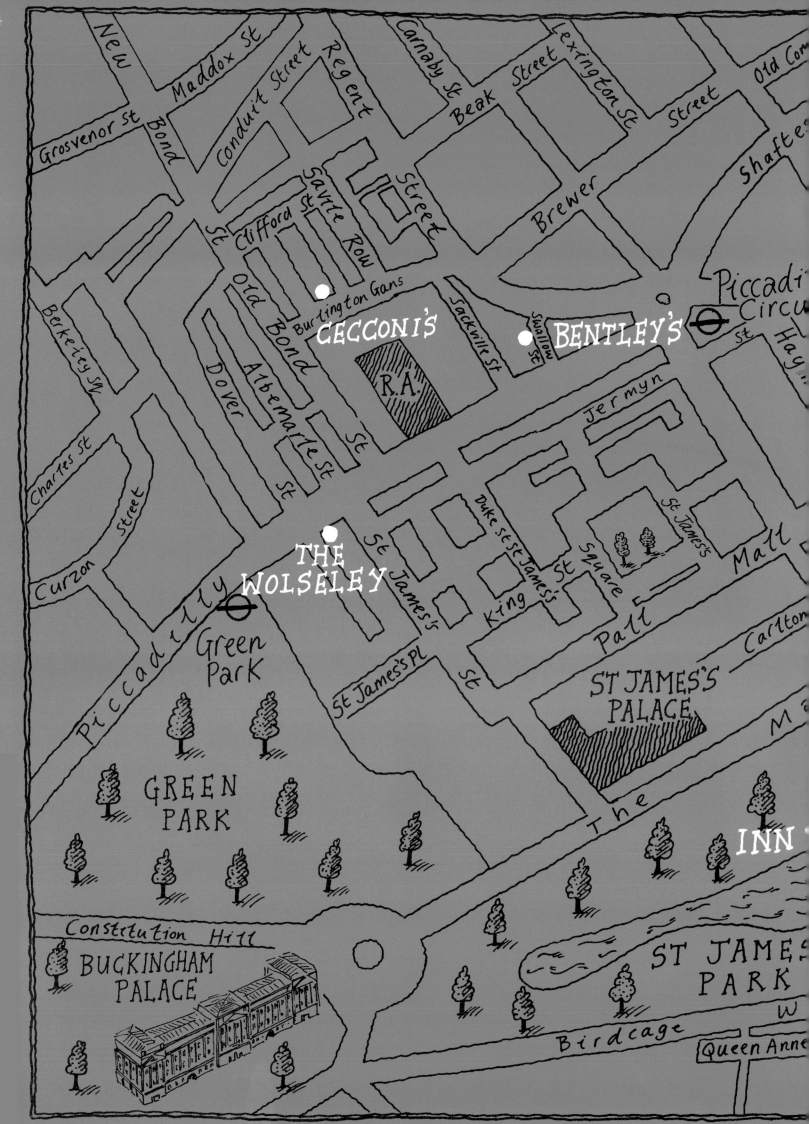

Restaurants

©MICHAELA HILL

The Wolseley

160 Piccadilly, London W1J 9EB
☎ +44 20 7499 6996
www.thewolseley.com
Tube: Green Park

Since its opening in 2003, the great and good of London have descended in droves. The Venetian/Florentine influences of this 1921 building (a car showroom, originally) was respected when, in 2003, designer David Collins converted it into a grand, chandeliered space. It's hard to get a dinner booking but drop in for breakfast or afternoon tea. Be nice to staff: they are British politeness personified.

Seit der Eröffnung von 2003 pilgert ganz London hierher. Designer David Collins hat die venezianischen und florentinischen Elemente des Gebäudes bewahrt und aus dem ehemaligen Auto-Showroom einen prachtvollen Raum gestaltet. Eine Reservierung für ein Dinner zu erhalten ist praktisch unmöglich; für ein Frühstück oder einen Afternoon Tea sollte es allerdings klappen. Das Personal ist übrigens die Verkörperung britischer Höflichkeit.

Depuis son ouverture en 2003, le tout Londres s'y rue. Les influences vénitiennes et florentines de cet ancien showroom de voitures bâti en 1921 ont été préservées par David Collins qui l'a converti en espace grandiose orné de lustres. Obtenir une table pour dîner est difficile mais passez donc prendre le petit-déjeuner ou le thé. Soyez gentil avec le personnel : ils sont la politesse anglaise incarnée.

Interior: In 1921 Wolseley Motors Limited commissioned the architect William Curtis Green to design a luxurious showroom. The flamboyant pillars, arches and staircases exhibit Venetian and Florentine influences.
Open: Mon–Fri 7am–midnight, Sat 8am–midnight, Sun 8am–11pm.
Prices: Meals £6–22.
X-Factor: The delicious Wolseley English Breakfast Tea and Afternoon Blend can be ordered online.

Interieur: 1921 beauftragte Wolseley Motors William Curtis Green, einen luxuriösen Showroom zu entwerfen: Venezianisch-florentinische Einflüsse zeigen sich in den grandiosen Säulen, Bögen und Treppen.
Öffnungszeiten: Mo–Fr 7–24, Sa 8–24, So 8–23 Uhr.
Preise: Gerichte 6–22 £.
X-Faktor: Man kann den köstlichen English Breakfast Tea und Afternoon Blend online bestellen.

Intérieur : En 1921, Wolseley Motors demanda à William Curtis Green de créer un showroom luxueux. Les influences vénitiennes et florentines se constatent dans les colonnes, arcs et escaliers grandioses.
Horaires d'ouverture : Lun–Ven 7h–24h, Sam 8h–24h, Dim 8h–23h.
Prix : Plats 6–22 £.
Le « petit plus » : Il est possible de commander en ligne le délicieux English Breakfast Tea et Afternoon Blend de Wolseley.

Inn The Park

St James's Park
Lakeside, London SW1A 2BJ
☎ +44 20 7451 9999
www.innthepark.com
Tube: St James's Park/Charing Cross

The lakeside Inn The Park (owned by Oliver Peyton) offers the experience of dining in one of the loveliest parks in London without ever having to leave the comfort of the Tom Dixon-designed restaurant. The restaurant is open for breakfast, lunch, tea and dinner and the focus is on British cuisine.

Das Inn The Park von Oliver Peyton liegt direkt am See. Hier kann man mitten in einem der schönsten Parks Londons essen gehen, und trotz Nähe zur Natur muss man im von Designer Tom Dixon gestalteten Restaurant auf Komfort nicht verzichten. Für Frühstück, Mittagessen, Tee und Abendessen geöffnet. Die Küche ist hauptsächlich britisch.

Appartenant à Oliver Peyton, ce restaurant au bord du lac vous permet de dîner dans un des plus beaux parcs de Londres sans quitter le confort d'un décor signé Tom Dixon. Ouvert pour le petit-déjeuner, le déjeuner, le goûter et le dîner, avec une cuisine typiquement british.

Interior: This building of naturally-weathered larch wood, designed by Hopkins Architects, fits harmoniously into the park, which was laid out in 1828.
Open: Mon–Fri 8–11 am (Sat/Sun from 9am); Mon–Fri midday–3pm (Sat/Sun till 4pm); Tues–Sun 5–10pm.
Prices: Dishes £6–18.50.
X-Factor: The café offers take-away snacks for a picnic in the park.

Interieur: Das von Hopkins Architects entworfene Gebäude aus natürlich verwitterndem Lärchenholz fügt sich harmonisch in dem 1828 angelegten Park ein.
Öffnungszeiten: Mo–Fr 8–11 (Sa/So ab 9); Mo–Fr 12–15 (Sa/So bis 16); Di–So 17–22 Uhr.
Preise: Gerichte 6–18,50 £.
X-Faktor: Das Café bietet Snacks zum Mitnehmen für ein Picknick im Park an.

Intérieur : Conçu par Hopkins Architects, le bâtiment en bois de mélèze, naturellement rongé par le temps, s'harmonise avec le parc aménagé en 1828.
Horaires d'ouverture : Lun–Ven 8h–11h (Sam/Dim à partir de 9h) ; Lun–Ven 12h–15h (Sam/Dim jusqu'à 16h) ; Mar–Dim 17h–22h.
Prix : Plats 6–18,50 £.
Le « petit plus » : Le café propose des snacks à emporter pour un pique-nique dans le parc.

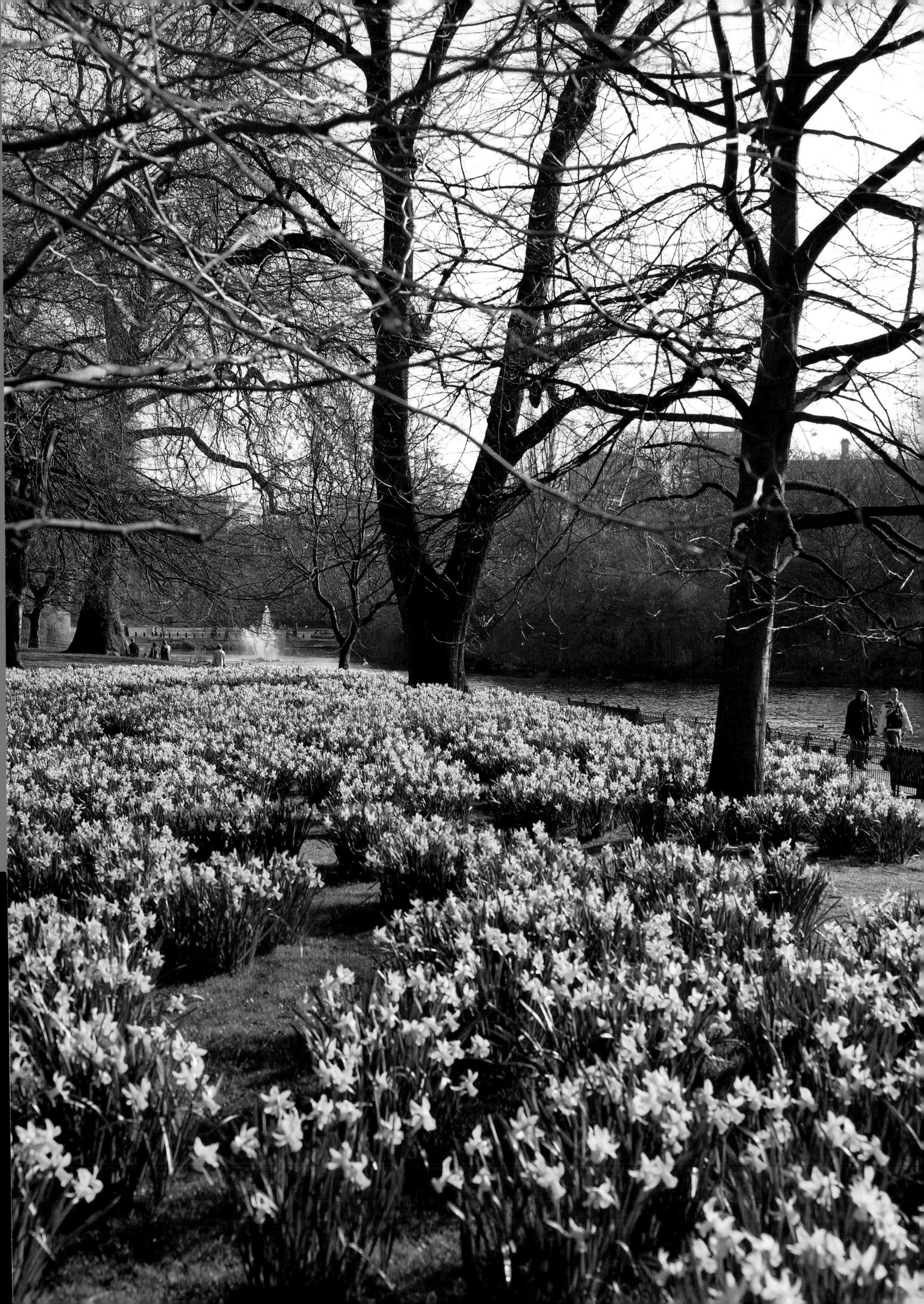

Cecconi's

5a Burlington Gardens, London W1S 3EP
☎ +44 20 7434 1500
www.cecconis.co.uk
Tube: Piccadilly Circus/Green Park

When Enzo Cecconi, formerly manager of the restaurant Cipriani in Venice, came to London in 1978 and set up Cecconi's, it became a favourite among the rich, the beautiful and the aristocracy. They were as enthusiastic for his food as for his show cooking. During Ascot Week in the 1980s it was quite possible to encounter several royal families at lunch there at one time. Today the restaurant is no longer owned by the Cecconi family, but still serves classic Italian cuisine. The "cicchetti", which are similar to tapas, taste especially good.

Als Enzo Cecconi, einst Manager des Restaurants Cipriani in Venedig, 1978 nach London kam, schuf er mit dem Cecconi's einen Lieblingsplatz der Reichen, Schönen und Adligen – sie waren von seiner Küche ebenso begeistert wie von seinem Showcooking. Während der Ascot-Wochen in den 1980ern konnte man hier durchaus gleich mehrere Königsfamilien beim Lunch antreffen. Heute ist das Lokal nicht mehr in Familienbesitz, aber noch immer klassisch italienisch; besonders köstlich sind die den Tapas verwandten „Cicchetti".

Lorsqu'Enzo Cecconi, l'ancien manager du restaurant Cipriani à Venise, est arrivé à Londres en 1978, il a créé le Cecconi's et avec lui le rendez-vous préféré d'une clientèle aristocratique et huppée, ravie par sa cuisine autant que par son show-cooking. Durant le meeting annuel du Royal Ascot au cours des années 1980, on pouvait rencontrer ici plusieurs familles royales en train de déjeuner. Si le restaurant a cessé d'être une propriété familiale, sa cuisine est restée classiquement italienne ; les « cicchetti » qui rappellent les tapas espagnoles sont délicieuses.

Interior: The whole restaurant was renovated in 2005 and re-designed by Ilse Crawford with a view to its Venetian roots.
Open: Mon–Fri 7–1am, Sat 8–1am, Sun 8–12.30am.
Prices: Coffee £2.50, dishes £4–35.
X-Factor: The Bellinis.

Interieur: 2005 wurde das gesamte Restaurant renoviert und von Ilse Crawford im Hinblick auf seine venezianischen Wurzeln neu gestaltet.
Öffnungszeiten: Mo–Fr 7–1, Sa 8–1, So 8–0.30 Uhr.
Preise: Kaffee 2,50 £, Gerichte 4–35 £.
X-Faktor: Die Bellinis.

Intérieur : Complètement rénové en 2005, le restaurant a été redécoré par Ilse Crawford qui s'est inspirée de ses racines vénitiennes.
Horaires d'ouverture : Lun–Ven 7h–1h, Sam 8h–1h, Dim 8h–0h30.
Prix : Café 2,50 £, plats 4–35 £.
Le « petit plus » : Les Bellinis.

Bentley's

11–15 Swallow Street, London W1B 4DG
☎ +44 20 7734 4756
www.bentleys.org
Tube: Piccadilly Circus

The 1916 Oyster Bar was bought, refurbished and opened in 2005 by one of London's most renowned chefs, Richard Corrigan, who also has his hands on the Michelin-starred Lindsay House in Soho. This acquisition is rightly famous for its oysters. The downstairs bar is also perfect for relaxing with a drink if dinner seems a bit much. This is one of London's fantastic fish restaurants: both in terms of ambience and clientele.

Die seit 1916 bestehende Austernbar hat Richard Corrigan 2005 gekauft, umgebaut und wiedereröffnet. Er gehört zu den renommiertesten Küchenchefs Londons – ihm gehört auch das mit einem Michelin-Stern ausgezeichnete Lindsay House in Soho. Für Gäste ohne Hunger gibt's im Untergeschoss eine Bar, an der man sich bei einem Drink entspannen kann. Bentley's ist eines der klassischen Londoner Fischrestaurants – mit entsprechendem Ambiente.

L'établissement datant de 1916 a été racheté et restauré en 2005 par l'un des chefs les plus réputés de Londres, Richard Corrigan (également à l'œuvre à la Lindsay House à Soho, distinguée par Michelin), Il est célèbre à juste titre pour ses huîtres. Si vous ne voulez pas dîner, le bar au sous-sol est très agréable. Ambiance et clientèle distinguées, un classique en matière de restaurants de poissons.

Interior: Luxurious understatement.
Open: Mon–Sat midday–midnight, Sun till 10pm.
Prices: 6 oysters from £9.25.
X-Factor: For guests who wish to imitate his creations, Richard Corrigan's best recipes are available in two cookery books.

Interieur: Luxuriöses Understatement.
Öffnungszeiten: Mo–Sa 12–24, So bis 22 Uhr.
Preise: 6 Austern ab 9,25 £.
X-Faktor: Gästen, die seine Kreationen nachkochen möchten, verrät Richard Corrigan die besten Rezepte in zwei Kochbüchern.

Intérieur : Understatement luxueux.
Horaires d'ouverture : Lun–Sam 12h–24h, Dim jusqu'à 22h.
Prix : 6 huîtres à partir de 9,25 £.
Le « petit plus » : À ses clients qui ont aimé ses créations Richard Corrigan révèle ses meilleures recettes dans deux livres de cuisine.

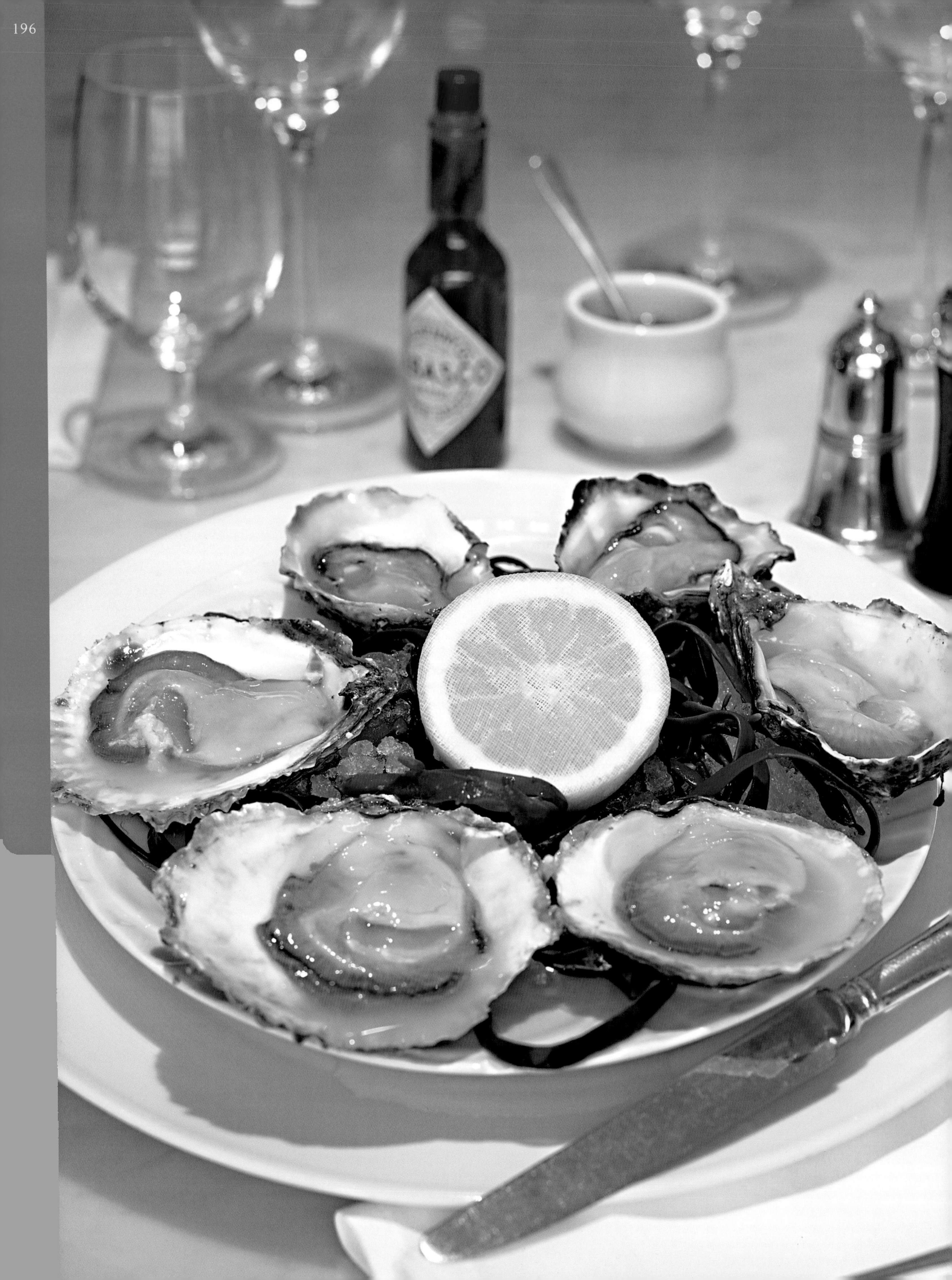

Andrew Edmunds

46 Lexington Street, London W1F 0LP
☎ +44 20 7437 5708
Tube: Piccadilly Circus/Oxford Circus

Unpretentious and reliable, this long-running bistro is many Londoners' favourite restaurant. From the cream-coloured walls and chalkboard menus to the pew seating and small vases of flowers on the tables, every detail is seen to. The menu focuses on high-quality seasonal produce, simply and expertly prepared. Leave room for the traditional English desserts, such as sticky toffee pudding.

Null Attitüde, gute Qualität: Dieses Bistro ist das Lieblingslokal vieler Londoner. Mit cremefarbenen Wänden, Schiefertafeln, auf denen die Menüs aufgelistet sind, alten Kirchenbänken zum Sitzen und kleinen Vasen mit Blumensträußchen auf den Tischen zeigt es zudem viel Liebe zum Detail. Hier kommen saisonale Qualitätsprodukte auf den Tisch, einfach aber gekonnt umgesetzt. Unbedingt die traditionell englischen Nachspeisen, wie den Karamellpudding, kosten.

Sans prétention et fiable, ce bistrot est depuis longtemps un chéri des Londoniens. Tous les détails sont soignés : murs beiges, bancs d'église, menus sur ardoise, petits bouquets de fleurs sur les tables. La cuisine à base de produits de saison de qualité est préparée avec art et simplicité. Laissez de la place pour les desserts traditionnels comme le pudding au caramel mou.

Interior: Very romantic: a perfect place for a country-style candle-light dinner.
Open: Mon–Fri 12.30–3pm, Sat 1– 3pm, Sun 1–3.30pm; Mon–Sat 6–10.45pm (Sun till 10.30pm).
Prices: Dishes £3–18.50.
X-Factor: The excellent wine list and the salads are particularly good, for example, artichokes and feta cheese or chorizo and squid.

Interieur: Sehr romantisch: ein perfekter Platz für ein Candle-Light-Dinner im Countrystil.
Öffnungszeiten: Mo–Fr 12.30–15, Sa 13–15, So 13–15.30; Mo–Sa 18–22.45 Uhr (So bis 22.30).
Preise: Gerichte 3–18,50 £.
X-Faktor: Die hervorragende Weinkarte. Und besonders gut sind die Salate – zum Beispiel mit Artischoke und Feta oder Chorizo und Tintenfisch.

Intérieur : Très romantique : un endroit idéal pour un dîner aux chandelles dans le style country.
Horaires d'ouverture : Lun–Ven 12h30–15h, Sam 13h–15h, Dim 13h–15h30 ; Lun–Sam 18h–22h45 (Dim jusqu'à 22h30).
Prix : Plats 3–18,50 £.
Le « petit plus » : L'excellente carte des vins. Les salades sont exquises, comme celle aux artichauts et à la féta ou celle au chorizo et au poulpe.

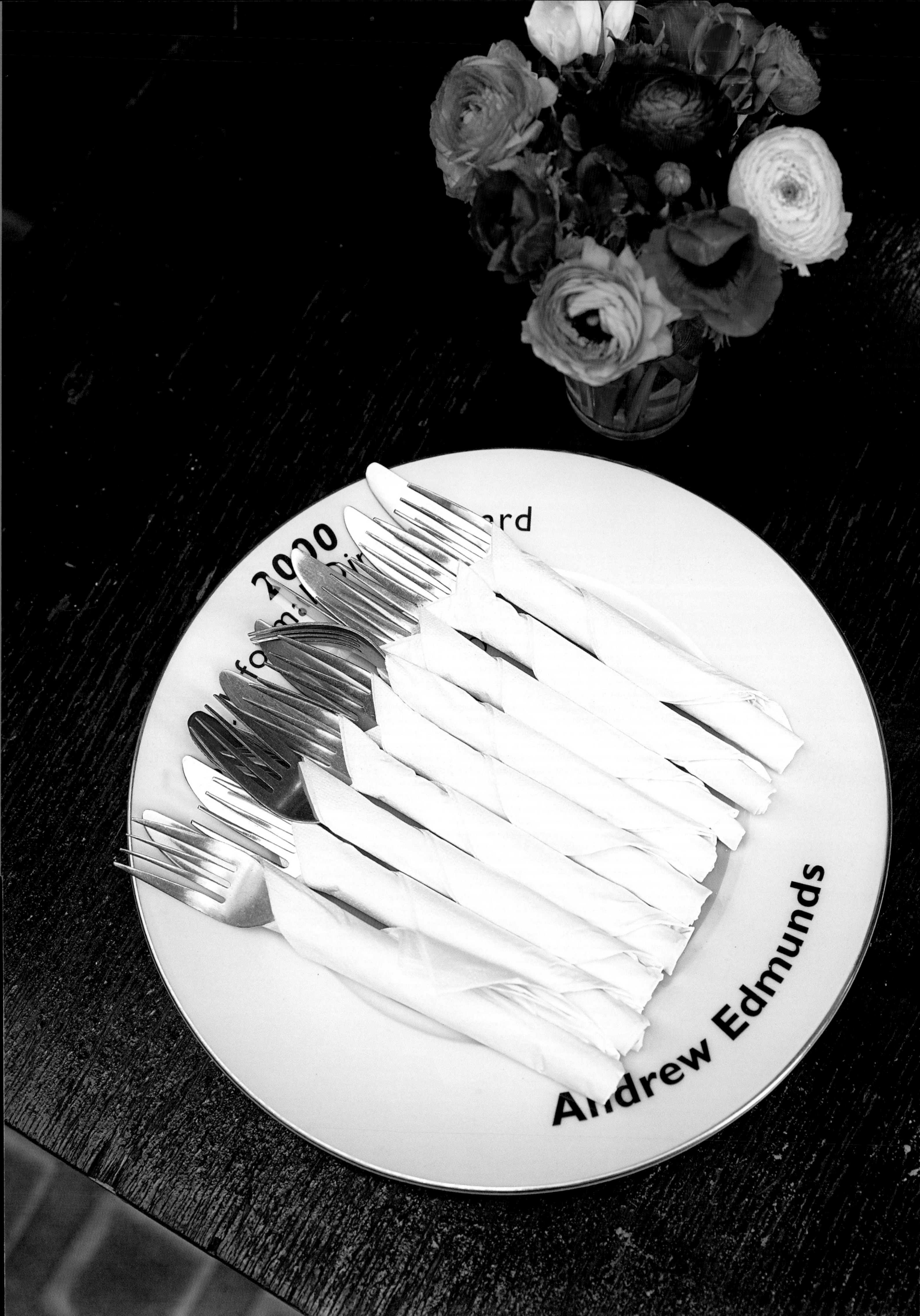
Andrew Edmunds

Patisserie Valerie

44 Old Compton Street, London W1D 5JX
☎ +44 20 7437 3466
www.patisserie-valerie.co.uk
Tube: Leicester Square

Though this mini-chain now has branches all over the city, the original opened in nearby Frith Street in 1926 and moved to Old Compton Street during the Second World War. The décor is pure 1950s Soho, and the café is still popular with art students from nearby Central Saint Martins College. Along with the luscious pastries and coffees, Patisserie Valerie is considered the best place in Soho to get breakfast.

Patisserie Valerie gibt's bereits seit 1926. Heute sind die Patisserien über ganz London verstreut. Das erste Geschäft eröffnete an der nahe gelegenen Frith Street, doch nachdem es im Zweiten Weltkrieg ausgebombt wurde, zog Valerie an die Old Compton Street. Im 1950er-Dekor des Cafés tummeln sich viele Kunststudenten des nahe gelegenen Central Saint Martins College. Das Gebäck ist deliziös, der Kaffee köstlich, und hier gibt's das beste Frühstück in Soho.

Cette chaîne qui possède des enseignes dans toute la ville a vu le jour sur Frith Street en 1926 avant de déménager sur Old Compton Street pendant la Seconde Guerre mondiale. Avec son décor pur Soho années 1950, c'est la cantine des étudiants de l'école d'art voisine, Central Saint Martins College. Outre ses délicieuses pâtisseries, le café est réputé pour servir les meilleurs petits-déjeuners de Soho.

Interior: The wonderful atmosphere is reminiscent of the 1950s – not only because of the Terroni cartoons in the style of Toulouse-Lautrec.
Open: Mon/Tue 7.30am–8pm, Wed–Sat 7.30am–11pm, Sun 9am–8pm.
Prices: Coffee from £2.30, cake from £2.75.
X-Factor: The heavenly éclairs au chocolat.

Interieur: Die schöne Atmosphäre erinnert an die 1950er-Jahre – nicht nur dank der Terroni-Cartoons im Stil von Toulouse-Lautrec.
Öffnungszeiten: Mo/Di 7.30–20, Mi–Sa 7.30–23, So 9–20 Uhr.
Preise: Kaffee ab 2,30 £, Kuchen ab 2,75 £.
X-Faktor: Die zarten Eclairs au Chocolat.

Intérieur : La belle atmosphère rappelle les années 1950, pas seulement à cause des cartoons de Terroni dans le style de Toulouse-Lautrec.
Horaires d'ouverture : Lun–Mar 7h30–20h, Mer–Sam 7h30–23h, Dim 9h–20h.
Prix : Café à partir de 2,30 £, gâteau à partir de 2,75 £.
Le « petit plus » : Les moelleux éclairs au chocolat.

Maison Bertaux

28 Greek Street, London W1D 5DQ
☎ +44 20 7437 6007
Tube: Leicester Square

In the age of Starbucks and other homogenized coffee-and-muffin chains, this old-established patisserie, sandwiched between a strip club and a pub, is a Soho treasure. The window is filled with authentically French, lovingly made gateaux, flans, mille-feuilles, éclairs and cream cakes, and the décor, which runs to dark wood tables and chairs, hasn't changed in 50 years.

Diese alteingesessene Patisserie, eingeklemmt zwischen einem Strip-Club und einem Pub, ist ein Juwel, das man im Zeitalter von Starbucks besonders zu schätzen weiß. Im Schaufenster türmen sich Kuchen, Flans, Mille-feuilles und Eclairs nach original französischen Rezepten. Innen hat sich seit 50 Jahren nichts verändert – die dunklen Holztische und -stühle sind immer noch dieselben.

À l'ère des Starbucks et autres chaînes homogénéisées, cette pâtisserie établie depuis longtemps, coincée entre une boîte de strip-tease et un pub, est un véritable trésor. Sa vitrine regorge de flans, millefeuilles, éclairs, choux à la crème et autres pâtisseries françaises confectionnées avec amour. Le décor, avec son mobilier en bois sombre, n'a pas changé depuis 50 ans.

Interior: This patisserie has been exuding its French flair since 1871.
Open: Mon–Sat 8.30am–11pm, Sun 9am–9pm.
Prices: Coffee and snacks from £1.50.
X-Factor: You can also sit outside in summer and do some people watching over coffee.

Interieur: Seit 1871 verströmt die Patisserie französisches Flair.
Öffnungszeiten: Mo–Sa 8.30–23, So 9–21 Uhr.
Preise: Kaffee und Snacks ab 1,50 £.
X-Faktor: Im Sommer kann man auch draußen sitzen und beim Kaffee herrlichstes People-Watching betreiben.

Intérieur : Depuis 1871, la pâtisserie est un petit coin de France.
Horaires d'ouverture : Lun–Sam 8h30–23h, Dim 9h–21h.
Prix : Café et snacks à partir de 1,50 £.
Le « petit plus » : En été, on peut aussi s'asseoir dehors et déguster son café en s'amusant à regarder les passants.

Norman's Coach & Horses

29 Greek Street, London W1D 5DH
☎ +44 20 7437 5920
www.normanscoachandhorses.com
Tube: Leicester Square

Norman's Coach & Horses is a proper Soho boozer, and that's just how the patrons like it. Because of its association with journalists – the staff of Private Eye and the late columnist Jeffrey Bernard were amongst the regulars – it's something of a local legend. Its former owner Norman Balon (he retired in May 2006) was the self-proclaimed "rudest landlord in London".

So stellt man sich eine typische Kneipe vor. In Norman's Coach & Horses verkehren vor allem Journalisten, etwa die Macher des Satiremagazins „Private Eye". Auch der verstorbene Kolumnist Jeffrey Bernard gehörte zu den Stammgästen. Norman's Coach & Horses ist eine lokale Legende, zu der auch der ehemalige Besitzer Norman Balon, der sich im Mai 2006 zur Ruhe setzte, beigetragen hat. Er bezeichnete sich als „den ruppigsten Gastgeber Londons".

Norman's Coach & Horses est un troquet de Soho pur jus et ses clients tiennent à ce qu'il le reste. Fréquenté par des journalistes (notamment ceux du « Private Eye » et feu le chroniqueur Jeffrey Bernard), c'est une légende locale. Son ancien propriétaire Norman Balon (à la retraite depuis mai 2006), se vantait d'être « le bistrotier le plus grossier de Londres ».

Interior: Unchanged since the 1930s – but with a new dining room on the first floor.
Open: Mon–Thur 11am–11.30pm, Fri/Sat 11am–midnight, Sun midday–10.30pm.
Prices: Beer £3.40.
X-Factor: A legend – always frequented by actors from the theatres nearby.

Interieur: Seit den 1930ern unverändert – aber es gibt einen neuen Dining Room im 1. Stock.
Öffnungszeiten: Mo–Do 11–23.30, Fr/Sa 11–24, So 12–22.30 Uhr.
Preise: Bier 3,40 £.
X-Faktor: Eine Legende – schon immer geschätzt von den Schauspielern der nahen Theater.

Intérieur : Inchangée depuis les années 1930, mais il y a une nouvelle salle au 1er étage.
Horaires d'ouverture : Lun–Jeu 11h–23h30, Ven/ Sam 11h–24h, Dim 12h–22h30.
Prix : Bière 3,40 £.
Le « petit plus » : Légendaire, l'établissement est prisé depuis toujours des comédiens du théâtre tout proche.

Hakkasan

8 Hanway Place, London W1T 1HD
☎ +44 20 7927 7000
www.hakkasan.com
Tube: Tottenham Court Road

Hakkasan is centrally located near Tottenham Court Road. The restaurant was opened in 2001 by Alan Yau, who also owns the successful, reasonably priced Wagamama und Busaba Eathai restaurants, but it is decidedly swish, with dim sum to die for and cocktails from classic to exotic, such as the Lychee Martini. The atmosphere is dark and dreamy with Asian touches, and the prizewinning cuisine is innovative.

Hakkasan liegt zentral in der Nähe der Tottenham Court Road. Das Lokal wurde 2001 von Alan Yau eröffnet, dem auch die erfolgreichen und preiswerten Restaurants Wagamama und Busaba Eathai gehören. Die Dim Sums hier sind himmlisch, und die Auswahl an Cocktails reicht von klassisch bis exotisch, wie zum Beispiel der Lychee-Martini. Das Interieur mit asiatischen Akzenten ist dunkel und etwas verträumt. Die preisgekrönte Küche ist innovativ.

Hakkasan est situé à deux pas de Tottenham Court Road. Il a été ouvert en 2001 par Alan Yau, à qui appartiennent aussi les restaurants bon marché à succès Wagamama et Busaba Eathai. Chic, à l'atmosphère tamisée et onirique saupoudrée de touches asiatiques, sa cuisine innovante et primée est exquise (le Dim Sum est à mourir !). Les cocktails vont du classique à l'exotique, comme le martini aux lychees.

Interior: This sophisticated Asian design is by Christian Liaigre.
Open: Restaurant: Mon–Fri midday–3pm (Sat/Sun till 4.30pm), Sun–Wed 6pm–11pm, Thu–Sat 6pm–12pm; bar: Mon–Wed midday–12.30am, Thu–Sat midday–1.30am, Sun midday–midnight.
Prices: Menu from £20 (lunch) and £40 (dinner).
X-Factor: First-class cocktails mixed at the long bar with the blue lighting.

Interieur: Das Design von Christian Liaigre ist asiatisch-sophisticated.
Öffnungszeiten: Restaurant: Mo–Fr 12–15 (Sa/So bis 16.30), So–Mi 18–23, Do–Sa 18–24 Uhr; Bar: Mo–Mi 12–0.30, Do–Sa 12–1.30, So 12–24 Uhr.
Preise: Menü ab 20 £ (Lunch) und 40 £ (Dinner).
X-Faktor: Erstklassige Cocktails, die an der langen, blau beleuchteten Bar gemixt werden.

Intérieur : Le design de Christian Liaigre est asiatique et sophistiqué.
Horaires d'ouverture : Restaurant : Lun–Ven 12h–15h (Sam/Dim jusqu'à 16h30), Dim–Mer 18h–23h, Jeu–Sam 18h–24h ; bar : Lun–Mer 12h–0h30, Jeu–Sam 12h–1h30, Dim 12h–24h.
Prix : Menu à partir de 20 £ (déjeuner) et 40 £ (dîner).
Le « petit plus » : Cocktails de qualité mixés au grand comptoir éclairé en bleu.

VitaOrganic

74 Wardour Street, London W1F 0TE
☎ +44 20 7734 8986
www.vitaorganic.co.uk
Tube: Tottenham Court Road/Leicester Square

If you're vegan or vegetarian, travelling can present difficulties. VitaOrganic is one of the more delicious solutions to a veggie's food search. A light and airy café, it features communal tables and a self-serve buffet. Both vegans and vegetarians are catered for, with a wide selection of hot and cold dishes, a juice bar and a separate raw menu. VitaOrganic is open for lunch and dinner.

Veganer und Vegetarier haben es beim Reisen auf der Suche nach dem richtigen Essen nicht immer einfach. Bei VitaOrganic, einem hellen, offenen Café mit Gemeinschaftstischen und Selbstbedienungsbüfett, finden sie eine köstliche Auswahl an warmen und kalten Gerichten, Rohkost und eine Saftbar. Das Lokal ist mittags und abends geöffnet.

Quand vous êtes végétalien ou végétarien, voyager n'est pas toujours facile. VitaOrganic offre la plus délicieuse des solutions à votre quête de nourriture. Ce café lumineux propose des tables communes et un buffet self-service avec une vaste sélection de plats chauds et froids ainsi qu'un menu cru séparé. VitaOrganic est ouvert midi et soir.

Interior: Straight-lined and functional.
Open: Mon–Sat midday–10pm, Sun 1pm–8pm.
Prices: Juice from £2.50, dishes £2.50–8.90.
X-Factor: Dishes prepared according to ayurvedic and enzyme-preserving principles, with no additives or preservatives.

Interieur: Geradlinig und zweckmäßig.
Öffnungszeiten: Mo–Sa 12–22, So 13–20 Uhr.
Preise: Saft ab 2,50 £, Gerichte 2,50–8,90 £.
X-Faktor: Nach ayurvedischen Prinzipien, enzymschonend zubereitete Speisen, ohne Zusatz- und Konservierungsstoffe.

Intérieur : Lignes droites et fonctionnalité.
Horaires d'ouverture : Lun–Sam 12h–22h, Dim 13h–20h.
Prix : Jus de fruits à partir de 2,50 £, plats 2,50–8,90 £.
Le « petit plus » : Plats préparés suivant les principes ayurvédiques, préservant les enzymes, sans additifs ni produits de conservation.

Monmouth Coffee Company

27 Monmouth Street, Covent Garden, London WC2H 9EU
☎ +44 20 7379 3516
www.monmouthcoffee.co.uk
Tube: Covent Garden

The best coffee in London is found at the heart of Covent Garden. The Monmouth Coffee Company installed its first roasting machine in 1978 in the cellar of a 17th-century house. The fair-trade beans come from plantations in South and Central America, as well as from Asia and Africa. Customers can order a croissant to go with the perfectly roasted and brewed coffee. It is worth making a detour to try the Monmouth coffee.

Londons besten Kaffee gibt es im Herzen von Covent Garden. Im Keller dieses Hauses aus dem 17. Jahrhundert stellte die Monmouth Coffee Company 1978 die erste Röstmaschine auf. Die Bohnen sind fair gehandelt und stammen von Plantagen in Mittel- und Südamerika sowie Asien und Afrika. Zum perfekt gerösteten und zubereiteten Kaffee kann man Croissants bestellen. Ein Kaffee von Monmouth ist eine Reise wert.

C'est au cœur de Covent Garden que l'on peut déguster le meilleur café de Londres. En 1978, la Monmouth Coffee Company a installé le premier torréfacteur dans la cave de cette maison du XVIIᵉ siècle. Le café issu du commerce équitable provient de plantations d'Amérique centrale et d'Amérique du Sud, d'Asie et d'Afrique. Parfaitement torréfié et préparé, il peut être accompagné de croissants. Un café de Monmouth vaut le déplacement.

Interior: Dignified-rustic – with a lot of wood.
Open: Mon–Sat 8am–6.30pm.
Prices: Coffee £1–2.
X-Factor: Pastries by Villandry and Paul to go with your coffee and in winter fine chocolate by Pralus and pralines by Sally Clarke.

Interieur: Edel-rustikal – mit viel Holz.
Öffnungszeiten: Mo–Sa 8–18.30 Uhr.
Preise: Kaffee 1–2 £.
X-Faktor: Zum Kaffee gibt es Gebäck von Villandry und Paul, und im Winter erhält man auch feine Schokolade von Pralus und Trüffelpralinen von Sally Clarke.

Intérieur : Noblesse rustique, avec moultes boiseries.
Horaires d'ouverture : Lun–Sam 8h–18h30.
Prix : Café 1–2 £.
Le « petit plus » : Des biscuits de Villandry et Paul sont servis avec le café et, en hiver, on peut aussi déguster les chocolats de Pralus et les truffes de Sally Clarke.

Rules

35 Maiden Lane, London WC2E 7LB
☎ +44 20 7836 5314
www.rules.co.uk
Tube: Leicester Square/Covent Garden

Established in 1798, Rules is London's oldest restaurant and it specialises in British cookery, with game from the restaurant's own estate in the Pennines. The décor is English country house, making it the ideal setting in which to try the tasty fish 'n' chips, which come wrapped in the day's newspaper and served with silver cutlery. The service is polished and discreet.

Londons ältestes Restaurant, das es seit 1798 gibt, konzentriert sich auf britische Küche und Wild vom eigenen Gutshof in den Pennines. Das Dekor im englischen Landhausstil macht Lust auf die leckeren Fish 'n' Chips, die hier in Zeitungspapier eingewickelt und mit Silberbesteck serviert werden. Der Service ist gepflegt und diskret.

Établi en 1798, Rules est le plus vieux restaurant de Londres. Il est spécialisé dans la cuisine britannique et son gibier provient de son domaine privé dans les Pennines. Le décor très maison de campagne anglaise en fait le lieu idéal où goûter le délicieux et léger fish 'n' chips présenté dans le quotidien du jour. Service courtois et discret.

Interior: More than 200 years of history are always in the air: the walls are covered in countless historical paintings, drawings and cartoons.
Open: Daily midday–11.30pm (Sun till 10.30pm).
Prices: Dishes £3.50–27.95.
X-Factor: Charles Dickens once ate here. Rules is also described in novels by Evelyn Waugh, Graham Greene and John Le Carré.

Interieur: Die mehr als 200 Jahre umfassende Geschichte ist immer präsent: An den Wänden hängen ungezählte historische Gemälde, Zeichnungen und Cartoons.
Öffnungszeiten: Täglich 12–23.30 Uhr (So bis 22.30).
Preise: Gerichte 3,50–27,95 £.
X-Faktor: Schon Charles Dickens speiste hier. Rules wird auch in Romanen von Evelyn Waugh, Graham Greene oder John Le Carré beschrieben.

Intérieur : Le passé vieux de plus de deux siècles est toujours présent : d'innombrables tableaux historiques, dessins et cartoons sont accrochés au mur.
Horaires d'ouverture : Tous les jours 12h–23h30 (Dim jusqu'à 22h30).
Prix : Plats 3,50–27,95 £.
Le « petit plus » : Déjà fréquenté par Charles Dickens. Rules est décrit dans les romans d'Evelyn Waugh, Graham Greene ou John Le Carré.

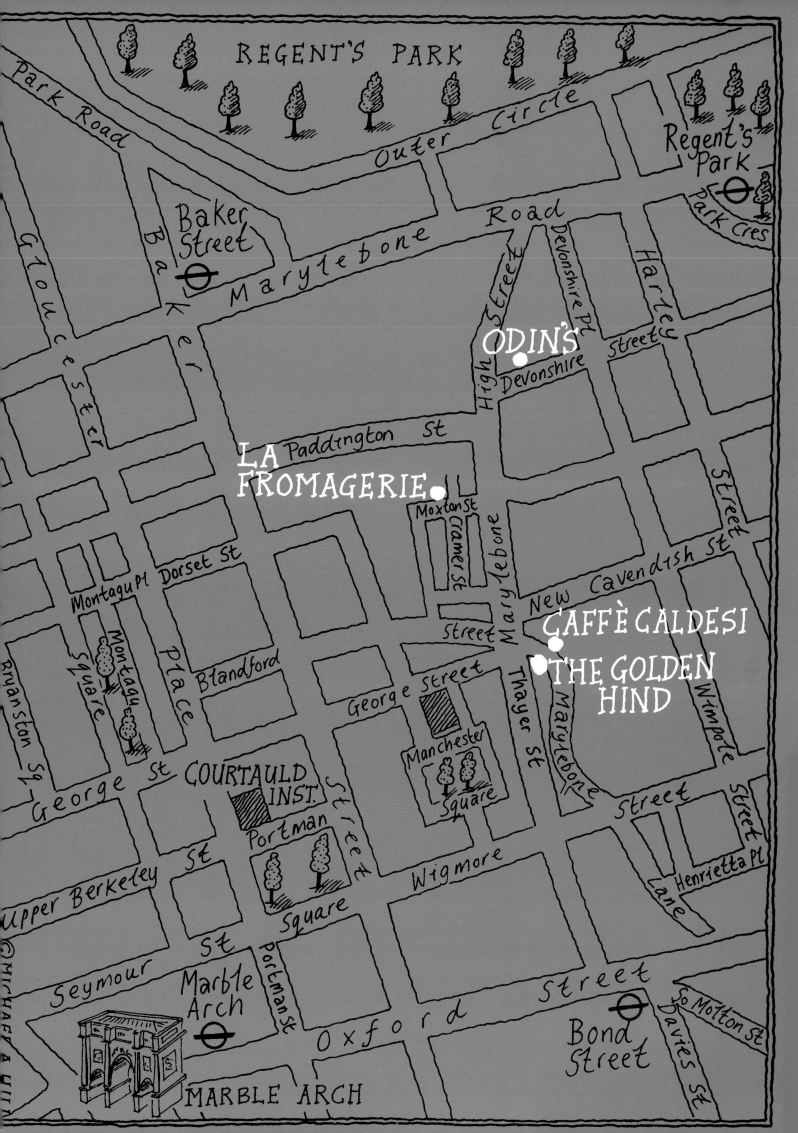

La Fromagerie

2–6 Moxon Street, London W1U 4EW
☎ +44 20 7935 0341
www.lafromagerie.co.uk
Tube: Baker Street/Bond Street

La Fromagerie is the perfect pit stop for when shopping in Marylebone starts hurting. Patricia Michelson is the brains behind this temple of cheese and wine and not only is it a delicatessen with fresh groceries, but a gorgeous lunch is served in the petite dining room to showcase the quality food. French cheeses prevail here and you can taste before you buy if you're not sure which sort you'd like best.

Shopping in Marylebone kann sehr anstrengend sein, und da kommt ein Lokal wie La Fromagerie gerade recht. Im Käse- und Weinparadies von Patricia Michelson gibt es nicht nur Feinkost und frische Lebensmittel, sondern auch köstliche Mittagsmahlzeiten, die in einem Café serviert werden. Große Auswahl an Käsesorten, die man vor dem Kauf probieren kann.

Quand vos pieds crient au secours après des heures de shopping dans Marylebone, c'est qu'il est temps de faire une halte à la Fromagerie. Conçu par Patricia Michelson, ce temple du fromage (surtout français) et du vin est aussi une épicerie fine et un traiteur. Testez les produits au cours d'un délicieux déjeuner dans la petite salle à manger.

Interior: French country-house style: home-made jams, chutneys and freshly-baked bread everywhere.
Open: Mon 10.30am– 7.30pm, Tue–Fri 8am–7.30pm, Sat 9am–7pm, Sun 10am–6pm.
Prices: Dishes £6–15.
X-Factor: The cheeses are supplied by small cheese-makers, most of them in France and Italy, but the British Isles are also well represented.

Interieur: Französischer Landhausstil: überall sieht man selbst gemachte Marmeladen, Chutneys und frisch gebackenes Brot.
Öffnungszeiten: Mo 10.30–19.30, Di–Fr 8–19.30, Sa 9–19, So 10–18 Uhr.
Preise: Gerichte 6–15 £.
X-Faktor: Die Käsesorten stammen von kleinen Handwerksbetrieben – die meisten liegen in Frankreich und Italien, aber auch die Britischen Inseln sind stark vertreten.

Intérieur : Style campagnard français : partout on voit des confitures maison, des chutneys et du pain frais.
Horaires d'ouverture : Lun 10h30–19h30, Mar–Ven 8h–19h30, Sam 9h–19h, Dim 10h–18h.
Prix : Plats 6–15 £.
Le « petit plus » : Les variétés de fromage viennent de petites exploitations artisanales. La plupart sont en France ou en Italie, mais les Îles britanniques sont bien représentées.

MASCARPONE

The Golden Hind

73 Marylebone Lane, London W1U 2PN
☎ +44 20 7486 3644
Tube: Bond Street

A chippie that is reminiscent of another era altogether, The Golden Hind has been a fixture on Marylebone Lane since 1914. Locals are religious followers and Londoners travel from far and wide to come and try its trademark cod and chips. The restaurant itself has an Art Deco fish fryer, the wooden tables are simple and sparse, and the vibe is pure London.

Die Fish 'n' Chips-Bude erinnert an längst vergangene Zeiten. Seit 1914 ist The Golden Hind fester Bestandteil der Marylebone Lane, und die Bewohner des Viertels haben eine fast religiöse Beziehung zu dem Lokal. Es gibt sogar Londoner, die quer durch die Stadt fahren, um in den Genuss der Hausspezialität, frittierten Kabeljau und Pommes frites, zu kommen. Typisches Londoner Lokal mit einfachen Holztischen und original Art-déco-Fritteuse.

Vrai fish'n'chips qui rappelle un autre temps, le Golden Hind existe sur Marylebone Lane depuis 1914. Les gens du quartier le vénèrent et les Londoniens viennent de loin pour savourer sa fameuse morue agrémentée de frites. Avec sa friteuse Art Déco, ses tables en bois, son décor dépouillé et son ambiance bon enfant, c'est du Londres pur jus.

Interior: Visually prominent: the pastel Art Deco deep-fryer.
Open: Mon–Fri midday–3pm and 6–10pm, Sat 6–10pm.
Prices: Dishes £5–17.
X-Factor: If you don't like the ginger-beer served here, you can bring along your own wine to go with your quick snack.

Interieur: Optisch herausragend: die pastelfarbene Art-déco-Fritteuse.
Öffnungszeiten: Mo–Fr 12–15 und 18–22, Sa 18–22 Uhr.
Preise: Gerichte 5–17 £.
X-Faktor: Wer das hier ausgeschenkte Ingwerbier nicht mag, kann zum schnellen Essen auch seinen eigenen Wein mitbringen.

Intérieur : Saute tout de suite aux yeux : la friteuse Art Déco de couleur pastel.
Horaires d'ouverture : Lun–Ven 12h–15h et 18h–22h, Sam 18h–22h.
Prix : Plats 5–17 £.
Le « petit plus » : Si vous n'aimez pas la bière au gingembre, vous pouvez apporter votre bouteille de vin.

Caffè Caldesi

118 Marylebone Lane, London W1U 2QF
☎ +44 20 7935 1144
www.caffe.caldesi.com
Tube: Bond Street

Caffè Caldesi is the only place to go to in Marylebone for Saturday and Sunday brunch (have the Big Tuscan) or lunch. This place is staffed by proper Italians so you could just as well be in a square somewhere in Tuscany for all you know. The coffees are divine, the service brisk and the people-watching provides countless hours of entertainment. Dinners upstairs are also worth a look-in, too.

Ein besseres Lokal für den Wochen-end-Brunch (empfehlenswert ist The Big Tuscan) oder -Lunch als das Caffè Caldesi gibt's nirgends in Marylebone. Hier wird man von echten Italienern bedient, und so fühlt man sich wie in der Toskana. Der Kaffee schmeckt zudem himmlisch. Nicht zu schlagen ist das Lokal auch als Beobachtungsposten: Man kann hier locker stundenlang People-Watching betreiben. Im oberen Stock gibt's übrigens auch Abendessen.

C'est le seul endroit à Marylebone où prendre son brunch ou déjeuner le samedi et le dimanche (optez pour le Big Tuscan). Avec son personnel entiè-rement italien, on se croirait sur une petite place toscane. Les cafés sont divins, le service rapide et on ne se lasse pas d'observer la clientèle. Les salles à l'étage valent également le coup d'œil.

Interior: A breath of Italy.
Open: Mon–Fri 10am–11pm (Sat from 9.30am).
Prices: Dishes £6.50–19.50.
X-Factor: Like a short trip to the South: real Italians serving cucina alla mamma and first-class espresso.

Interieur: Italienisch inspiriert.
Öffnungszeiten: Mo–Fr 10–23 Uhr (Sa ab 9.30).
Preise: Gerichte 6,50–19,50 £.
X-Faktor: Wie ein Kurztrip in den Süden: Echte Italiener servieren Cucina alla Mamma und erstklassigen Espresso.

Intérieur : D'inspiration italienne.
Horaires d'ouverture : Lun–Ven 10h–23h (Sam à partir de 9h30).
Prix : Plats 6,50–19,50 £.
Le « petit plus » : Une excursion dans le Sud : de vrais Italiens vous servent une cuci-na alla mamma et un excellent expresso.

Odin's

27 Devonshire Street, London W1G 6PL
☎ +44 20 7935 7296
www.langansrestaurants.co.uk
Tube: Baker Street

The first thing that you should know about Odin's is that it is closed on Sunday. It has been around since 1966 so, really, it doesn't need to worry. Odin's is as perfect for a serious business meeting as for a romantic dinner à deux. The food is beautifully prepared English fare (beef, oysters, game) and puddings are not to be missed. Service is impeccable.

Das Wichtigste, das man über Odin's wissen sollte: Sonntags bleibt das Restaurant geschlossen. Das ist bereits seit 1966 so und hat seinem Erfolg keinen Abbruch getan. Perfekt für ein geschäftliches Treffen, aber auch für ein romantisches Dinner zu zweit. Hier gibt's schön zubereitete englische Gerichte mit Rind, Austern und Wild, und natürlich Puddings. Nicht nur das: Der Service ist tadellos.

Avant tout, sachez qu'Odin's est fermé le dimanche ; toutefois, pas de panique, ce restaurant existe depuis 1966. C'est l'endroit idéal pour un rendez-vous d'affaires sérieux comme pour un dîner romantique en tête à tête. La cuisine anglaise (bœuf, huîtres, gibier) est superbement présentée et les puddings sont un must. Le service est impeccable.

Interior: The restaurant is also an art gallery – some of the paintings on the walls are by David Hockney.
Open: Mon–Fri midday–2.30pm and 6.30pm–11pm, Sat 6.30pm–11pm.
Prices: Two-course menu £31, three courses £35.
X-Factor: Mrs. Langan's Chocolate Pudding.

Interieur: Das Restaurant ist zugleich eine Kunstgalerie – einige der Gemälde an den Wänden stammen von David Hockney.
Öffnungszeiten: Mo–Fr 12–14.30 und 18.30–23, Sa 18.30–23 Uhr.
Preise: Menü mit 2 Gängen 31 £, mit 3 Gängen 35 £.
X-Faktor: Mrs. Langan's Chocolate Pudding.

Intérieur : Restaurant mais aussi galerie d'art – certains tableaux accrochés au mur sont de David Hockney.
Horaires d'ouverture : Lun–Ven 12h–14h30 et 18h30–23h, Sam 18h30–23h.
Prix : Menu à 2 plats 31 £, 3 plats 35 £.
Le « petit plus » : Mrs. Langan's Chocolate Pudding.

THE GRENADIER↗

Hans Crescent

Hans Rd

Basil St

Pont Street

Hans Place

Pont Street

Sloane Street

Pavilion Road

Cadogan Place

Cadogan Lane

Lowndes St

Chesham St

Belgrave Square

Upp Belgrave St

Belgrave Pl

Eaton Place

Belgrave Sq

King's Road

Eaton Sq

Eaton Square

Elizabeth Street

Lyall St

Cadogan Street

Draycott Place

Avenue

enue

Road

Smith Street

Tedworth Sq

St Leonard's Terr

Cheltenham Terrace

Franklin's Row

Royal Hospital Road

Sloane Square

Lower Sloane Street

•ORIEL

Sloane Square

Eaton Terr

Chester Row

Ebury

Pimlico Rd

Bloomfield Terrace

Ranelagh Gr

Chelsea Bridge Road

Ebury Bridge Road

ROYAL HOSPITAL CHELSEA

©MICHAEL A HILL

Restaurants

Daquise

20 Thurloe Street, London SW7 2LT
☎ +44 20 7589 6117
Tube: South Kensington

Daquise is the kind of restaurant that makes eating out fun. This Polish eatery has been in South Kensington since 1947 and its popularity – with Poles and non-Poles alike – has not abated. Go on a busy Friday night and try the pierogi, the potato pancakes, dumplings and finish off with apple cake. (Those on an Atkins diet need not enter the doors.) Best of all, prices are reasonable.

Hier macht es richtig Spaß, auswärts zu essen. Das polnische Restaurant Daquise in South Kensington gibt es seit 1947 und ist bei Polen und Nicht-Polen genauso beliebt. Am besten an einem Freitag hingehen, dann ist besonders viel los, und Pirog- gen, Kartoffelpuffer, Knödel und zum Abschluss Apfelkuchen kosten. Wer sich einer Atkins-Diät verschrieben hat, bleibt besser draußen. Und: Die Preise sind durchaus vernünftig.

Dîner chez Daquise est une vraie fête. Depuis son ouverture en 1947, ce restaurant polonais ne désemplit pas de Polonais comme de non Polonais. Allez-y un vendredi soir, quand il y a foule. Goinfrez-vous de pierogi, de galettes de pommes de terre, de boulettes et finissez avec un gâteau aux pommes. Si vous êtes au régime, n'entrez pas ! En outre, les prix sont raisonnables.

Interior: Rustically rural – with waxed check tablecloths and simple crockery.
Open: Daily midday–11pm.
Prices: Dishes £6.50–14.50.
X-Factor: The menu even includes varieties of beer and vodka from Poland and a "Polish platter" – for those who like to try everything.

Interieur: Bäuerlich – mit karierten Wachs- tuch-Tischdecken und schlichtem Porzellan.
Öffnungszeiten: Täglich 12–23 Uhr.
Preise: Gerichte 6,50–14,50 £.
X-Faktor: Die Karte umfasst sogar Bier- und Wodkasorten aus Polen und eine „Polish platter" – für alle, die von allem kosten möchten.

Intérieur : Campagnard, avec des nappes cirées à carreaux et de la porcelaine toute simple.
Horaires d'ouverture : Tous les jours 12h– 23h.
Prix : Plats 6,50–14,50 £.
Le « petit plus » : La carte comprend même des variétés de bière et de vodka polonai- ses ainsi qu'une « polish platter » si vous dé- sirez goûter à tout.

Oriel

50–51 Sloane Square, London SW1W 8AX
☎ +44 20 7730 2804
Tube: Sloane Square

With a perfect view of Sloane Square and all around it, it's no wonder that Oriel is almost always full to the hilt. This café/restaurant is as close you get to a French brasserie in London – grumpy service included – and is very popular with locals and tourists alike. Opt for a big English breakfast, or just go for coffee. Either way, there is plenty to look at.

Vom Oriel hat man einen tollen Blick auf den Sloane Square. Kein Wunder, ist das Café-Restaurant meist zum Bersten voll. Es ist genau so, wie man sich in London eine französische Brasserie vorstellt; dazu gehört auch der unfreundliche Service. Bei Einheimischen und Besuchern ist es dennoch beliebt. Unbedingt das große englische Frühstück ausprobieren – oder einfach einen Kaffee genießen. Egal was, zu sehen gibt es hier allemal viel.

Avec sa vue imprenable sur Sloane Square, il ne faut pas s'étonner qu'Oriel soit toujours bondé. Ce café/restaurant, très prisé des locaux et des touristes, est ce qui se rapproche le plus d'une brasserie parisienne à Londres, les serveurs grognons inclus. Que vous preniez un copieux breakfast anglais ou un simple café, vous ne vous y ennuierez pas.

Interior: The elegant lower floor was designed by the British interior designer Lawrence Llewelyn-Bowen.
Open: Mon–Sat 8.30am–11pm, Sun 9am–10.30pm.
Prices: Lunch approx. £15, dinner approx. £ 25.
X-Factor: This is how England sees France.

Interieur: Das elegante Untergeschoss wurde vom britischen Interiordesigner Lawrence Llewelyn-Bowen entworfen.
Öffnungszeiten: Mo–Sa 8.30–23, So 9–22.30 Uhr.
Preise: Lunch um 15 £, Dinner um 25 £.
X-Faktor: So stellt man sich Frankreich in England vor.

Intérieur : L'élégant souterrain a été décoré par le designer britannique Llewelyn-Bowen.
Horaires d'ouverture : Lun–Sam 8h30–23h, Dim 9h–22h30.
Prix : Déjeuner env. 15 £, dîner env. 25 £.
Le « petit plus » : C'est ainsi qu'on s'imagine la France en Angleterre.

ORIEL

GRANDE BRASSERIE DE LA PLACE

Bibendum

Michelin House
81 Fulham Road, London SW3 6RD
☎ +44 20 7581 5817
www.bibendum.co.uk
Tube: South Kensington

In 1909 the French tyre manufacturer Michelin founded its first English headquarters here. When the company moved out in 1985, Sir Terence Conran bought the striking building and opened Bibendum, which not only bears the name of the Michelin man, but adorns the floors, windows and plates with his corpulent outline. For guests in a hurry there is also an oyster bar in the building, as well as a seafood stall where Londoners queue on Saturday mornings from 9am for lobster with homemade mayonnaise.

1909 gründete der französische Reifenhersteller Michelin hier das erste Hauptquartier in England. Nach dem Auszug des Unternehmens 1985 kaufte Sir Terence Conran das markante Gebäude und eröffnete das Bibendum – es trägt nicht nur den Namen des Michelin-Männchens, sondern schmückt mit dessen korpulenter Silhouette Böden, Fenster und Teller. Für eilige Gäste sind im selben Haus eine Austernbar sowie der Crustaceen-Stand untergebracht, wo die Londoner am Samstagmorgen ab 9 Uhr für den Hummer mit hausgemachter Mayonnaise Schlange stehen.

Le fabricant de pneus français Michelin a créé ici en 1909 son premier quartier général en Angleterre. Lorsque l'entreprise a quitté les lieux en 1985, Sir Terence Conran a acheté le bâtiment de caractère et ouvert le Bibendum. Celui-ci ne porte pas seulement le nom du bonhomme Michelin – la silhouette reconnaissable entre toutes décore aussi les sols, les fenêtres et les assiettes. Les clients pressés peuvent se restaurer au bar à huîtres ou au stand de crustacés. Ici les Londoniens font la queue le samedi matin à partir de 9h pour acheter du homard à la mayonnaise maison.

Interior: In this Michelin building, dated 1909, the legendary Michelin Man turns up as a decorative element on floors, windows and tables.
Open: Mon–Fri midday–2.30pm and 7–11pm, Sat/Sun 12.30–3pm, Sat 7–11.30pm, Sun 7–10.30pm.
Prices: Lunch from £25.
X-Factor: The oyster bar is particularly en vogue.

Interieur: Im Michelin-Haus von 1909 taucht das legendäre Michelin-Männchen als Boden-, Fenster- und Tischschmuck auf.
Öffnungszeiten: Mo–Fr 12–14.30 und 19–23, Sa–So 12.30–15, Sa 19–23.30, So 19–22.30 Uhr.
Preise: Lunch ab 25 £.
X-Faktor: En vogue ist vor allem die Austernbar.

Intérieur : Dans la maison Michelin de 1909, le bonhomme Michelin apparaît en décoration sur les sols, les fenêtres et les tables.
Horaires d'ouverture : Lun–Ven 12h–14h30 & 19h–23h, Sam/Dim 12h30–15h, Sam 19h–23h30, Dim 19h–22h30.
Prix : Déjeuner à partir de 25 £.
Le « petit plus » : Le bar aux huîtres est particulièrement en vogue.

The Grenadier

18 Wilton Row, London SW1X 7NR
☎ +44 20 7235 3074
Tube: Hyde Park Corner/Knightsbridge

For a pub with local history, look no further than The Grenadier, which sits in very posh Wilton Row and is painted British red, white and blue. The interior pays homage to its military past: the Duke of Wellington's troops used it as their mess.

The Grenadier, in den britischen Farben Rot, Weiß und Blau, ist ein Pub voller Lokalgeschichte. Die Einrichtung ist eine Hommage an die militärische Vergangenheit des Lokals: Es diente den Truppen des Duke of Wellington als Messe.

Pour un pub chargé d'histoire locale, rendez-vous au Grenadier peint aux couleurs du drapeau britannique. Le décor rend hommage à son passé militaire : c'était autrefois le mess des troupes du duc de Wellington.

Interior: Outside red, white and blue, inside rustic, with numerous militaria.
Open: Daily midday–11pm.
Prices: Dishes £6–17.
X-Factor: According to a creepy legend there is even a pub ghost – an officer who cheated at cards and had to die as a result.

Interieur: Außen in Rot, Weiß und Blau, innen urig mit zahlreichen Militär-Memorabilien.
Öffnungszeiten: Täglich 12–23 Uhr.
Preise: Gerichte 6–17 £.
X-Faktor: Laut einer schaurigen Legende soll es sogar einen Pub-Geist geben – einen Offizier, der beim Kartenspiel schummelte und dafür sterben musste.

Intérieur : L'extérieur en rouge, blanc et bleu, l'intérieur très pittoresque avec les nombreux souvenirs militaires.
Horaires d'ouverture : Tous les jours 12h–23h.
Prix : Plats 6–17 £.
Le « petit plus » : D'après la légende, le pub aurait son fantôme : un officier qui avait triché aux cartes et avait dû mourir pour cela.

Souveniers
Champagne
RUGBY SHIRTS
POLO SHIRTS
SWEAT SHIRTS
TANKARDS
BASEBALL CAPS
SILK SCARVES
GRENADIER
HIP FLASK
MOET & CHANDON
VEUVE CLICQUOT BRUT
LAURENT PERRIER CUVÉE ROSÉ BRUT
DOM PERIGNON - VINTAGE
HENRIOT
RUM
WHISKY
NO SMOKING

TANGIERS 1680
SOMME 1916
MARNE 1914

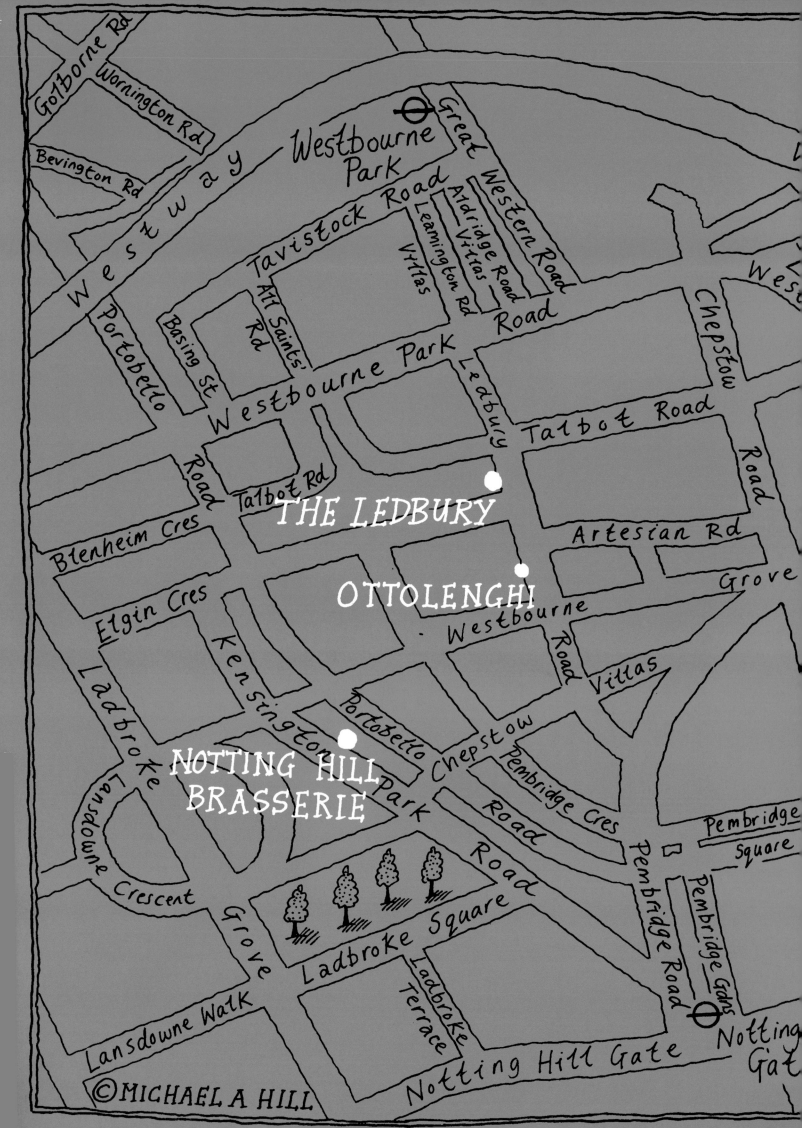

THE LEDBURY

OTTOLENGHI

NOTTING HILL BRASSERIE

©MICHAEL A HILL

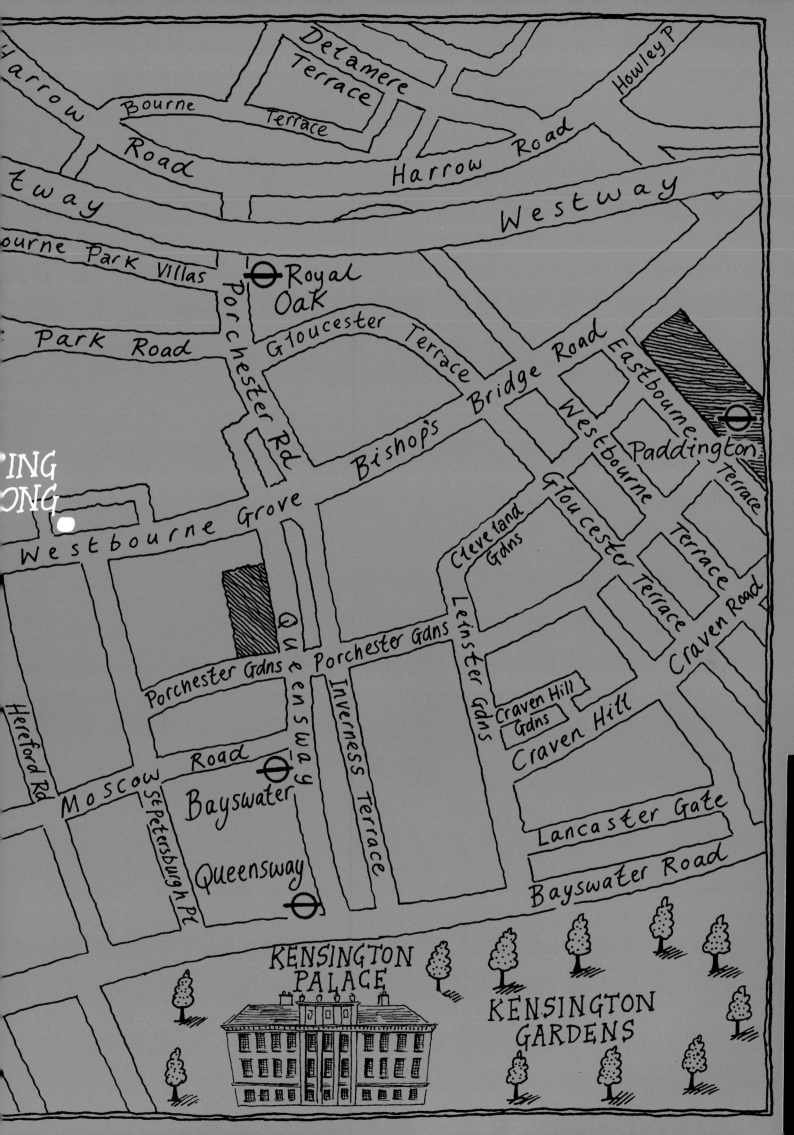

Notting Hill Brasserie

92 Kensington Park Road, London W11 2PN
☎ +44 20 7229 4481
www.nottinghillbrasserie.com
Tube: Notting Hill Gate

Popular with Notting Hill residents and Holland Park dwellers alike, the Notting Hill Brasserie housed in three converted Edwardian townhouses provides a touch of French elegance in the chicest part of west London. Yet, although it caters to a sophisticated crowd, the vibe is very laid-back and staff are super friendly. Duck, fish and seafood, done contemporary French-style, feature heavily on the menu.

Die Notting Hill Brasserie, die bei den Bewohnern von Notting Hill und Holland Park sehr beliebt ist, bringt ein Stück französische Eleganz ins schicke Westlondon. Dafür wurden drei nebeneinanderliegende Stadthäuser aus der Zeit Eduards VII. umgebaut. Die Gäste sind zwar mondän, dennoch ist das Ambiente sehr entspannt und das Personal außergewöhnlich freundlich. Ente, Fisch und Meeresfrüchte nach moderner französischer Art dominieren die Speisekarte.

Très prisée des habitants de Notting Hill et d'Holland Park, cette brasserie occupant trois maisons édouardiennes constitue une élégante touche française dans la partie la plus chic de l'ouest de Londres. La clientèle est sophistiquée mais l'ambiance très décontractée et le personnel adorable. La carte, très moderne, met à l'honneur le canard, les poissons et les fruits de mer.

Interior: A modern classic – with high windows, stucco and shining parquet flooring.
Open: Mon/Tue 7pm–11pm, Wed–Sat midday–3pm and 7pm–11pm, Sun midday–3pm and 7pm–10.30pm.
Prices: Dishes £5.50–23.50.
X-Factor: The cocktail bar with refined live jazz music.

Interieur: Ein moderner Klassiker – mit hohen Fenstern, Stuck und glänzendem Parkett.
Öffnungszeiten: Mo/Di 19–23, Mi–Sa 12–15 und 19–23, So 12–15 und 19–22.30 Uhr.
Preise: Gerichte 5,50–23,50 £.
X-Faktor: Die Cocktailbar mit gepflegtem Live-Jazz.

Intérieur : Un classique moderne avec ses hautes fenêtres, ses stucs et son parquet brillant.
Horaires d'ouverture : Lun/Mar 19h–23h, Mer–Sam 12h–15h et 19h–23h, Dim 12h–15h et 19h–22h30.
Prix : Plats 5,50–23,50 £.
Le « petit plus » : Le cocktail bar et sa musique de jazz live en sourdine.

NOTTING HILL
BRASSERIE

BAR & RESTAURANT

92 KENSINGTON PARK ROAD
020 7229 4481

Ottolenghi

63 Ledbury Road, London W11 2AD
☎ +44 20 7727 1121
www.ottolenghi.co.uk
Tube: Notting Hill Gate

Is it a café or a deli? Who cares as long as it's this yummy. Ottolenghi is like a boudoir of delicious, hand-crafted food. From the pastries displayed like jewels to the delicious fresh salads overflowing in huge white bowls, it's difficult to know where to start. Or finish. Get a selection of salads and quiche as a takeaway or jostle with the Notting Hill yummy mummies for a seat in the café section.

Café oder Delikatessengeschäft? Das Ottolenghi ist nicht nur beides, sondern auch ein Schlaraffenland mit köstlichen, von Hand zubereiteten Spezialitäten. Die Feingebäckteile werden wie Schmuckstücke ausgestellt, die frischen Salate in großen, weißen Schüsseln präsentiert. Alles sieht so lecker aus, dass die Wahl schwer fällt. Im Café angelt man sich einen Tisch neben all den schicken Notting-Hill-Bewohnern. Für ein Take-away empfiehlt sich Salat mit Quiche.

Café ou traiteur ? Peu importe tant que c'est bon. Ottolenghi est un boudoir de mets divins faits maison. Des pâtisseries présentées comme des bijoux aux immenses bols blancs débordant de salades exquises, on ne sait plus où donner de la tête. Emportez un choix de salades et une quiche ou battez-vous avec les jolies jeunes mamans de Notting Hill pour une table dans le coin café.

Interior: Puristically white, and always decorated with opulent bouquets of flowers.
Open: Mon–Fri 8am–8pm, Sat 8am–7pm, Sun 8.30am–6pm.
Prices: Dishes £9.50–14.50.
X-Factor: The cookery courses, where you can learn the fantastic vegetable, herb and spice combinations used for the salads.

Interieur: Puristisch in Weiß, immer mit wunderschönen, prächtigen Blumensträußen geschmückt.
Öffnungszeiten: Mo–Fr 8–20, Sa 8–19, So 8.30–18 Uhr.
Preise: Gerichte 9,50–14,50 £.
X-Faktor: Die Kochkurse, bei denen man die fantastischen Gemüse-, Kräuter- und Gewürzkombinationen der Salate lernen kann.

Intérieur : Puriste en blanc, toujours décorée de magnifiques bouquets de fleurs.
Horaires d'ouverture : Lun–Ven 8h–20h, Sam 8h–19h, Dim 8h30–18h.
Prix : Plats 9,50–14,50 £.
Le « petit plus » : Les cours de cuisine où l'on peut apprendre de fantastiques combinaisons de légumes, d'herbes et d'épices pour les salades.

CHOCOLATE
and ESPRESSO
TART
£ 2.60

The Ledbury

127 Ledbury Road, London W11 2AQ
☎ +44 20 7792 9090
www.theledbury.com
Tube: Westbourne Park

It was given a Michelin star and several other awards in 2006 but if that isn't enough to convince you of how fabulous this elegant restaurant is, then let it be known that the chic customers have to book months in advance to get in here. Opened in 2005 by Nigel Platts-Martin and Philip Howard, the French-influenced cooking by Australian chef Brett Graham has won fans far and wide.

Das elegante Ledbury konnte 2006 einen Michelin-Stern und zahlreiche andere Auszeichnungen entgegennehmen, und selbst die schicke Stammkundschaft muss Monate auf einen freien Tisch warten. Nigel Platts-Martin und Philip Howard haben das fantastische Lokal 2005 eröffnet. Küchenchef ist der Australier Brett Graham. Mit seiner französisch inspirierten Küche hat er sich einen Namen gemacht.

Il a reçu une étoile Michelin et plusieurs autres prix en 2006 mais si cela ne suffit pas à vous convaincre que cet élégant restaurant est fabuleux, sachez qu'il faut réserver des mois à l'avance. Ouvert en 2005 par Nigel Platts-Martin et Philip Howard, la cuisine aux accents français du chef australien Brett Graham a fait des adeptes dans le monde entier.

Interior: The elegant interior in shades of cream and brown is by Nelson Design.
Open: Mon–Sat midday–2.30pm and 6.30pm–10.30pm, Sun midday–2.45pm and 6.30pm–10pm.
Prices: Menu from £19.50 (lunch) and £50 (dinner).
X-Factor: The vegetarian degustation menu.

Interieur: Das edle Interieur in Crème- und Schokotönen stammt von Nelson Design.
Öffnungszeiten: Mo–Sa 12–14.30 und 18.30–22.30, So 12–14.45 und 18.30–22 Uhr.
Preise: Menü ab 19,50 £ (Lunch) und 50 £ (Dinner).
X-Faktor: Das vegetarische Degustations-Menü.

Intérieur : L'élégant intérieur dans les tons crème et chocolat a été aménagé par Nelson Design.
Horaires d'ouverture : Lun–Sam 12h–14h30 et 18h30–22h30, Dim 12h–14h45 et 18h30–22h.
Prix : Menu à partir de 19,50 £ (déjeuner) et 50 £ (dîner).
Le « petit plus » : Le menu végétarien de dégustation.

Ping Pong

74–76 Westbourne Grove, London W2 5SH
☎ +44 20 7313 9832
www.pingpongdimsum.com
Tube: Bayswater/Royal Oak

Dim sum and cocktails sound like a rather strange combination but, at Ping Pong, it somehow works. Dim sum is essentially a steamed dumpling filled with meat, seafood or vegetables and a staple Chinese dish. Ping Pong employs the best dim sum chefs and barstaff in London who prepare zingy cocktails to accompany the food. The simple, modern design of the restaurant also adds to the experience.

Dim Sum und Cocktails klingt nach einer seltsamen Kombination. Doch im Ping Pong geht das ganz gut zusammen. Chinesische Dim Sum sind gedämpfte Teigtaschen mit Fleisch-, Fisch- oder Gemüsefüllung. Bei Ping Pong arbeiten die besten Dim-Sum-Köche und Barkeeper Londons – ein Besuch im Restaurant mit dem einfachen, modernen Look ist ein wahres Erlebnis.

L'association de dim sum et de cocktails peut surprendre mais chez Ping Pong, elle marche. Ces raviolis à la vapeur au porc, aux crevettes ou aux légumes, plat de base de la cuisine chinoise, sont préparés par les meilleurs spécialistes de Londres et accompagnés de cocktails détonants mixés par des barmen experts. Le décor design simple et moderne ajoute à l'expérience.

Interior: Architect David Marquardt and designer Niclas Sellebråten have created a chic Asian interior with a twist.
Open: Mon–Wed midday–11pm, Thu–Sat till midnight, Sun till 10.30pm.
Prices: Dim sum from £2.99.
X-Factor: Dim Sum means "small heart-warmers" – and for the chefs here they are child's play.

Interieur: Architekt David Marquardt und Designer Niclas Sellebråten entwarfen ein schickes asiatisches Interieur mit Twist.
Öffnungszeiten: Mo–Mi 12–23, Do–Sa bis 24, So bis 22.30 Uhr.
Preise: Dim Sum ab 2,99 £.
X-Faktor: Dim Sum bedeutet „kleine Herzwärmer" – das gelingt den Chefs hier spielend.

Intérieur : L'architecte David Marquardt et le designer Niclas Sellebråten ont réalisé un intérieur asiatique chic.
Horaires d'ouverture : Lun–Mer 12h–23h, Jeu–Sam jusqu'à 24h, Dim jusqu'à 22h30.
Prix : Dim sum à partir de 2,99 £.
Le « petit plus » : Dim Sum signifie « réchauffe le cœur » et les chefs y parviennent aisément.

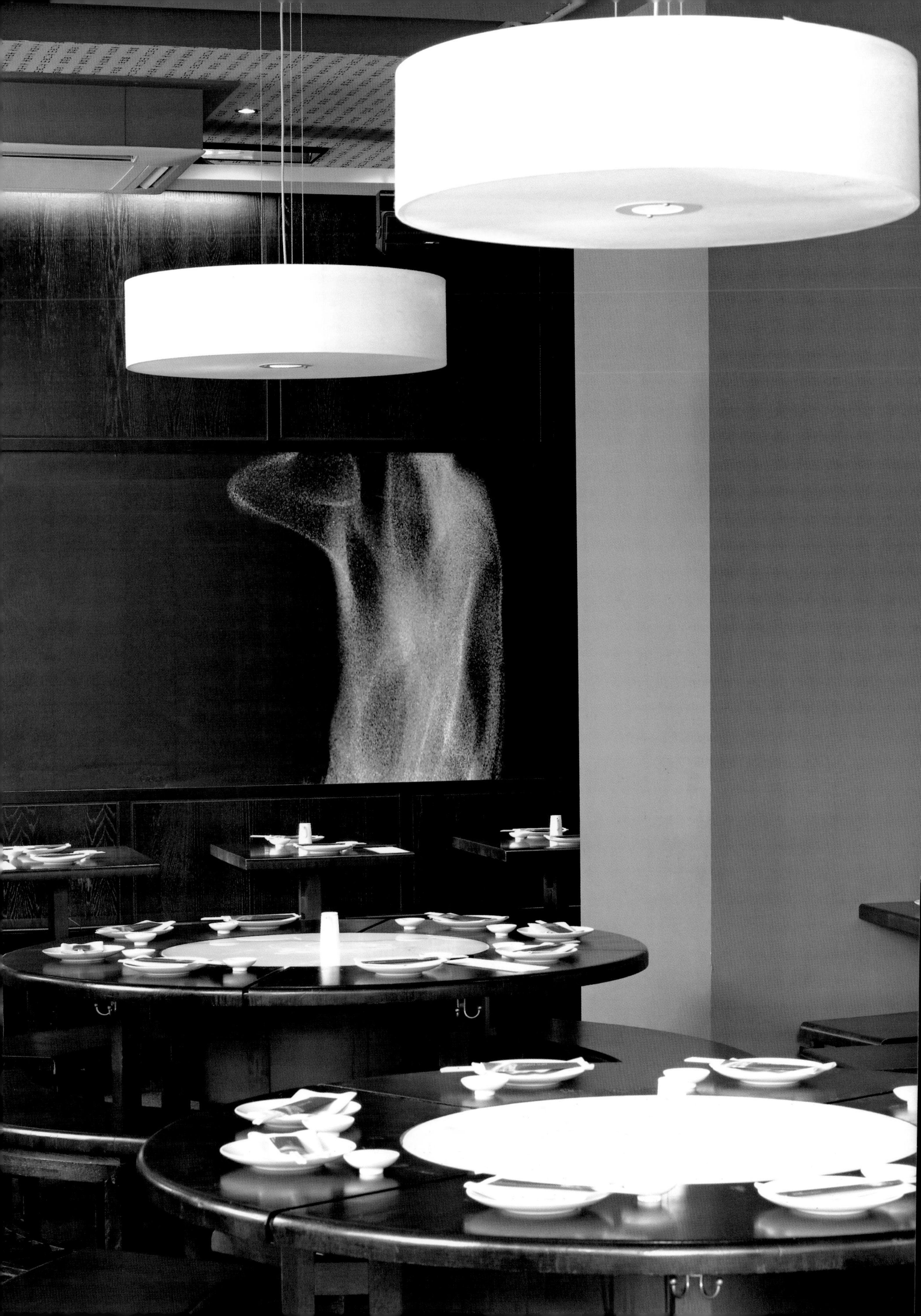

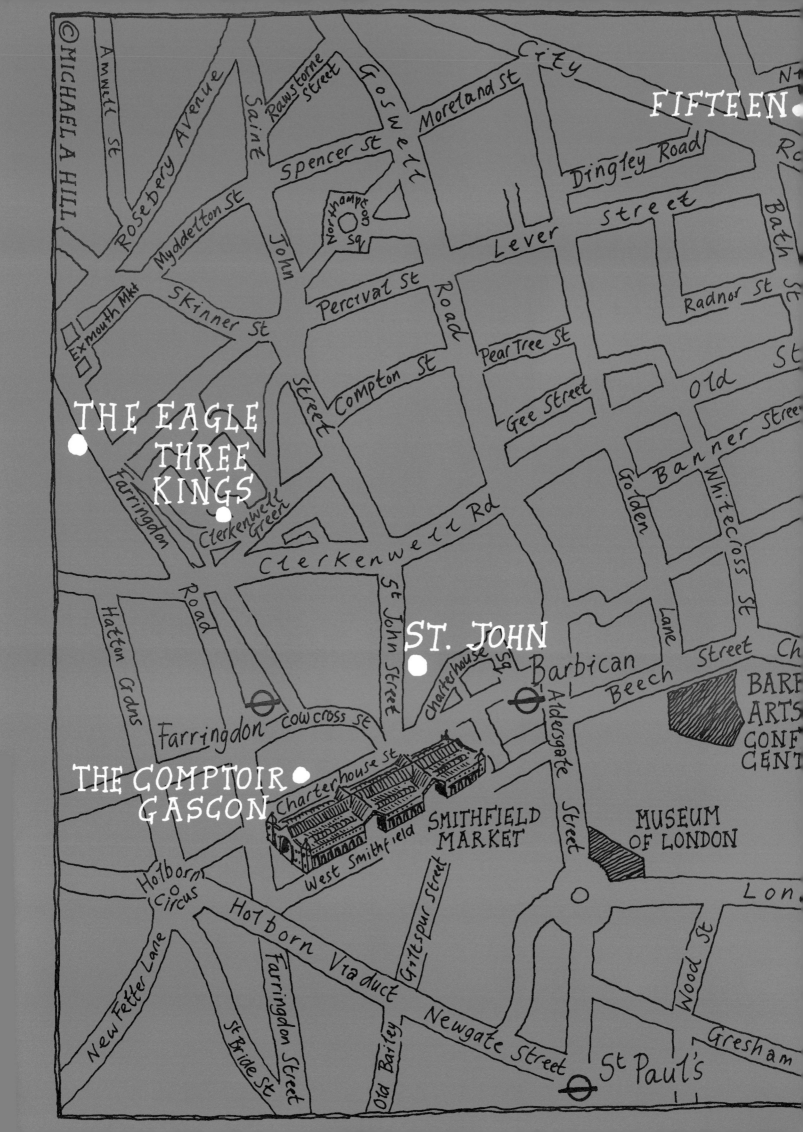

© MICHAEL A HILL

FIFTEEN

THE EAGLE
THREE
KINGS

ST. JOHN

THE COMPTOIR
GASCON

Amwell St

Rosebery Avenue

Rawstorne Street

Saint

Spencer St

Goswell

Northampton Sq

John

Myddelton St

Skinner St

Exmouth Mkt

Farringdon

Clerkenwell Green

Street

Percival St

Compton St

Moreland St

City

Dingley Road

street

Lever

Road

Pear Tree St

Gee Street

Clerkenwell Rd

CLERKENWELL Rd

St John Street

Charterhouse Sq

Barbican

Beech Street

Aldersgate

Street

Radnor St

Bath St

Old

St

Banner Street

Golden

Lane

Whitecross St

BARB
ARTS
CONF
CENT

MUSEUM
OF LONDON

Hatton Gdns

Road

Farringdon

Cow cross St

Charterhouse St

West Smithfield

SMITHFIELD
MARKET

Holborn
Circus

Holborn Viaduct

New Fetter Lane

St Bride St

Farringdon Street

Old Bailey

Giltspur Street

Newgate Street

Wood St

St Paul's

Gresham

Lon

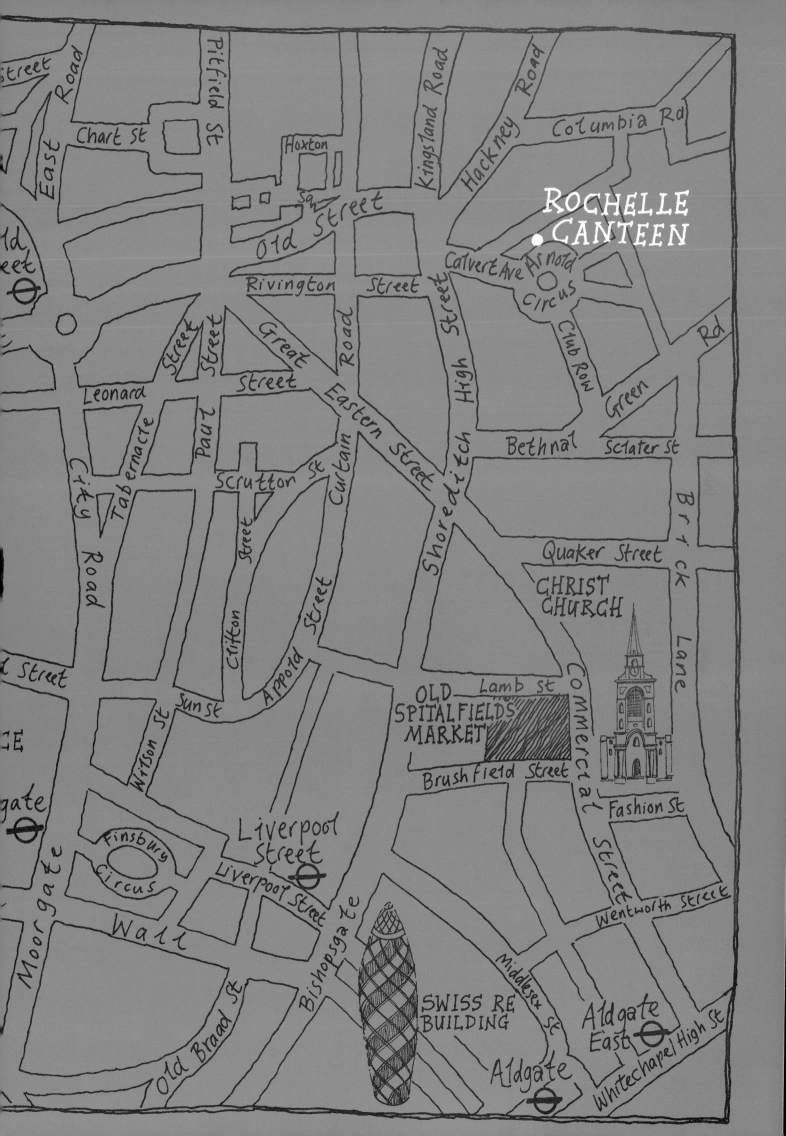

ROCHELLE
CANTEEN

St. John

26 St John Street, London EC1M 4AY
☎ +44 20 7251 0848
www.stjohnrestaurant.com
Tube: Farringdon/Barbican

Fergus Henderson's former smoke-house put St John Street on the culinary map. When he launched St. John in 1994, this Clerkenwell thoroughfare got very little evening trade and this city had little reliable nose-to-tail eating. But Henderson made offal cool during the 1990s, and that's some accomplishment. But just because cows and pigs are sold nearby does not mean you'll get a simple chop here.

Fergus Henderson machte 1994 aus dieser ehemaligen Räucherei an der St John Street einen kulinarischen Begriff. Damals war an dieser Durchgangsstraße in Clerkenwell nicht sehr viel los. Auch bodenständiges Essen, wie Henderson es auf den Tisch brachte, kannte man in London damals noch nicht. Dank ihm wurde ein neues Bewusstsein geschaffen – eine respektable Leistung. Einfache Küche auf hohem Niveau.

En transformant cet ancien fumoir en 1994, Fergus Henderson a placé St John Street sur la carte des gastronomes. Jusque là, Clerkenwell ne disposait pas de bonne table digne de ce nom et les bonnes tripes étaien rares à Londres. Henderson a su rendre les abats chics pendant les années 1990, et ce n'est pas parce que le marché aux bestiaux est à côté qu'on vous servira une simple côtelette.

Interior: Unpretentious loft atmosphere in a former smokehouse.
Open: Mon–Fri midday–3pm, Mon–Sat 6–11pm.
Prices: Dishes £6–29.
X-Factor: The home-made breads are particularly popular with the many regulars and can be bought and taken home.

Interieur: Unprätentiöses Loft-Ambiente in einer ehemaligen Räucherei.
Öffnungszeiten: Mo–Fr 12–15, Mo–Sa 18–23 Uhr.
Preise: Gerichte 6–29 £.
X-Faktor: Die selbst gebackenen Brotsorten sind bei den vielen Stammgästen besonders beliebt und können gekauft und mit nach Hause genommen werden.

Intérieur : Ambiance de loft son prétentieuse dans un ancien fumoir.
Horaires d'ouverture : Lun–Ven 12h–15h, Lun–Sam 18h–23h.
Prix : Plats 6–29 £.
Le « petit plus » : On peut acheter et emporter chez soi les pains maison, très appréciés des habitués du restaurant.

3) CHATEAU DE LASCAUX Btl 17-
COTEAUX DU LANGUEDOC Gls 4.50
2005 Shop 6.65
4) VIN DE PAYSDE MONT CAUME Btl. 17-
DOMAINE LE LUQUETTES Gls. 4.30
2005 Shop 6.99
5) MUSCAT SEC Btl. 18-
COTEAUX DU LIBRON Gls. 4.60
DOMAINE LA COLOMBETTE Shop 7.20
2005
6) COTEAUX D'AIX EN PROVENCE Btl 20.40
CHATEAU REVELETTE 2005 Gls 5.10
Shop 8.30
MEANTIME
GUINNESS
DOUBLE STOUT
6X

CAUTION

Rochelle Canteen

Rochelle School
Arnold Circus, London E2 7AS
☏ +44 20 7729 5677
Tube: Shoreditch

Run by Margot Henderson, who has her own catering company, this lovely lunchtime venue serves the creative workers (think art, fashion, music) whose offices, workshops and studios occupy this former school. It looks like a proper school canteen but the food is British with a European edge – seasonal, simple (that is the secret), always fresh and changing daily.

Die Rochelle Canteen liegt in einem ehemaligen Schulhaus und wird von der Catering-Unternehmerin Margot Henderson geführt. Das reizende Mittagslokal sieht zwar immer noch wie eine Schulkantine aus, wird aber heute von Gästen aus Kunst, Mode und Musik besucht, die hier ihre Büros, Ateliers und Studios eingerichtet haben. Die Küche ist britisch mit kontinentaleuropäischem Einschlag: saisonal, einfach und stets frisch. Das Menü wechselt täglich.

Dirigée par la traiteuse Margot Henderson, c'est la cantine des créatifs (de l'art, de la mode et de la musique) dont les bureaux et ateliers se trouvent dans cette ancienne école. La salle rappelle toujours un réfectoire mais la cuisine (anglaise avec une touche européenne) est saisonnière, simple et toujours fraîche. Le menu change quotidiennement.

Interior: Chic canteen-style in an old schoolhouse.
Open: Mon–Fri midday–3pm.
Prices: Menu approx. £20.
X-Factor: The cook, Margot Henderson.

Interieur: Schicker Kantinenstil in einem alten Schulhaus.
Öffnungszeiten: Mo–Fr 12–15 Uhr.
Preise: Menü um 20 £.
X-Faktor: Die Chefin Margot Henderson.

Intérieur : Cantine chic dans une ancienne école.
Horaires d'ouverture : Lun–Ven 12h–15h.
Prix : Menu env. 20 £.
Le « petit plus » : Le chef Margot Henderson.

The Comptoir Gascon

63 Charterhouse Street, London EC1M 6HJ
☎ +44 20 7608 0851
www.comptoirgascon.com
Tube: Farringdon

The English may still pretend to hate the French, but they will always admit to liking their food. Hence the success of this little gem of a restaurant that has garnered positive commentary from even the most jaded of reviewers. In typical French style, duck and pig feature heavily on the menu as do delicious after-dinner treats like apricot tarts and home-made ice cream.

Zwar kokettieren die Engländer immer noch damit, die Franzosen nicht zu mögen. Doch gegen ihr Essen haben sie überhaupt nichts einzuwenden. Das Comptoir Gascon, ein kleines Juwel, wird selbst von den snobistischsten Restaurantkritikern gelobt. Auf der Menükarte findet man typisch französische Gerichte mit viel Ente und Schwein. Auch die Nachspeisen, wie Aprikosen-Tarte und hausgemachtes Eis, sind köstlich.

Les Anglais ont beau prétendre détester les Français, ils ne peuvent résister à leur cuisine. D'où le succès de ce petit bijou qui s'est attiré les éloges des critiques les plus blasés. La carte typiquement française met l'accent sur le canard et le porc et inclut de délicieux desserts comme les tartes aux abricots et les crèmes glacées faites maison.

Interior: French country-house style.
Open: Bistro: Tue–Sat midday–2pm (lunch) and 7pm–10pm (dinner), Fri/Sat till 11pm; takeaway: Tue–Sat 9am–11pm.
Prices: Dishes £7.50–13.50.
X-Factor: The Cassoulet and duck confit. The wine cellar is well-stocked with vintages from south-western France.

Interieur: Französischer Landhausstil.
Öffnungszeiten: Bistro: Di–Sa 12–14 (Lunch) und 19–22 (Dinner), Fr/Sa bis 23 Uhr; Take-away: Di–Sa 9–23 Uhr.
Preise: Gerichte 7,50–13,50 £.
X-Faktor: Das Cassoulet und Entenconfit. Im Weinkeller lagern sehr gute Sorten und Jahrgänge aus dem Südwesten Frankreichs.

Intérieur : Style campagnard français.
Horaires d'ouverture : Bistro : Mar–Sam 12h–14h (déjeuner) et 19h–22h (dîner), Ven/Sam jusqu'à 23h ; plats à emporter : Mar–Sam 9h–23h.
Prix : Plats 7,50– 13,50 £.
Le « petit plus » : Le cassoulet et le confit de canard. La cave abrite de très bons crus du sud-ouest de la France.

Fifteen

15 Westland Place, London N1 7LP
☎ +44 87 1330 1515
www.fifteen.net
Tube: Old Street

This is fine dining Jamie Oliver-style, meaning the walls are coated with retro mosaics and the dishes have names like "Fantastic Salad." The open kitchen (you may catch Oliver on one of his few days in) serves a six-course tasting menu and a set lunch, with vegetarian options. If you're passing through town without a reservation, you might get a shot at a table in the casual main-floor trattoria.

So wird bei Jamie Oliver diniert: Die Wände sind mit Retromosaiken verziert, und auf den Tisch kommen Gerichte mit Namen wie „Fantastic Salad". In der offenen Küche (mit etwas Glück kann man einen Blick von Oliver erhaschen) werden das sechsgängige Tasting-Menü und ein Lunchmenü mit vegetarischer Alternative zubereitet. Ohne Tischreservation wird man am einfachsten in der schlichten Trattoria im Hauptgeschoss einen Platz finden.

L'esprit de Jamie Oliver règne partout : les murs sont tapissés de mosaïques rétro, les plats portent des noms genre « la salade fantastique ». La cuisine ouverte (vous y apercevrez peut-être Oliver en personne) offre un menu dégustation de six plats ou des menus simples avec options végétariennes. Si vous n'avez pas réservé, tentez quand même d'obtenir une table à la charmante trattoria.

Interior: Retromix by Bobby Desai.
Open: Trattoria: Mon–Sat 7.30am–11am, midday–3pm and 6pm–10pm, Sun 8am–11am, midday–3.30pm and 6pm–9.30pm; Dining Room: Mon–Sun midday–3pm and 6.30pm–9.45pm.
Prices: Dishes £6–24.
X-Factor: The restaurant is also a help project: young people from the social periphery work in the kitchen and serving.

Interieur: Retromix von Bobby Desai.
Öffnungszeiten: Trattoria: Mo–Sa 7.30–11, 12–15 und 18–22, So 8–11, 12–15.30 und 18–21.30 Uhr; Dining Room: Mo–So 12–15 und 18.30–21.45 Uhr.
Preise: Gerichte 6–24 £.
X-Faktor: Das Lokal ist zugleich ein Hilfsprojekt: In Küche und Service arbeiten Jugendliche aus sozialen Randgruppen.

Intérieur : Mélange rétro de Bobby Desai.
Horaires d'ouverture : Trattoria : Lun–Sam 7h30–11h, 12h–15h et 18h–22h, Dim 8h–11h, 12h–15h30 et 18h–21h30 ; Dining Room : Lun–Dim 12h–15h et 18h30– 21h45.
Prix : Plats 6–24 £.
Le « petit plus » : L'établissement est aussi un projet social : des jeunes défavorisés travaillent dans la cuisine et au service.

Three Kings

7 Clerkenwell Close, London EC1R 0DY
☎ +44 20 7253 0483
Tube: Farringdon

You won't notice the Three Kings pub walking around old, industrial Clerkenwell – and they like it that way. The cosy old-school hideaway in a romantic street corner opposite an old church has a loyal clientele from the local film and fashion houses, who gather outside. Its gypsy-chic look and flair with papier-mâché decorations set it apart from the £10 Martini lounges.

Wer durchs alte, industrielle Clerkenwell spaziert, wird den Pub Three Kings ziemlich sicher übersehen. So bleibt dieser Pub an einer romantischen Straßenecke gegenüber einer Kirche ein behaglicher, altmodischer Zufluchtsort für die Stammkunden aus der lokalen Film- und Modebranche. Der Zigeunerschick und die Papiermaschee-Dekorationen sind ein Kontrastprogramm zu den schicken Lounges, in denen ein Martini locker zehn Pfund kostet.

En vous promenant dans le vieux quartier industriel de Clerkenwell vous ne remarquerez sans doute pas The Three Kings mais sa clientèle de gens du cinéma et de mode l'aime pour ça. Situé dans un petit coin romantique en face d'une vieille église, ce pub douillet à l'ancienne a un parfum chic bohème avec des décorations en papier mâché qui le distinguent des bars design à 10 £ le martini.

Interior: Ideal, if you are not looking for a well-styled cool cocktail bar.
Open: Mon–Fri midday–11pm (Sat from 5.30pm).
Prices: Beer from £3.
X-Factor: These Three Kings are no saints – the pub's name pays homage to King Kong, Elvis and Henry VIII.

Interieur: Ideal, wenn es mal keine cool gestylte Cocktailbar sein soll.
Öffnungszeiten: Mo–Fr 12–23 Uhr (Sa ab 17.30).
Preise: Bier ab 3 £.
X-Faktor: Die „Drei Könige" sind hier keine Heiligen – der Name des Pubs ist eine Hommage an King Kong, Elvis und Heinrich VIII.

Intérieur : Plaira à ceux qui n'aiment pas les bars à cocktails stériles.
Horaires d'ouverture : Lun–Ven 12h–23h (Sam à partir de 17h30).
Prix : Bière à partir de 3 £.
Le « petit plus » : Les « Trois Rois » ne sont pas les rois mages. Le nom rend hommage à King Kong, Elvis et Henri VIII.

The Eagle

---

159 Farringdon Road, London EC1R 3AL
☎ +44 20 7837 1353
Tube: Farringdon

By most accounts, The Eagle was London's first gastropub, opened by the Eyre brothers in 1991 and it set the precedent for quality British fare in an honest pub. It has a perennial buzz and the excellent food has kept it at the top of the gastropub rankings all these years: comfort food made with fresh seasonal ingredients.

The Eagle, Londons erster Gastropub, wurde von den Gebrüdern Eyre 1991 eröffnet und gilt als Vorbild für einfache, gute britische Pub-Qualitätskost. Seit Jahren steht das viel beachtete Lokal dank seines exzellenten Essens ganz oben auf der Liste der Gastropubs. Hier gibt's Hausmannskost, zubereitet aus frischen, saisonalen Zutaten.

Ouvert par les frères Eyre en 1991, The Eagle aurait été le premier pub gastronomique de Londres, inaugurant l'ère de la nourriture de qualité dans un pub authentique, brouhaha inclus. Depuis toutes ces années, sa réputation ne s'est pas démentie. La cuisine excellente est à base de produits frais de saison.

Interior: Pleasantly unpretentious. Bistro tables and chair of the most varied styles – the window seats are the best.
Open: Mon–Sat midday–11pm, Sun midday–5pm.
Prices: Dishes approx. £10.
X-Factor: British beer is served with hearty meals, such as the fabulous steak sandwich.

Interieur: Angenehm unprätentiös. Man sitzt an Bistrotischchen auf Stühlen unterschiedlichster Stilrichtungen – am schönsten sind die Fensterplätze.
Öffnungszeiten: Mo–Sa 12–23, So 12–17 Uhr.
Preise: Gerichte um 10 £.
X-Faktor: Zu deftigen Gerichten wie dem herrlichen Steak-Sandwich bestellt man britisches Bier.

Intérieur : Sans prétention. On est assis à des tables de bistro sur des chaises de différents styles. Les meilleures places sont à la fenêtre.
Horaires d'ouverture : Lun–Sam 12h–23h, Dim 12h–17h.
Prix : Plats env. 10 £.
Le « petit plus » : On commandera une bière anglaise pour accompagner les plats goûteux comme le succulent sandwich au steak.

THE EAGLE

BAR

Shops

STELLA McCARTNEY

Jimmy Choo

Agent Provocateur

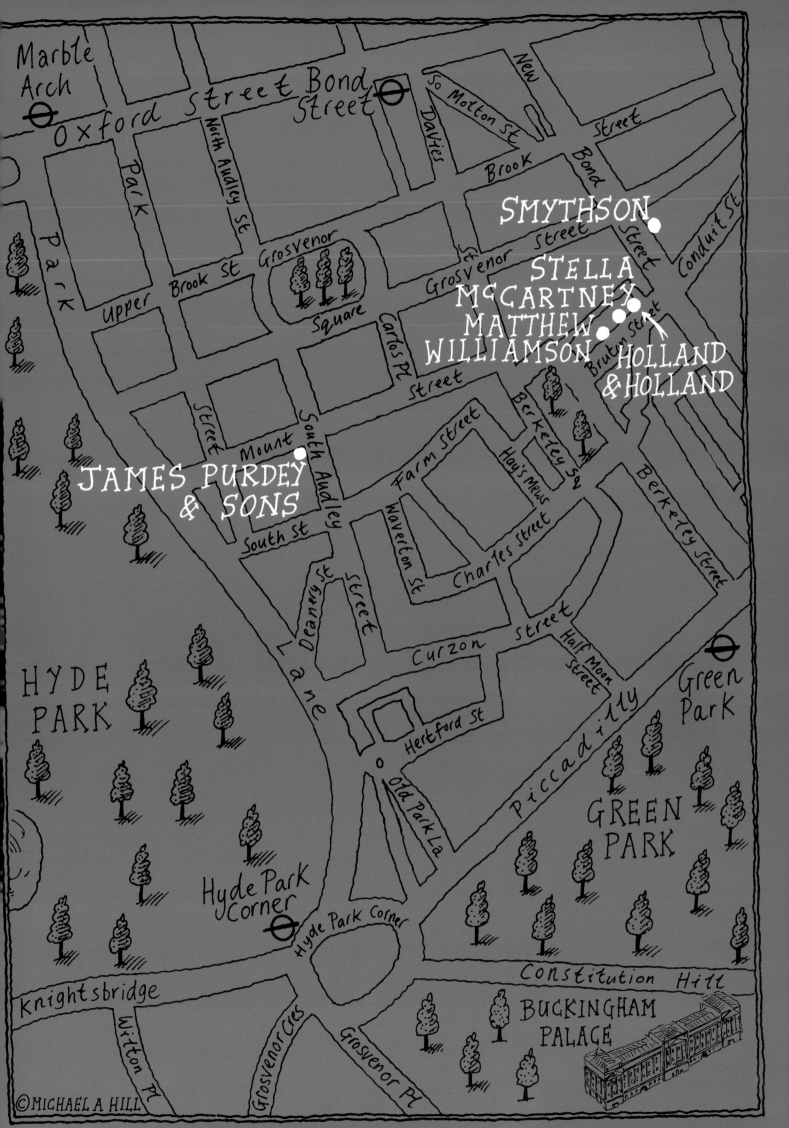

SMYTHSON

STELLA
McCARTNEY
MATTHEW
WILLIAMSON
HOLLAND
& HOLLAND

JAMES PURDEY
& SONS

©MICHAEL A HILL

James Purdey & Sons

Audley House
57–58 South Audley Street, London W1K 2ED
☎ +44 20 7499 1801
www.purdey.co.uk
Tube: Bond Street/Green Park

Hunting may not be a palatable activity to some of us, but there are still plenty of Brits who take the sport very seriously, and Purdey has been around to indulge them since 1814 (the store has been on this site since 1882). Who knew there were so many types of game guns and rifles? Those with a weak stomach can leave the guns on the shelves and instead buy lots of tweed and some Wellingtons.

Nicht jedem sagt die Jagd zu. Doch viele Briten nehmen diesen Sport sehr ernst, und für sie ist Purdey das Paradies schlechthin. Seit 1814 gibt es dieses Geschäft bereits, allerdings erst seit 1882 an dieser Adresse. Man wird hier staunen, wie viele verschiedene Jagdgewehre es überhaupt gibt. Achtung: Wer schwache Nerven hat, sollte unverzüglich zu der zeitlosen Tweedbekleidung und den Gummistiefeln weiterziehen.

Tout le monde n'apprécie pas la chasse mais de nombreux Britanniques prennent encore ce sport très au sérieux. Purdey est leur fournisseur depuis 1814 (la boutique actuelle existe depuis 1882). Qui aurait imaginé qu'il puisse y avoir une telle variété de fusils de chasse ? Les âmes sensibles préféreront sans doute se concentrer sur les beaux tweeds et les bottes en caoutchouc.

Interior: Tastefully conservative – with hunting trophies, oil paintings and old photographs of English gentlemen on the (genuine) fireplace mantelpiece.
Open: Mon–Fri 9.30am–5.30pm, Sat 10am–5pm.
X-Factor: Bespoke shotguns and rifles, such as the Purdey Sporter, as well as exclusive shooting clothing and accessories, e.g. tweeds, cashmere pullovers and safari fashion.

Interieur: Gediegen konservativ – mit Jagdtrophäen, Ölgemälden und alten Fotos englischer Gentlemen auf dem (echten!) Kamin.
Öffnungszeiten: Mo–Fr 9.30–17.30, Sa 10–17 Uhr.
X-Faktor: Maßangefertigte Jagdgewehre, wie den Purdey Sporter, außerdem exklusive Jagdkleidung und -accessoires, wie Tweedjacken, Kaschmirpullover und Safarimode.

Intérieur : Solidité et conservatisme, avec trophées de chasse, tableaux à l'huile et anciennes photos de gentilhommes anglais sur la (vraie !) cheminée.
Horaires d'ouverture : Lun–Ven 9h30–17h30, Sam 10h–17h.
Le « petit plus » : Fabrication de fusils de chasse personnalisés. Également vêtements et accessoires de chasse, comme les vestes en tweed, les pullovers en cachemire et la mode safari.

MOUNT
STREET W1
CITY OF WESTMINSTER
BY APPOINTMENT TO H.M. QUEEN ELIZABETH II
1881
AUDLEY
MANUFACTURERS
PURDEY

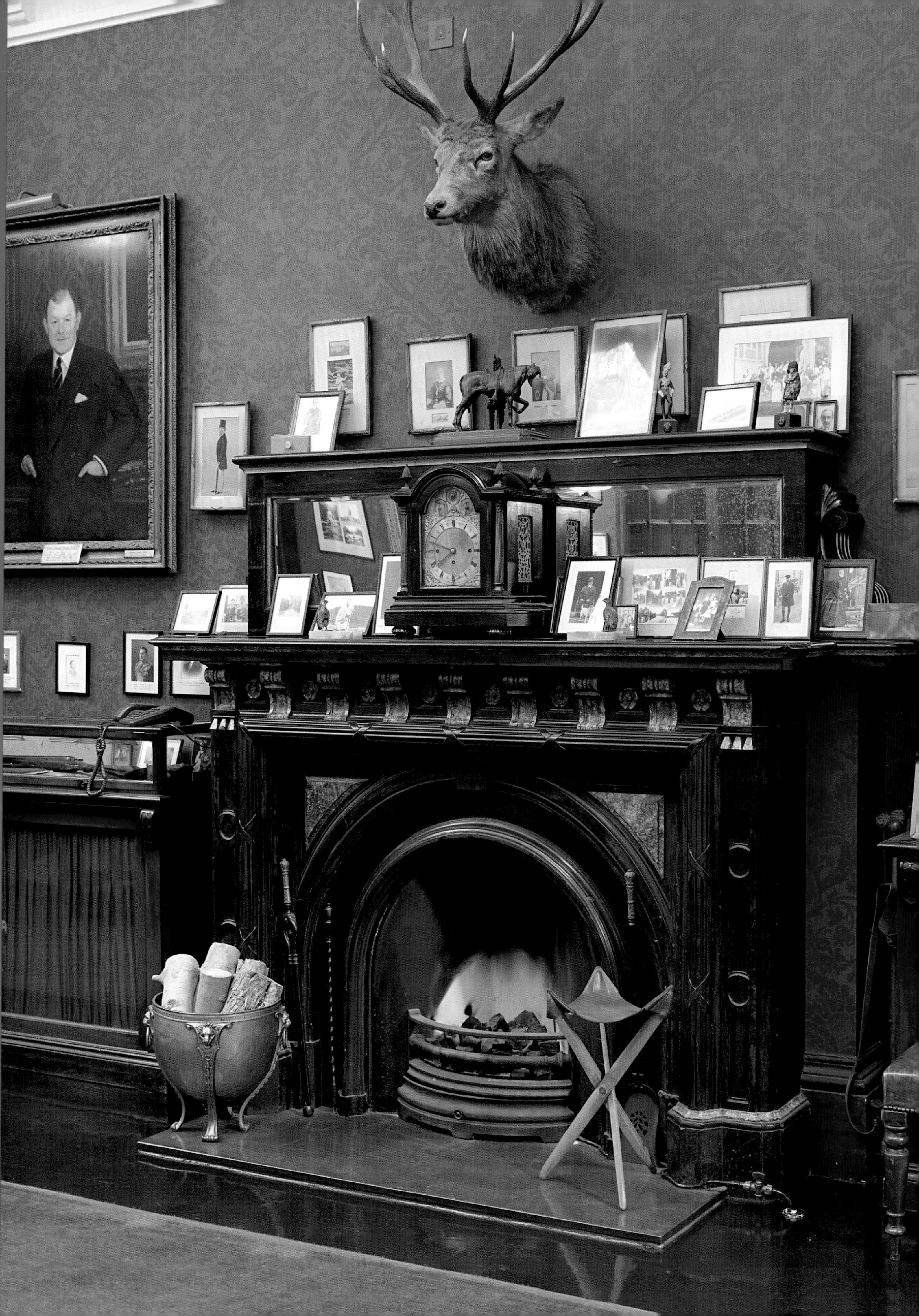

Stella McCartney

30 Bruton Street, London W1J 6LG
☎ +44 20 7518 3100
www.stellamccartney.com
Tube: Bond Street/Green Park

She is the cool princess of the London fashion scene and what Stella McCartney sells in her shop is very much a reflection of her own personal style: a little bit sassy, a bit eclectic and very, very London. Her flattering tailored suits are hugely popular as are her feminine chiffon dresses, which normally come in very pale pinks and other neutrals. Also great are the leather-free handbags and shoes designed by the vegetarian. Lingerie, fragrances and an eco collection can also be found here.

Sie ist das Coolste, was die Londoner Modeszene zu bieten hat. Die Kleider und Accessoires, die Stella McCartney in ihrer Boutique verkauft, entsprechen genau ihrem persönlichen Stil: frech, eklektisch und typisch für London. Genauso beliebt wie die figurschmeichelnden Anzüge sind die femininen Chiffonkleider in Blassrosa und anderen neutralen Tönen. Fantastisch auch die Taschen und Schuhe, die die Vegetarierin McCartney ohne Leder herstellen lässt. Außerdem findet man hier Parfüme, Dessous und eine Ökokollektion.

Dans sa boutique londonienne, la petite princesse de la mode anglaise présente des vêtements qui reflètent son propre sens du style : un peu provocants, éclectiques et très, très british. On s'arrache ses tailleurs impeccables et flatteurs ainsi que ses robes ultra féminines en mousseline de soie rose pâle ou dans d'autres couleurs neutres. Ses sacs et souliers sans cuir valent aussi le détour. On trouve ici aussi des parfums, de la lingerie et une collection écologique.

Interior: The shop interior, perfectly in keeping with the fashion, was designed by Universal Design Studio.
Open: Mon–Sat 10am–6pm, Thur till 7pm.
X-Factor: The organic skin care line Care.

Interieur: Das perfekt zur Mode passende Shop-Interieur wurde von Universal Design Studio entworfen.
Öffnungszeiten: Mo–Sa 10–18, Do bis 19 Uhr.
X-Faktor: Die organische Hautpflegelinie Care.

Intérieur : Universal Design Studio a conçu l'intérieur de la boutique en parfaite harmonie avec la mode présentée.
Horaires d'ouverture : Lun–Sam 10h–18h, Jeu jusqu'à 19h.
Le « petit plus » : La ligne de soins organique Care.

Holland & Holland

33 Bruton Street, London W1J 6HH
☏ +44 20 7499 4411
www.hollandandholland.com
Tube: Bond Street/Green Park

Harris Holland was originally a tobac-
conist – but in 1835 he made his
hobby into his business and started
producing firearms; he was so successful at this that he was permitted
to include the word "royal" in the
company name in 1885. Hand-made
rifles are still sold here, but the stylish
country pursuit and safari fashion
that was added to the portfolio in the
1990s is more suitable for everyday
purposes. The ideal way to take the
cashmere pullovers and tweed jackets
home in style is to buy one of the
elegant leather bags.

Eigentlich war Harris Holland Tabak-
händler – doch 1835 machte er sein
Hobby zum Beruf und gründete eine
Manufaktur für Schusswaffen; er war
damit so erfolgreich, dass er den
Firmennamen 1885 um den Zusatz
„Royal" ergänzen durfte. Handgefer-
tigte Gewehre gibt es hier noch immer – etwas alltagstauglicher ist aber
die schicke Safari- und Countrystyle-
Mode, die in den 1990ern ins Portfolio aufgenommen wurde. Um die
Kaschmirpullis und Tweedjacken stilvoll nach Hause zu bringen, ersteht
man am besten auch eine der eleganten Ledertaschen.

Harris Holland était marchand de ta-
bac mais il aimait la chasse. En 1835,
faisant de son violon d'Ingres un mé-
tier, il fonda une manufacture d'armes
à feu. Celle-ci connut un tel succès
qu'il put accoler en 1885 l'adjectif
« Royal » au nom de sa maison. On
trouve encore ici des fusils fabriqués
à la main, mais la ligne de vêtements
chics de style safari et country, déve-
loppée au cours des années 1990, est
plus adaptée à la vie de tous les jours.
Pour rapporter chez soi les pulls en
cachemire et les vestes en tweed, un
des élégants sacs en cuir s'impose.

Interior: The stuffed animals, oil paintings
and historical photographs in the salesrooms
recall British heritage.
Open: Mon–Fri 9am–6pm, Sat 10am–5pm.
X-Factor: The legendary "Paradox" gun. The
luxury bespoke service.

Interieur: In den Verkaufsräumen erinnen
ausgestopfte Tiere, Ölbilder und historische
Fotos an die britische Kolonialgeschichte.
Öffnungszeiten: Mo–Fr 9–18, Sa 10–
17 Uhr.
X-Faktor: Das legendäre „Paradox"-Gewehr.
Die luxuriösen Maßanfertigungen.

Intérieur : Dans les pièces, les animaux em-
paillés, les toiles et les photos historiques
rappellent le passé colonial de l'Angleterre.
Horaires d'ouverture : Lun–Ven 9h–18h,
Sam 10h–17h.
Le « petit plus » : L'arme légendaire
« Paradox ». Les sur-mesure luxeux.

Matthew Williamson

28 Bruton Street, London W1J 6QH
☎ +44 20 7629 6200
www.matthewwilliamson.com
Tube: Bond Street/Green Park

Matthew Williamson is one of the darlings of the British fashion landscape. He burst on to the scene in the late 1990s with his Indian-inspired colourful fabrics worn by model friends such as Jade Jagger. His look has moved on but his popularity hasn't diminished. His jewel box of a store with his rich colours and striking details is an ode to his particular – and lasting – sense of style.

Matthew Williamson gehört zu den Lieblingen der britischen Modeszene. Auf ihn aufmerksam wurde sie in den späten 1990ern, als Leute wie Jade Jagger anfingen, seine bunten, damals indisch angehauchten Kreationen zu tragen. Sein Look hat sich weiterentwickelt, angesagt ist er genauso wie damals. Seine farbenfrohe Boutique mit vielen interessanten Details erinnert an eine Schmuckschatulle und ist eine Ode an seine eigenwillige Ästhetik.

Matthew Williamson est un des chouchous de la mode anglaise. Il a fait sensation à la fin des années 1990 avec ses tissus aux couleurs indiennes portés par ses amies mannequins comme Jade Jagger. Son style a changé mais pas sa popularité. Sa boutique, un petit bijou rempli de couleurs et de détails, est un hommage à son sens esthétique unique.

Interior: According to Suzy Menkes, this boutique is like a bird of paradise – the interior is as wonderfully colourful as the collections.
Open: Mon–Sat 10am–6pm.
X-Factor: Helena Christensen and Sienna Miller are regular clients here.

Interieur: Diese Boutique gleiche einem Paradiesvogel, schrieb Suzy Menkes – das Interieur ist so fantastisch bunt wie die Kollektionen.
Öffnungszeiten: Mo–Sa 10–18 Uhr.
X-Faktor: Helena Christensen und Sienna Miller sind Stammkundinnen.

Intérieur : Suzy Menkes a écrit que cette boutique ressemblait à un oiseau de paradis, sa décoration est aussi colorée que ses collections.
Horaires d'ouverture : Lun–Sam 10h–18h.
Le « petit plus » : Helena Christensen et Sienna Miller sont de fidèles clientes.

MATTHEW WILLIAMSON
SPICE
scented candle
MATTHEW WILLIAMSON
CITRUS
scented candle
MATTHEW WILLIAMSON
FIG
scented candle
MATTHEW WILLIAMSON
MATTHEW WILLIAMSON
MATTHEW WILLIAMSON

Smythson

40 New Bond Street, London W1S 2DE
☎ +44 20 7629 8558
www.smythson.com
Tube: Bond Street/Oxford Circus

Started in 1887, Smythson has been the purveyor of fine products for those who love stationery. It is the most quintessentially English place in London to get your thank-you cards, bespoke stationery, beautiful pens, leather goods, travel and business accessories. Do not leave the premises without a Classic Travel Wallet. It's as beautiful as it is practical.

Smythson ist seit 1887 Lieferant für edle Schreibwaren und Briefpapiere. Hier kann man Dankeskarten, individuell bedrucktes Briefpapier, edle Schreibstifte und Lederwaren sowie Reise- und Business-Accessoires beziehen – alles in feinster englischer Tradition. Unbedingt eine der Classic-Travel-Brieftaschen erstehen: Sie sind nicht nur schön zum Anschauen, sondern auch äußerst praktisch.

Depuis 1887, Smythson approvisionne les amateurs de beau papier. C'est l'endroit à Londres où acheter ses cartes de remerciement, son papier à en-tête, de beaux stylos et des articles en cuir, ainsi que des accessoires de voyage et de business. Ne repartez pas sans un portefeuille de voyage, ils sont aussi beaux que pratiques.

Interior: Classical elegance, in timeless black, gray and white.
Open: Mon, Tue, Wed, Fri 9.30am–6pm, Thu 10am–7pm, Sat 10am–6pm.
X-Factor: The attractive souvenirs: little notebooks with names like "Happiness is Shopping", "Dreams & Thoughts" or "Me Me Me" printed on them.

Interieur: Klassisch elegant; in zeitlosem Schwarz-Grau-Weiß gehalten.
Öffnungszeiten: Mo, Di, Mi, Fr 9.30–18, Do 10–19, Sa 10–18 Uhr.
X-Faktor: Schöne Souvenirs sind die Notizbüchlein mit Titeln wie „Happiness is Shopping", „Dreams & Thoughts" oder „Me Me Me".

Intérieur : Élégante et classique ; en couleurs intemporelles de noir, gris, blanc.
Horaires d'ouverture : Lun, Mar, Mer, Ven 9h30–18h, Jeu 10h–19h, Sam 10h–18h.
Le « petit plus » : Les calepins aux titres de « Happiness is Shopping », « Dreams & Thoughts » ou « Me Me Me » seront de jolis souvenirs.

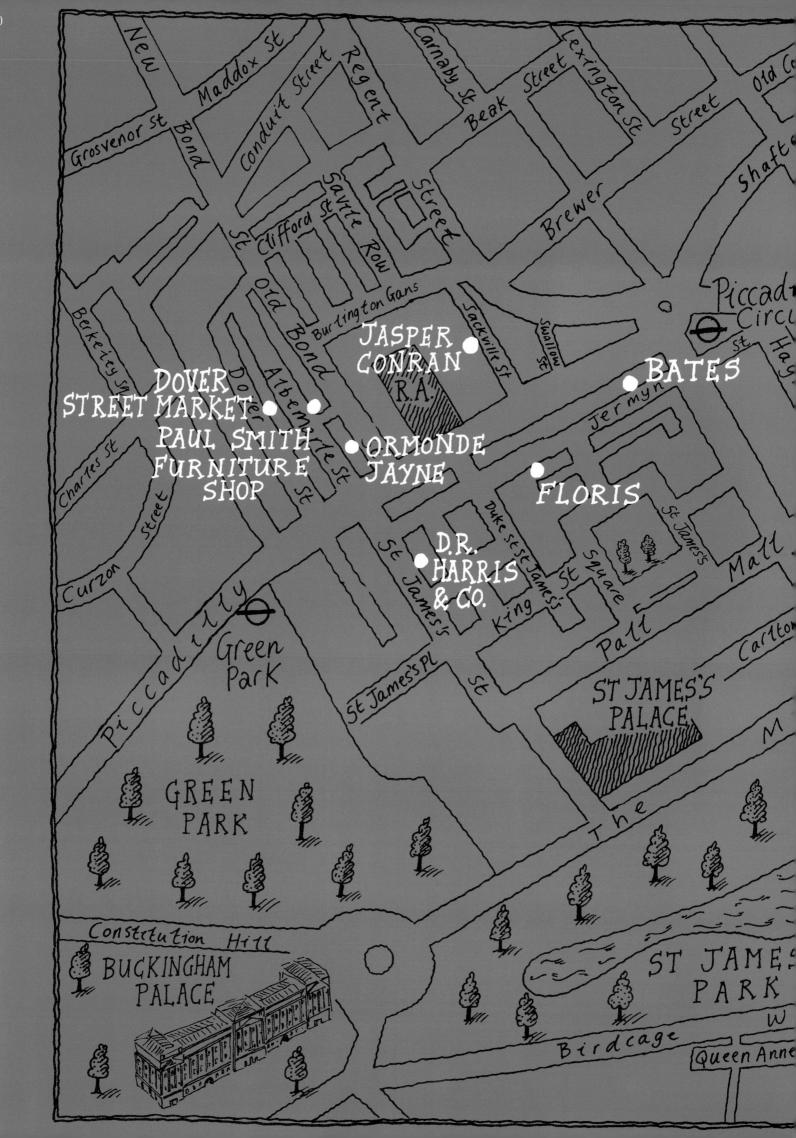

Avenue

Charing Cross

Leicester
Square

Long Acre

Covent
Garden

COVENT
GARDEN

Aldwych

Wellington St

● PENHALIGON'S

Cranbourn St

New Row

Bedford St

Maiden Lane

Strand

St Martins Lane

Road

Cockspur St

Terrace

mb St

William IV St

NATIONAL
GALLERY

Trafalgar Square

Cockspur St

John Adam St

Savoy Pl

Embankment

Waterloo Bridge

Charing
Cross

Villiers St

● Embankment

Northumberland
Ave

Whitehall Place

Whitehall Court

Hungerford Bridge

Hungerford Footbridges

ROYAL
FESTIVAL
HALL

Belvedere Road

Horse Guards Road

Whitehall

Victoria

R. THAMES

LONDON
EYE

Downing Street

Horseguards Ave

Parliament St

Gt George St

Parliament

Square

● Westminster

Westminster Bridge

York Road

HOUSES OF
PARLIAMENT

© MICHAELA HILL

Ormonde Jayne

The Royal Arcade
28 Old Bond Street, London W1S 4SL
☎ +44 20 7499 1100
www.ormondejayne.com
Tube: Green Park

Linda Pilkington founded this divine little perfumery in 2003 with an aim to sell gorgeous, luxury scents. The shop is located in the beautiful Victorian Royal Arcade built in the 1880s. All of her perfumes are made in London and her perfume library boasts scents inspired by her worldwide travels. Walk out with a new signature scent or just pick up perfumed candles as wonderful gifts.

Linda Pilkington bietet in dieser 2003 von ihr gegründeten reizenden, kleinen Parfümerie wunderbare Luxusdüfte an, und das mitten in dem wunderschönen Bau der viktorianischen Royal Arcade aus den 1880ern. Alle Parfüms werden in London hergestellt; dazu gibt es eine Parfüm-Bibliothek mit Düften, inspiriert von Pilkingtons Reisen rund um die Welt. Einen der neuen Düfte zu erwerben ist ein Muss, und die Duftkerzen geben schöne Geschenke her.

Linda Pilkington a ouvert cette charmante petite parfumerie en 2003 afin d'y vendre ses fragrances luxueuses. Elle est située dans les belles Royal Arcades victoriennes, une galerie bâtie vers 1880. Tous ses parfums sont fabriqués à Londres et beaucoup s'inspirent de ses voyages à travers le monde. Repartez avec votre nouveau parfum ou simplement des bougies parfumées qui font des cadeaux divins.

Interior: The luxuriously dramatic atmosphere conjured up by the brilliant black glass is the work of Caulder Moore.
Open: Mon–Sat 10am–6pm.
X-Factor: Even the shower creams and bath oils have exotic aromas – Frangipani being particularly fragrant.

Interieur: Das luxuriös-dramatische Ambiente aus glänzendem schwarzen Glas stammt von Caulder Moore.
Öffnungszeiten: Mo–Sa 10–18 Uhr.
X-Faktor: Auch die Duschcremes und Badeöle haben exotische Aromen – besonders gut riecht Frangipani.

Intérieur : Caulder Moore a créé cette ambiance luxueuse et dramatique en verre noir brillant.
Horaires d'ouverture : Lun–Sam 10h–18h.
Le « petit plus » : Les crèmes de douche et les huiles de bain ont elles aussi des arômes exotiques, celui à la frangipane sent particulièrement bon.

12
11
ORMONDE JAYNE
London Perfumery
CARROLL SECURITY GROUP
www.ormondejayne.com
ORMONDE JAYNE

EAU DE
PARFUM
£58.00

Paul Smith Furniture Shop

9 Albemarle Street, London W1S 4BL
☎ +44 20 7493 4565
www.paulsmith.co.uk
Tube: Green Park

As with Sir Paul Smith's fashion collections, the furniture he peddles has his quirky British modern twist (and humour) all over it. He opened this funky shop opposite Brown's Hotel in 2005 and he showcases pieces of contemporary furniture jazzed up with interesting fabrics or older pieces modernised with his own textiles. Colourful china, the ones in Smith's signature stripes, are also cool.

Genau wie seine Mode ist die Möbelkollektion von Sir Paul Smith eigenwillig britisch und humorvoll. Das unkonventionelle Geschäft gleich gegenüber dem Brown's Hotel eröffnete er 2005. Hier gibt es mit interessanten Stoffen aufgepeppte Möbel, aber auch gebrauchte Stücke, die mit Smith-Textilien zu neuem Leben erweckt wurden. Cool ist auch das bunte Porzellangeschirr mit den typischen Paul-Smith-Streifen.

Comme sa mode, les meubles choisis par Sir Paul Smith possèdent cette touche d'excentricité et d'humour toute britannique. Dans cette boutique ouverte en face du Brown's Hotel en 2005, il présente des meubles contemporains égayés par des tissus intéressants ou des pièces plus anciennes modernisées avec ses propres textiles. On y trouve aussi de jolies porcelaines aux rayures typiquement Paul Smith.

Interior: Two rooms that are entirely different in design – simplicity and minimalism vs. antique market.
Open: Mon, Tue, Wed, Fri 10.30am–6pm, Thu 10.30am–7pm, Sat 10am–6pm.
X-Factor: Rare and ever changing objects including antique furniture re-upholstered in Paul Smith fabrics. Sir Paul Smith offers a continually changing collection of extraordinary furniture, art and curios from around the world.

Interieur: Zwei Räume in völlig unterschiedlichen Designs – Schlichtheit und Minimalismus vs. Antikmarkt.
Öffnungszeiten: Mo, Di, Mi, Fr 10.30–18, Do 10.30–19, Sa 10–18 Uhr.
X-Faktor: Seltene und immer wechselnde Objekte, u. a. Vintage-Möbel, die mit Paul-Smith-Stoffen neu bezogen werden. Sir Paul Smith bietet eine Kollektion außergewöhnlicher Möbel, Kunstwerke und Kuriositäten aus der ganzen Welt.

Intérieur : Deux pièces au design complètement différent – sobriété et minimalisme contre marché d'antiquités.
Horaires d'ouverture : Lun, Mar, Mer, Ven 10h30–18h, Jeu 10h30–19h, Sam 10h–18h.
Le « petit plus » : Objets rares et meubles vintage retapissés avec des tissus Paul-Smith. Sir Paul Smith propose une collection exceptionnelle de meubles, œuvres d'art et curiosités venant du monde entier.

Dover Street Market

17–18 Dover Street, London W1S 4LT
☎ +44 20 7518 0680
www.doverstreetmarket.com
Tube: Green Park

Started by Comme des Garçons in 2004, it is more like a museum. In the so-called Tachiagari the interior is completely transformed by different designers to reflect the new collections of the season. Fashion is exhibited here, not merely hung up for customers to admire. This is where Raf Simons displayed his creations in an environment designed by Jan De Cock. Brands include big names such as Lanvin and John Galliano but more obscure labels (Sacai Gem, Ronnie Loves and Tabletop) are well served too.

Eigentlich ist Dover Street Market mehr ein Museum als ein Geschäft. Von Comme des Garçons 2004 ins Leben gerufen, werden hier Kleider wie Ausstellungsstücke präsentiert. Beim so genannten Tachiagari wird das Interieur von verschiedenen Designern komplett neu gestaltet, um die Ideen der aktuellen Kollektionen der Saison widerzuspiegeln. So zeigte Raf Simons seine Kreationen in einer vom Künstler Jan De Cock gestalteten Umgebung. Neben anderen großen Namen wie Lanvin und John Galliano findet man hier auch weniger bekannte Labels wie Sacai Gem, Ronnie Loves und Tabletop.

Lancé par Comme des Garçons en 2004, c'est plus un musée où les clients peuvent admirer la mode présentée dans différents environnements. Dans le fameux Tachiagari, l'intérieur est intégralement redécoré par différents designers afin de refléter les idées des collections de la saison actuelle. C'est ainsi que Raf Simons a montré ses créations dans un environnement aménagé par l'artiste Jan De Cock. On y trouve de grands créateurs comme Lanvin ou John Galliano mais aussi des marques plus obscures telles que Sacai Gem, Ronnie Loves ou Tabletop.

Interior: The original concept is by Rei Kawakubo, the alternating show areas are designed by people like Michael Howells (for John Galliano and YSL) and Alber Elbaz (for Lanvin), for example.
Open: Mon–Sat 11am–6pm, Thu till 7pm.
X-Factor: In the Rose Bakery on the fourth floor you can take a break from shopping and have a soup, risotto or a pastry.

Interieur: Das ursprüngliche Konzept stammt von Rei Kawakubo, die wechselnden Show-flächen werden z. B. von Designern wie Michael Howells (für John Galliano und YSL) und Alber Elbaz (für Lanvin) gestaltet.
Öffnungszeiten: Mo–Sa 11–18, Do bis 19 Uhr.
X-Faktor: In der Rose Bakery im 4. Stock kann man bei Suppen, Risottos und Gebäck eine Shoppingpause einlegen.

Intérieur : Le concept d'origine est de Rei Kawakubo, les espaces de présentation sont aménagés par des designers comme par exemple Michael Howells (pour John Galliano et YSL) et Alber Elbaz (pour Lanvin).
Horaires d'ouverture : Lun–Sam 11h–18h, Jeu jusqu'à 19h.
Le « petit plus » : Une pause shopping à la Rose Bakery (4e étage) s'impose pour déguster une soupe, un risotto ou des biscuits.

DOVER STREET MARKET

COMME des GARÇONS

Jasper Conran

36 Sackville Street, London W1S 3EQ
☎ +44 20 7292 9080
www.jasperconran.com
Tube: Piccadilly Circus

Jasper Conran's flagship store is a thing of beauty and impeccable taste. Housed in a Georgian building, the shop opened in 2005 and is the perfect environment in which to try on his luxurious pieces or just wander around feeling like a guest in a private home. Women can't go wrong with his flattering evening dresses, while men gravitate towards the well-cut suits. His home collection is also beautiful.

Jasper Conran hat 2005 in diesem Haus im georgianischen Stil seinen Flagship-Store eröffnet, der zum Inbegriff des guten Geschmacks geworden ist. Es ist der perfekte Ort, um seine Luxussachen anzuprobieren oder etwas herumzustöbern und sich dabei wie ein gern gesehener Gast in einem Privathaus zu fühlen. Die figurschmeichelnden Abendkleider und gut geschnittenen Anzüge sind immer richtig. Auch die Home Collection ist wunderbar.

Beauté et bon goût sont les mots d'ordre de la boutique phare de Jasper Conran, ouverte en 2005 dans un bâtiment du XVIIIᵉ siècle. On peut y essayer ses superbes vêtements ou se promener comme un invité dans une maison particulière. On ne peut pas se tromper avec ses robes du soir flatteuses et ses costumes d'hommes impeccablement coupés. Le linge de maison est également très beau.

Interior: Jasper Conran designed these rooms not like a classical shop, but more like a private house. The elegant interior is in white, grey and black.
Open: Mon–Fri 10.30am–6.30pm, Sat by appointment.
X-Factor: A made to measure brides and grooms collection is also offered.

Interieur: Jasper Conran hat die Räume nicht wie einen klassischen Shop, sondern eher wie ein Privathaus angelegt. Das elegante Interieur ist in Weiß, Grau und Schwarz gehalten.
Öffnungszeiten: Mo–Fr 10.30–18.30 Uhr, Sa nach Vereinbarung.
X-Faktor: Es werden auch maßgeschneiderte Kollektionen für Braut und Bräutigam angeboten.

Intérieur : Jasper Conran n'a pas décoré la boutique de manière classique, mais comme une résidence privée. L'élégant intérieur est tout en blanc, gris et noir.
Horaires d'ouverture : Lun–Ven 10h30–18h30, Sam sur rendez-vous.
Le « petit plus » : Propose également des collections mariage sur-mesure.

D.R. Harris & Co.

29 St James's Street, London SW1A 1HB
☎ +44 20 7930 3915
www.drharris.co.uk
Tube: Green Park

D.R. Harris has been established in St James's since 1790, when the area was known as Clubland because of the many gentlemen's clubs located there. This traditional pharmacy holds a royal warrant as chemist for HRH The Prince of Wales. Customers come in for the all-natural skincare products – some made from recipes that are 125 years old – and for badger-hair brushes.

Als D.R. Harris 1790 in St James's gegründet wurde, nannte man diese Gegend wegen der vielen ansässigen Herrenklubs „Clubland". Die traditionelle Apotheke ist königlicher Hoflieferant des Prinzen von Wales und hat sich vor allem mit natürlichen Hautpflegeprodukten, die heute noch aus zum Teil 125 Jahre alten Rezepten hergestellt werden, einen Namen gemacht. Bei D.R. Harris findet man auch Bürsten aus echtem Dachshaar.

D.R. Harris est établi à St James's depuis 1790 quand le quartier était surnommé Clubland en raison des nombreux clubs de gentlemen. Cette pharmacie traditionnelle est le fournisseur attitré de S.A.R. le prince de Galles. On vient y chercher ses cosmétiques 100% naturels (certains confectionnés à partir de recettes vieilles de 125 ans) et ses blaireaux de barbier.

Interior: In one of London's oldest pharmacies the products are still presented in ancient display cases and shelves.
Open: Mon–Fri 8.30am–6pm, Sat 9.30am–5pm.
X-Factor: The hand-made brushes, shaving sets, creams and soaps make charmingly old-fashioned gifts for the modern man.

Interieur: Die Nähe zum Adel verpflichtet: In einer der ältesten Pharmazien Londons werden die Produkte noch immer in den antiken Vitrinen und Regalen präsentiert.
Öffnungszeiten: Mo–Fr 8.30–18, Sa 9.30–17 Uhr.
X-Faktor: Die handgefertigten Bürsten, Rasiersets und -seifen und Cremes sind herrlich altmodische Geschenke für den modernen Mann.

Intérieur : Noblesse à proximité oblige : dans l'une des plus anciennes pharmacies de Londres on présente encore les articles dans des vitrines et des étagères surannées.
Horaires d'ouverture : Lun–Ven 8h30–18h, Sam 9h30–17h.
Le « petit plus » : Les brosses, trousses de rasages et savons maison sont de merveilleux cadeaux désuets pour l'homme d'aujourd'hui.

Floris

89 Jermyn Street, London SW1Y 6JH
☎ +44 20 7930 2885
www.florislondon.com
Tube: Green Park/Piccadilly Circus

Though the staff at Floris, founded in 1730, will no longer iron the bank notes before handing you your change, as they did in the 19th century, they will present it to you on a velvet-covered tray. Floris fragrances have been worn by British monarchs since 1820, as well as by such luminaries as Noël Coward and Eva Perón. The sandalwood scent is particularly lovely.

Im 19. Jahrhundert pflegte das Personal beim 1730 gegründeten Parfümeur Floris die Banknoten zu bügeln, bevor sie den Kunden überreicht wurden. Diese Zeiten sind zwar vorbei, doch das Wechselgeld wird heute – immer noch stilvoll – auf einem samtbezogenen Tablett übergeben. Seit 1820 haben britische Monarchen und auch illustre Namen wie Noël Coward und Eva Perón die Düfte von Floris getragen. Besonders fein riecht der Sandelholzduft.

On n'y repasse plus les billets avant de vous rendre la monnaie comme au XIXᵉ siècle mais elle vous est quand même tendue sur un plateau en velours. Fondé en 1730, Floris parfume les monarques britanniques depuis 1820 et a compté parmi ses clients des célébrités telles que Noël Coward et Eva Perón. Son santal est particulièrement divin.

Interior: The wonderful display cases are made of Spanish mahogany and were crafted in 1851 on the occasion of the First World Exhibition in London.
Open: Mon–Fri 9.30am–6pm, Sat 10am–6pm.
X-Factor: In 1730 Juan Famenias Floris left Menorca for England, where he opened a hair-dressing shop – which has become a perfume empire.

Interieur: Die wunderschönen Vitrinen sind aus spanischem Mahagoni und wurden 1851 anlässlich der ersten Weltausstellung in London gefertigt.
Öffnungszeiten: Mo–Fr 9.30–18, Sa 10–18 Uhr.
X-Faktor: 1730 kam Juan Famenias Floris aus Menorca nach England und eröffnete einen Friseurladen – daraus ist ein Duftimperium geworden.

Intérieur : Les magnifiques vitrines sont en acajou espagnoles et ont été fabriquées en 1851, à l'occasion de la la première Exposition universelle organisée à Londres.
Horaires d'ouverture : Lun–Ven 9h30–18h, Sam 10h–18h.
Le « petit plus » : En 1730, Juan Famenias Floris quitta Minorque pour l'Angleterre où il ouvrit un salon de coiffure devenu aujourd'hui un empire du parfum.

Bates

21a Jermyn Street, London SW1Y 6HP
☎ +44 20 7734 2722
www.bates-hats.co.uk
Tube: Piccadilly Circus

London's world-renowned black cabs are still designed to accommodate a man wearing a top hat. So why not stop by Bates and have one made to measure? This famous milliner, which has been outfitting gentlemen since the turn of the last century, can also supply such quintessentially British styles as the bowler and the deerstalker.

Die weltberühmten schwarzen Londoner Taxis sind so gebaut, dass man auch mit einem Hut auf dem Kopf Platz hat. Ein guter Grund, bei Bates vorbeizuschauen, um sich einen maßgefertigten Hut machen zu lassen. Der legendäre Hutmacher stattet seit der vorletzten Jahrhundertwende die eleganten Herren der Stadt aus, und hier findet man so typisch Britisches wie Melonen und Sherlock-Holmes-Kopfbedeckungen.

Les célèbres cabs noirs de Londres sont conçus pour accueillir un gentleman en haut-de-forme. Alors pourquoi ne pas commander le vôtre sur-mesure chez Bates ? Ce célèbre chapelier qui coiffe ces messieurs depuis un siècle peut aussi vous proposer d'autres classiques anglais comme le chapeau melon et la casquette à la Sherlock Holmes.

Interior: It would be impossible to fit more hats into so small a space! The items are packed in elegantly old-fashioned hat-boxes.
Open: Mon–Fri 9am–5pm, Sat 9.30am–1pm and 2pm–4pm.
X-Factor: This traditional shop is still run by the original family.

Interieur: Mehr Hüte sind auf kleinem Raum kaum möglich! Verpackt werden die Einkäufe in eleganten, altmodischen Hutschachteln.
Öffnungszeiten: Mo–Fr 9–17, Sa 9.30–13 und 14–16 Uhr.
X-Faktor: Der traditionsreiche Laden ist noch immer familiengeführt.

Intérieur : Impossible de placer un chapeau de plus sur un si petit espace ! À noter, les boîtes à chapeaux élégantes et surannées.
Horaires d'ouverture : Lun–Ven 9h–17h, Sam 9h30–13h et 14h–16h.
Le « petit plus » : La boutique riche en traditions est encore une entreprise familiale.

Penhaligon's

41 Wellington Street, London WC2E 7BN
☎ +44 20 7836 2150
www.penhaligons.co.uk
Tube: Covent Garden

Classic scents in beautiful packaging is the essence of what this shop is about. The company was founded in 1870 by William Henry Penhaligon, who came to London from Penzance to become a barber, but found himself selling perfumed waters and pomades to the aristocracy. Kate Moss' favourite is Bluebell. Treat yourself to the citrusy Blenheim Bouquet scent, created in 1902, in the beautiful glass bottle.

Penhaligon's, das sind klassische Düfte in wunderschöner Verpackung. Das Geschäft wurde 1870 von William Henry Penhaligon gegründet, der, weil er Friseur werden wollte, von Penzance, Cornwall, nach London zog. Friseur wurde er dann doch nicht. Stattdessen verkaufte er der Aristokratie parfümierte Wasser und Pomaden, und 1902 schuf er den Zitrusduft Blenheim Bouquet. Der Lieblingsduft von Kate Moss ist Bluebell. Wer sich verwöhnen will, sollte eines der traumhaft schönen Glasflakons erstehen.

Des fragrances classiques superbement présentées. La maison a été fondée par William Henry Penhaligon en 1870, venu de Penzance pour devenir barbier mais s'étant retrouvé vendant des eaux parfumées et des pommades à l'aristocratie de Londres. Le parfum favori de Kate Moss est Bluebell. Faites-vous plaisir avec le Blenheim Bouquet, aux senteurs citriques, créé en 1902 et vendu dans un magnifique flacon en verre.

Interior: Luxurious British understatement at its best: display cases, mirrors and parquet flooring all highly polished.
Open: Mon–Sat 10am–6pm (Thu till 7pm).
X-Factor: The Hammam Bouquet first created in 1872 is still on sale today.

Interieur: Luxuriös-britisches Understatement at its best: Vitrinen, Spiegel und Parkett sind auf Hochglanz poliert.
Öffnungszeiten: Mo–Sa 10–18 Uhr (Do bis 19).
X-Faktor: Bis heute kann man hier die erste Kreation Hammam Bouquet von 1872 kaufen.

Intérieur : Understatement luxueux et britannique dans toute sa splendeur : vitrines, miroirs et parquet brillent de mille feux.
Horaires d'ouverture : Lun–Sam 10h–18h (Jeu jusqu'à 19h).
Le « petit plus » : On peut encore acheter Hammam Bouquet, la toute première création de 1872.

HOICE PERFUMERY

Penhaligon's
ARTEMISIA
Eau de Parfum
PENHALIGON'S
LONDON
ARTEMISIA
BATH OIL
Penhaligon's
ARTEMISIA
Classic Candle
PENHALIGON'S
ARTEMISIA
500ml
ARTEMISIA
TESTER
PENHALIGON'S
LONDON

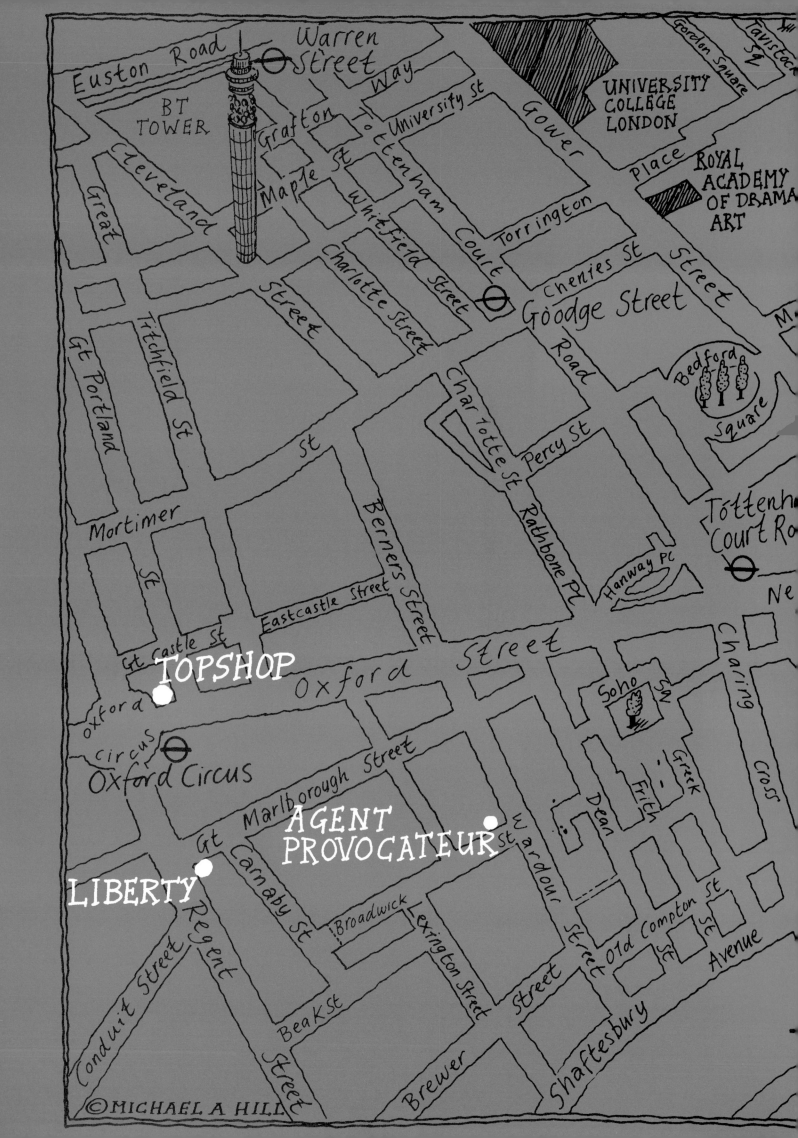

©MICHAEL A HILL

Agent Provocateur

6 Broadwick Street, London W1F 8HL
☎ +44 20 7439 0229
www.agentprovocateur.com
Tube: Tottenham Court Road/Oxford Circus

Soho has always had a risqué reputation, but it's seldom as stylishly executed as at Agent Provocateur, the lingerie shop opened by Joseph Corre and Serena Rees in 1994. The emphasis is on vintage styles and a saucy, tongue-in-cheek eroticism, as evidenced in the pale pink house coats worn by the sales girls and the naughty tableaux in the windows.

Gewagtes fand man in Soho schon immer. Doch so richtig stilvoll wird es erst beim Dessous-Geschäft Agent Provocateur, das von Joseph Corre und Serena Rees 1994 gegründet wurde. Vintage-Look wird hier mit frechironischer Erotik umgesetzt, kesse Verkäuferinnen tragen blassrosane Kittel, und im Schaufenster hängen leicht anzügliche Bilder.

Soho a toujours eu une réputation de quartier chaud mais le libertinage a rarement été aussi chic que chez Agent Provocateur, la boutique de lingerie ouverte par Joseph Corre et Serena Rees en 1994. Le style rétro est à l'honneur ainsi que l'érotisme coquin et ironique comme en attestent les blouses rose pâle des vendeuses et les tableaux grivois en vitrine.

Interior: The shop is in pale pink and black. The boudoir-style fitting rooms are a highlight.
Open: Mon–Wed, Fri/Sat 11am–7pm, Thu 11am–8pm, Sun midday–5pm.
X-Factor: The sales staffs' shop-coats were designed by Vivienne Westwood.

Interieur: Der Shop ist in Blassrosa und Schwarz gehalten; Highlights sind die Umkleidekabinen im Boudoir-Stil.
Öffnungszeiten: Mo–Mi, Fr/Sa 11–19, Do 11–20, So 12–17 Uhr.
X-Faktor: Die Kittelkleider der Verkäuferinnen entwarf Vivienne Westwood.

Intérieur : La boutique est tout en rose clair et noir ; les highlights sont les cabines d'essayage dans le style d'un boudoir.
Horaires d'ouverture : Lun–Mer, Ven/Sam 11h–19h, Jeu 11h–20h, Dim 12h–17h.
Le « petit plus » : C'est Vivienne Westwood qui a dessiné les blouses des vendeuses.

Liberty

Regent Street, London W1B 5AH
☎ +44 20 7734 1234
www.liberty.co.uk
Tube: Oxford Circus

With its Tudor façade, signature floral prints and mellow wood interior, Liberty is one of the more old-fashioned of London's department stores. But don't let that fool you: the shopping here is second to none. It has an ever-changing selection of new and exciting labels, as well as a fantastic interiors section with vintage and classic designs mixed in with newer ones.

Mit einer Fassade im Tudor-Stil und behaglichem Blumenmuster- und Holzdekor gehört Liberty zu den Kaufhäusern der altmodischen Sorte. Doch von solchen Äußerlichkeiten sollte man sich nicht täuschen lassen. Hier gibt's die neuesten und aufregendsten Labels und eine fantastische Interior-Abteilung mit Vintage-Möbeln und Designklassikern zusammen mit ein paar neuen Entwürfen.

Avec sa façade Tudor, ses imprimés fleuris et ses boiseries patinées, Liberty a un charme désuet mais ne vous y trompez pas : c'est un paradis du shopping. Sa sélection de nouvelles marques intéressantes est constamment renouvelée et son formidable rayon décoration mêle le classique et le vintage aux dernières créations.

Interior: The striking building dating from the 1920s is by Edwin T. Hall and his son Edwin S. Hall. The wood used for the magnificent panelling inside is from the two legendary ships HMS Impregnable and HMS Hindustan.
Open: Mon–Sat 10am–9pm, Sun midday–6pm.
X-Factor: The concierge at Liberty knows not only the shop but can also recommend the best restaurants and cafes nearby.

Interieur: Das markante Gebäude bauten Edwin T. Hall und sein Sohn Edwin S. Hall in den 1920ern. Für die herrliche Vertäfelung im Inneren verwendeten sie das Holz der beiden legendären Schiffe HMS Impregnable und HMS Hindustan.
Öffnungszeiten: Mo–Sa 10–21, So 12–18 Uhr.
X-Faktor: Der Liberty-Concierge kennt nicht nur das Kaufhaus sehr gut, sondern verrät auch die besten Restaurants und Cafés in der Nähe.

Intérieur : Ce remarquable bâtiment a été construit par Edwin T. Hall et son Fils Edwin S. Hall dans les années 1920. Pour les magnifiques boiseries à l'intérieur ils ont utilisé le bois des deux navires légendaires, le HMS Impregnable et le HMS Hindustan.
Horaires d'ouverture : Lun–Sam 10h–21h, Dim 12h–18h.
Le « petit plus » : Le concierge connaît non seulement le magasin, mais révèle aussi les meilleurs restaurants et cafés du quatier.

Topshop

214–216 Oxford Street, London W1D 1LA
☎ +44 20 7636 7700
www.topshop.com
Tube: Oxford Circus

No visit to London is complete without a stop at Topshop's flagship store. If it was on the runway, you'll find an affordable version of it here, along with a nail bar and a café. Expectant mothers can also keep up to date with Topshop's maternity range. If you're having trouble finding what you want, consult one of the resident style advisers, who'll be happy to scour the rails for you.

Ohne einen Abstecher in den Topshop-Flagship-Store gemacht zu haben, kann man London unmöglich verlassen. Hier findet man eine erschwingliche Version von Laufstegmode, eine Nagelpflege-Bar und ein Café. Auch werdende Mütter müssen nicht auf die letzten Trends verzichten: Die Umstandskleidung ist modisch. Praktisch: die Topshop-Style-Berater, die für ihre Kunden nach den passenden Stücken suchen.

Une visite à Londres ne serait pas complète sans un passage par la boutique phare de Topshop. Vous y trouverez toutes les nouvelles tendances à des prix abordables, ainsi qu'un nail bar et un café. Les futures mamans ne seront pas en reste grâce à une section maternité branchée. Si vous êtes perdu, des conseillers en style vous aideront à parcourir les rayons.

Interior: This flagship store is also the chain's largest: 90000 square feet presented in ever changing designs.
Open: Mon, Tue, Wed, Sat 9am–8pm, Thu/Fri 9am–10pm, Sun 11.30–6pm.
X-Factor: The online shop.

Interieur: Der Flagship-Store ist zugleich der größte der Kette – er umfasst 8400 immer wieder neu gestaltete Quadratmeter.
Öffnungszeiten: Mo, Di, Mi, Sa 9–20, Do/Fr 9–22, So 11.30–18 Uhr.
X-Faktor: Der Onlineshop.

Intérieur : Le Flagship Store est le plus grand de la chaîne avec ses 8400 mètres carrés constamment redécorés.
Horaires d'ouverture : Lun, Mar, Mer, Sam 9h–20h, Jeu/Ven 9h–22h, Dim 11h30–18h.
Le « petit plus » : La boutique Internet.

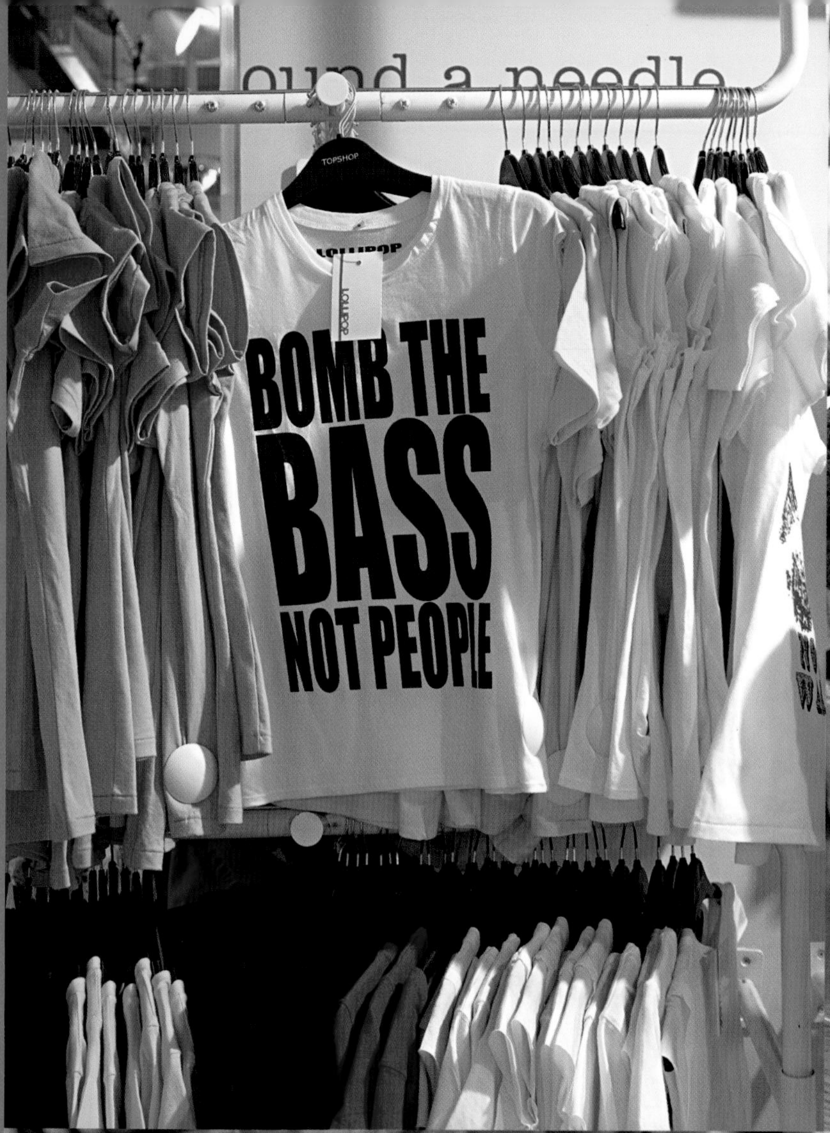

ound a needle

BOMB THE
BASS
NOT PEOPLE

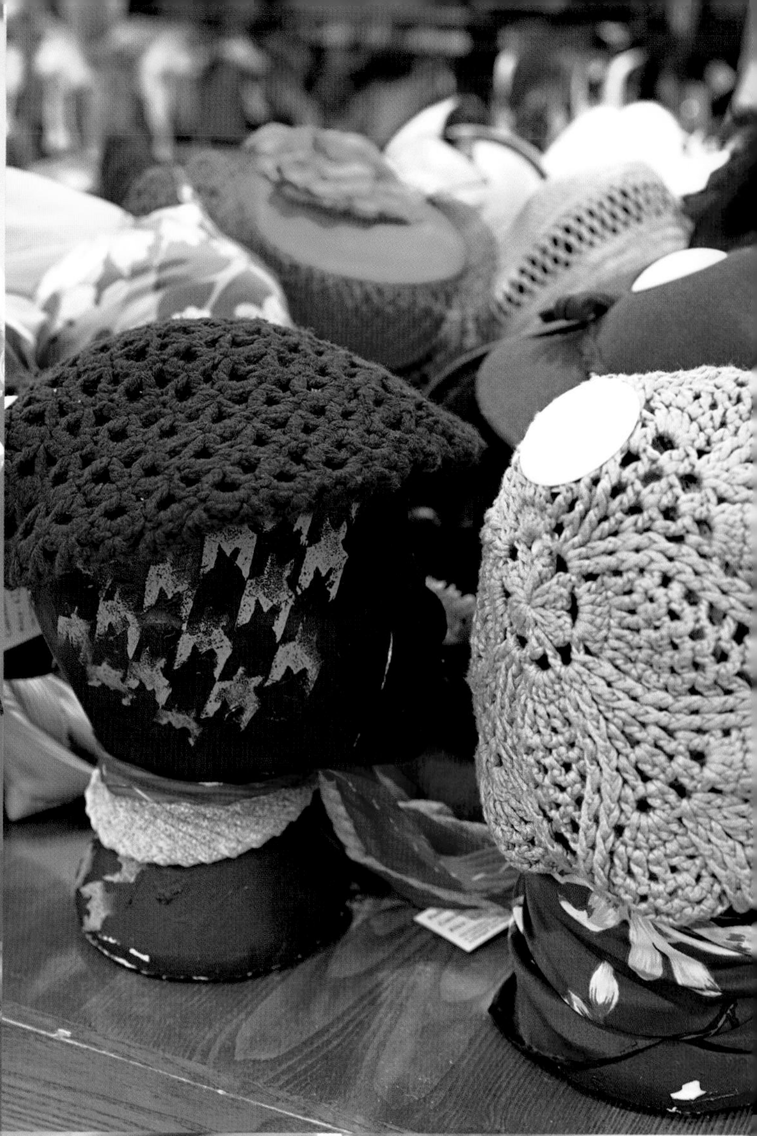

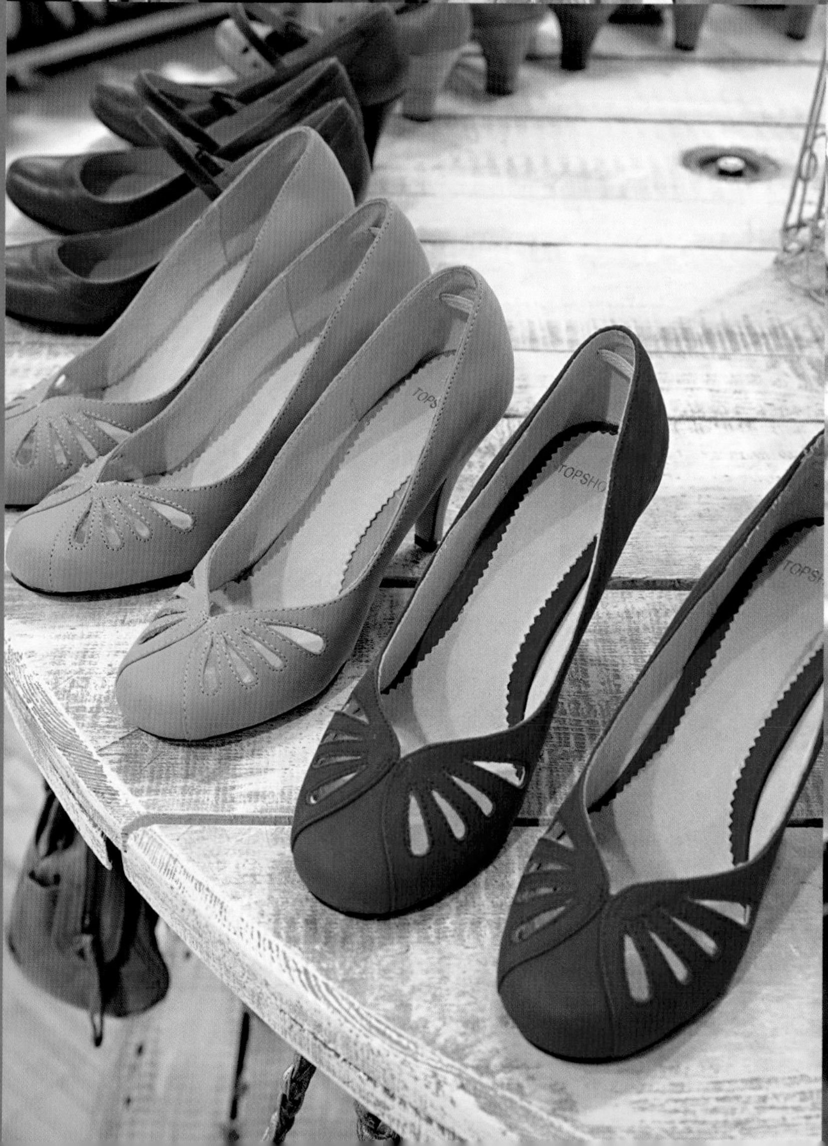

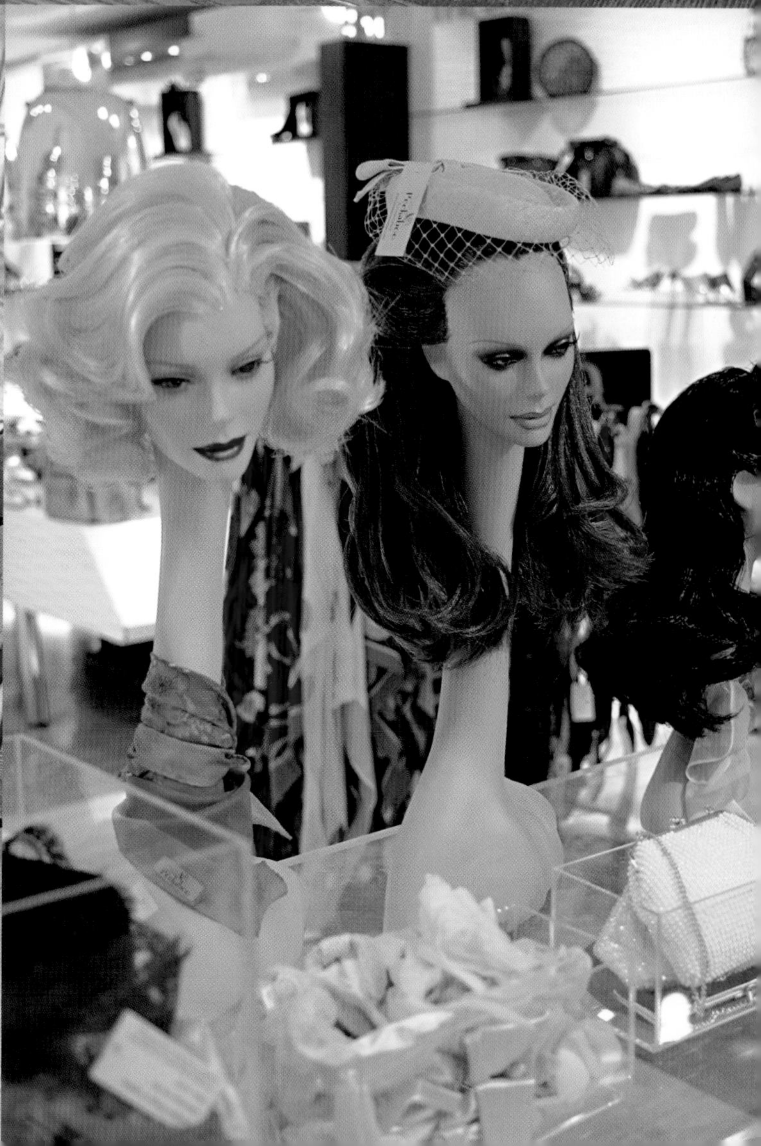

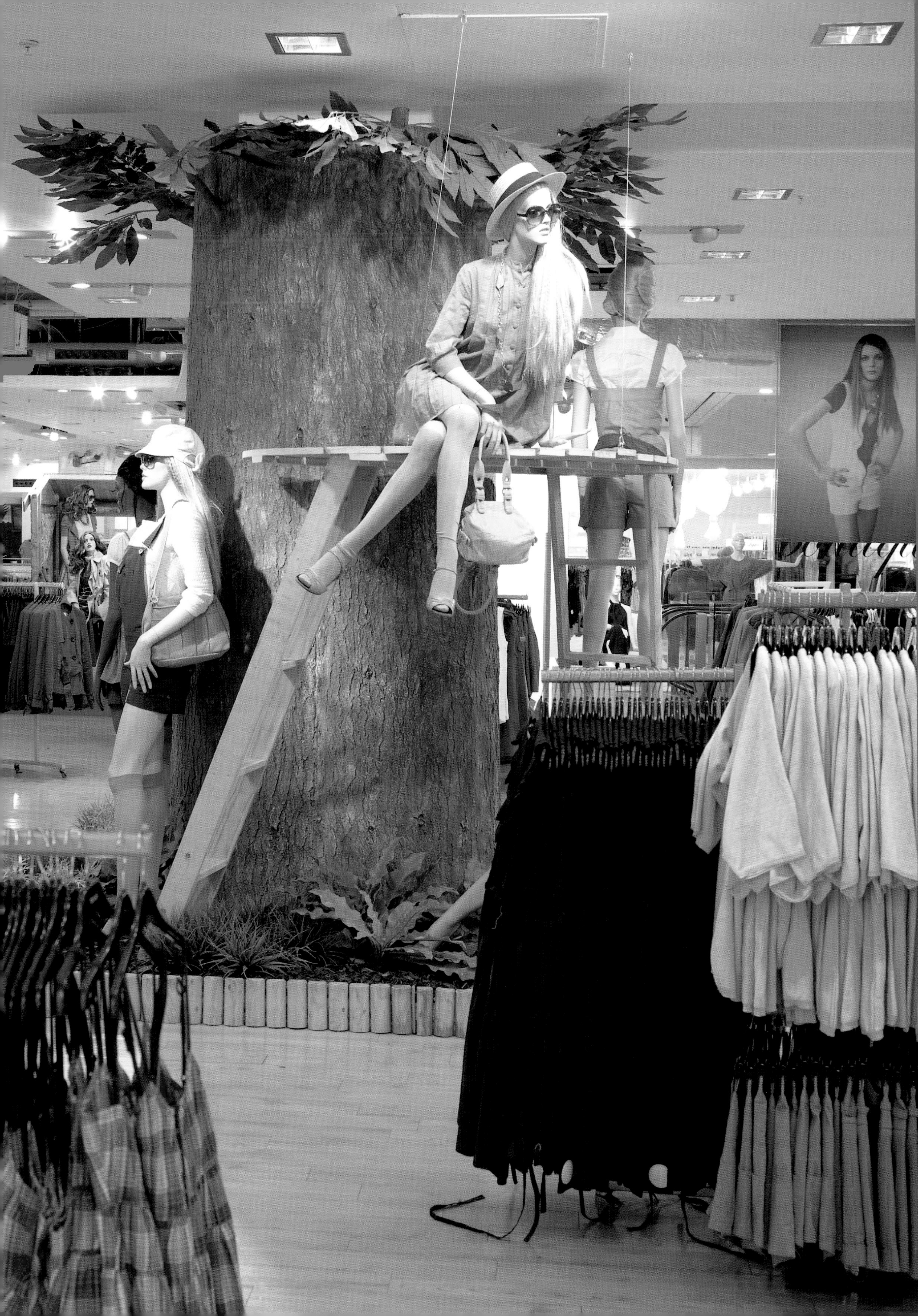

Neal's Yard Remedies

15 Neal's Yard, London WC2H 9DH
☎ +44 20 7379 7222
www.nealsyardremedies.com
Tube: Covent Garden

Neal's Yard Remedies, a charming little shop, was opened in a hippy dippy courtyard in1981. Surrounded by groovy hair salons, tattoo parlours and vegetarian restaurants, the company has stuck to its philosophy of providing natural, organic, handmade remedies and cosmetics using its own herbs grown in Dorset. The signature blue bottles are as practical as they are pretty: they cut down 97% of UV light and protect the sensitive herbal extracts.

Neal's Yard Remedies wurde 1981 in diesem alternativen Hinterhof gegründet und ist heute von coolen Hair-Salons, Tattoo-Shops und vegetarischen Restaurants umgeben. Das Unternehmen stellt natürliche, handgemachte Bio-Heilmittel und -Pflegeprodukte aus eigens dafür angebauten Kräutern in Dorset her. Die dunkelblauen Fläschchen sind praktisch – sie schützen die empfindlichen Kräuterextrakte vor UV-Strahlung – und sind schön anzuschauen.

Neal's Yard Remedies a ouvert sa charmante boutique en 1981 dans cette cour aux accents baba cool. Entourée de salons de coiffure branchés, d'échoppes de tatoueurs et de restaurants végétariens, elle est restée fidèle à sa philosophie : proposer des produits naturels, bios et artisanaux à base de ses propres herbes cultivées dans le Dorset. Aussi jolis que pratiques, ses flacons bleus protègent les extraits végétaux des UV.

Interior: The façade is colourful, while the shop interior is simple; the most important things here are the products. Good Feng Shui.
Open: Mon–Fri 10.30am–7pm, Sat 9.30am–7pm, Sun 11am–6pm.
X-Factor: The Therapy Rooms next door, where a wide range of massages, acupuncture, homeopathy and flower essence therapy are available.

Interieur: So bunt die Fassade ist, so schlicht gibt sich der Shop selbst – das Wichtigste sind hier die Produkte. Gutes Feng Shui.
Öffnungszeiten: Mo–Fr 10.30–19, Sa 9.30–19, So 11–18 Uhr.
X-Faktor: Die Therapy Rooms nebenan mit vielfältigem Angebot von Massagen über Akupunktur zu Homöopathie und Blütenessenz-Therapie.

Intérieur : Autant la façade est colorée, autant la boutique est sobre ; le plus important ici sont les produits. Bon Feng Shui.
Horaires d'ouverture : Lun–Ven 10h30–19h, Sam 9h30– 19h, Dim 11h–18h.
Le « petit plus » : Les Therapy Rooms avec leur offre diversifiée qui va des massages à l'homéopathie et l'aromathérapie en passant par l'acupuncture.

Neal's Yard Dairy

17 Shorts Gardens, London WC2H 9UP
☎ +44 20 7240 5700
www.nealsyarddairy.co.uk
Tube: Covent Garden

If you love cheese, you'll love Neal's Yard Dairy. Since opening in 1979, it's been providing Londoners with all-natural, hand-made cheeses and yoghurts by independent regional farmers. You can get everything here from Italian-style Mozzarella di Bufala to a Gloucestershire favourite known as Stinking Bishop. All the Dairy's cheeses are seasonal, so you may not find what you came in for – but you'll no doubt find something just as good.

Neal's Yard Dairy ist ein Schlaraffenland für Liebhaber britischer Käsesorten. Seit 1979 werden hier Londoner mit handgemachtem Käse und Joghurt aus natürlichen Zutaten von unabhängigen regionalen Farmern verwöhnt. Ob ein Mozzarella di bufala oder ein Stinking Bishop aus Gloucestershire – man findet so ziemlich alles. Die Käse werden saisonal hergestellt, deshalb findet man nicht immer, was man sucht. Ein Ersatz wird aber garantiert genauso gut schmecken.

Amateurs de fromages, Neal's Yard Dairy est faite pour vous. Depuis 1979, cette boutique approvisionne les Londoniens en fromages et yaourts naturels maison, provenant de fermes indépendantes de la région. Le choix va de la mozzarella de buffle à « l'évêque puant », une spécialité du Gloucestershire. Les produits étant saisonniers, vous n'y trouverez peut-être pas ce que vous cherchez mais vous ressortirez certainement avec autre chose d'aussi bon.

Interior: The cheeses are stacked on a simple counter – very picturesque and very enticing.
Open: Mon–Sat 10am–7pm.
X-Factor: Only regional cheeses from Great Britain and Ireland, which ripen in the rooms of Neal's Yard Dairy in Bermondsey under brick railway arches.

Interieur: Auf einer einfachen Theke stapeln sich die Käselaibe – sehr malerisch und sehr verlockend duftend.
Öffnungszeiten: Mo–Sa 10–19 Uhr.
X-Faktor: Ausschließlich regionale Käse aus Großbritannien und Irland, die in den Räumen von Neal's Yard Dairy unter Bahngleisbögen in Bermondsey reifen.

Intérieur : Les meules de fromages sont empilées sur un comptoir tout simple : très pittoresque et délicieusement odorant.
Horaires d'ouverture : Lun–Sam 10h–19h.
Le « petit plus » : Exclusivement des fromages régionaux de Grande-Bretagne et d'Irlande qui sont portés à maturité dans les locaux de Neal's Yard Dairy à Bermondsey.

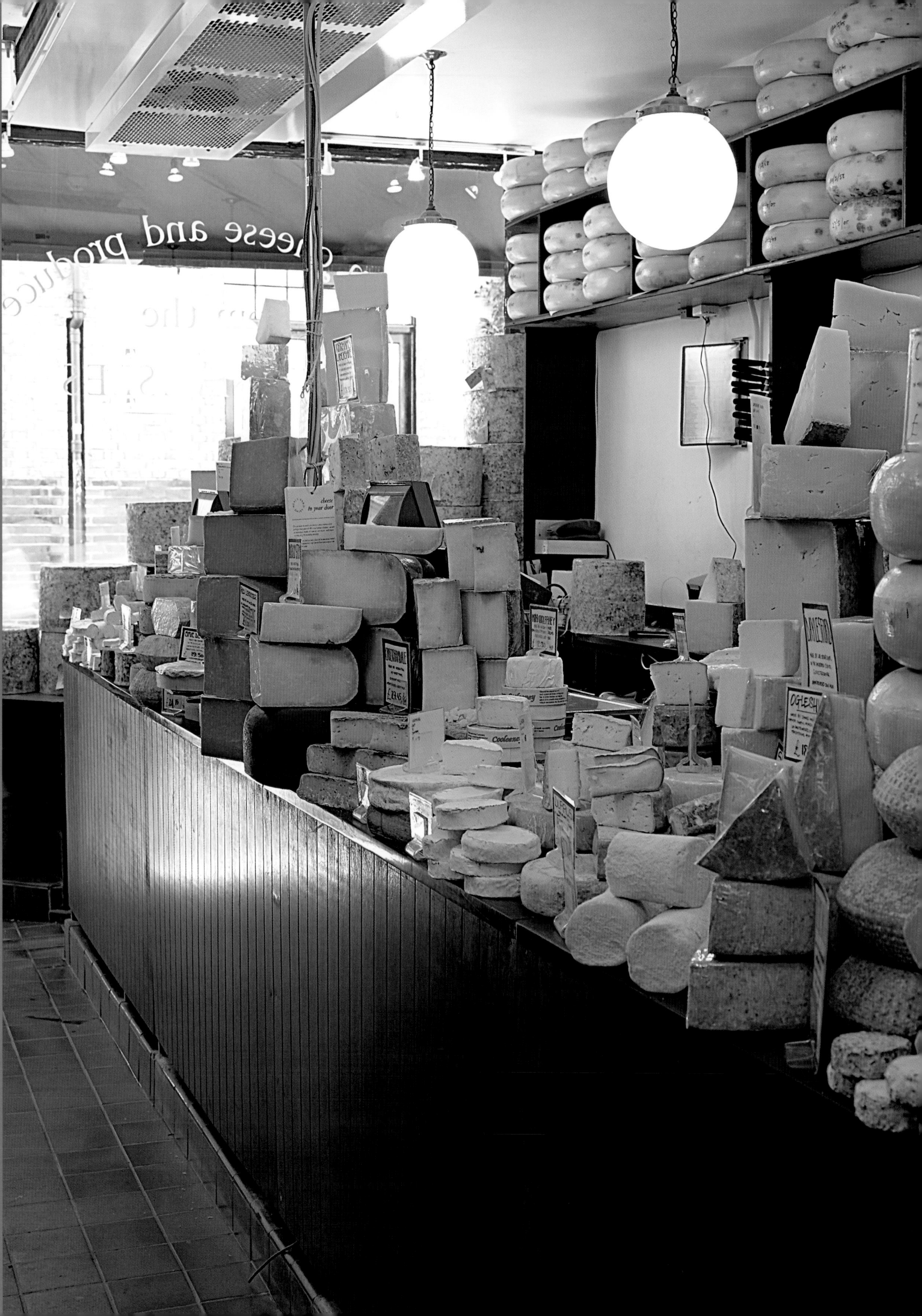
cheese to your door
Cooleeney

James Smith & Sons

Hazelwood House
53 New Oxford Street, London WC1A 1BL
☎ +44 20 7836 4731
www.james-smith.co.uk
Tube: Tottenham Court Road

James Smith & Sons, established in 1830, is where to turn when the British weather does what it does best: pour with rain. Locals go to this legendary shop – and have done so since 1857 – for the tried-and-tested brands of umbrellas, and some contemporary styles (the line by Paul Smith, for example). There are few London rituals so time-honoured as a visit to Smith's, rain or shine. And its classic walking sticks make great souvenirs.

Zeigt sich das britische Wetter von seiner besten Seite und schickt wieder mal Regen, sollte man James Smith & Sons, gegründet 1830, aufsuchen. In diesem legendären Geschäft decken sich die Londoner seit 1857 mit Schirmen ein. Neben altbewährten Modellen findet man auch neue, etwa solche von Paul Smith. Es gibt wenige Rituale, die den Lauf der Zeit so überstehen wie der Besuch bei Smith & Sons. Zu den Klassikern gehören die Gehstöcke: Sie sind super Geschenke.

Quand le climat anglais est fidèle à sa réputation, à savoir qu'il pleut, James Smith & Sons, fondé en 1830 est l'endroit où aller. Les Londoniens fréquentent cette boutique légendaire depuis 1857 pour s'équiper en parapluies solides ou en marques contemporaines (comme la ligne de Paul Smith). Même si le soleil est au rendez-vous, une visite chez Smith est un rituel londonien. Ses cannes classiques font de beaux cadeaux.

Interior: The interior is reminiscent of the Victorian era.
Open: Mon–Fri 9.30am–5.25pm, Sat 10am–5.25pm.
X-Factor: Used and broken umbrellas are expertly repaired and restored.

Interieur: Das Interieur lässt die viktorianische Epoche wiederaufleben.
Öffnungszeiten: Mo–Fr 9.30–17.25, Sa 10–17.25 Uhr.
X-Faktor: Gebrauchte und kaputte Schirme werden hier fachkundig aufpoliert und repariert.

Intérieur : L'intérieur fait revivre l'époque victorienne.
Horaires d'ouverture : Lun–Ven 9h30–17h25, Sam 10h–17h25.
Le « petit plus » : Les vieux parapluies retrouvent une seconde jeunesse et ceux qui sont cassés sont réparés avec compétence.

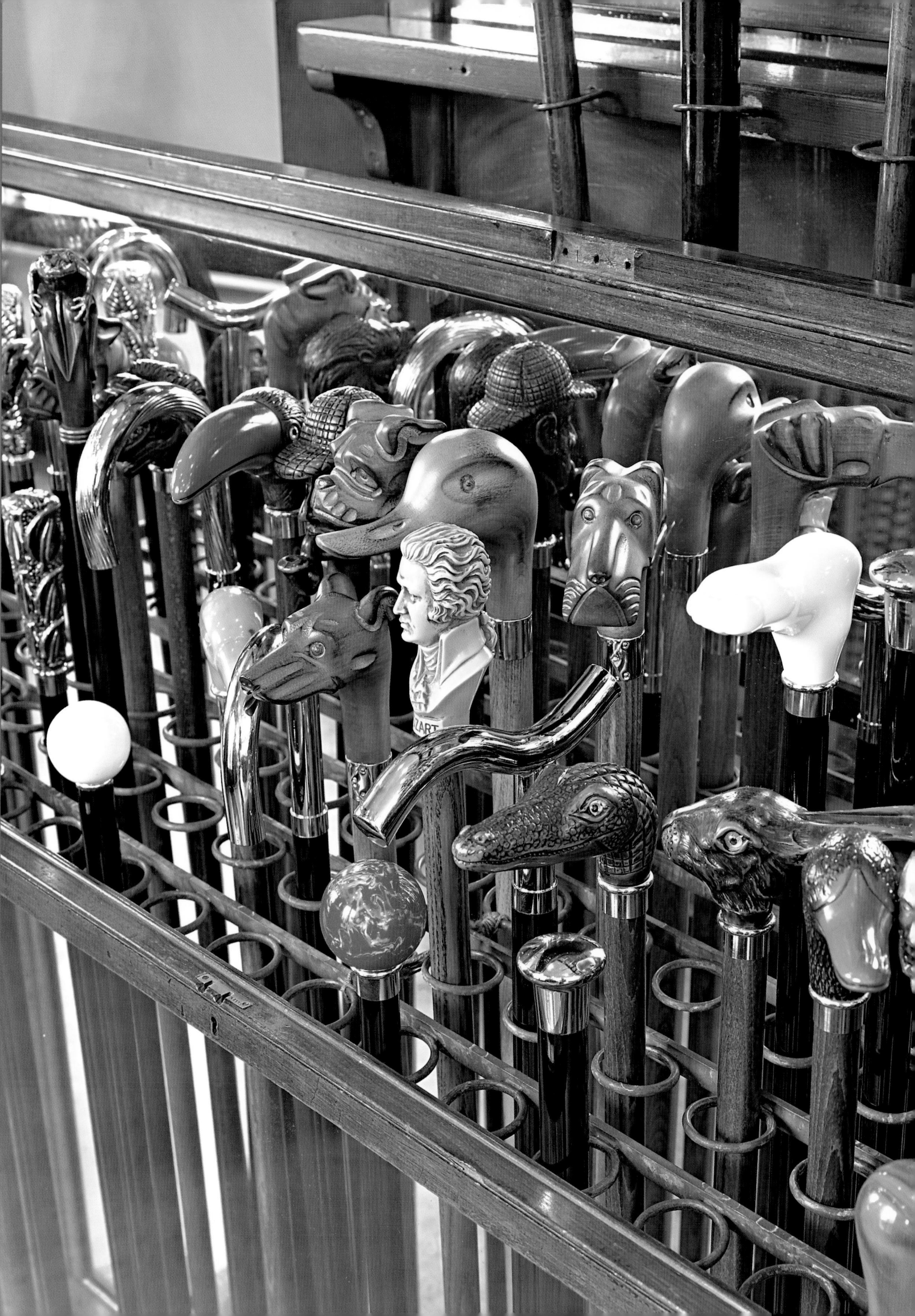

The London Silver Vaults

Chancery House
53–64 Chancery Lane, London WC2A 1QS
☎ +44 20 7242 3844
www.thesilvervaults.com
Tube: Chancery Lane

With more than 30 dealers hawking everything from thimbles to elaborate candelabra, you can bet that if it's made of silver, you'll find it here. This is the place embassies go to replace missing teapots and decorators go to find objets d'art for their celebrity clients. The emphasis is on household goods, but some dealers also sell jewellery.

Wer irgendetwas aus Silber sucht, wird hier fündig. Mehr als 30 Händler bieten zwischen Fingerhüten und elaborierten Kandelabern die ganze Palette an. In den Silver Vaults machen sich Botschaftsangestellte auf die Suche nach einem Ersatz für die verloren gegangene Teekanne, und Innendekorateure finden Objets d'Art für ihre prominenten Kunden. Die meisten Händler haben sich auf Haushaltswaren spezialisiert, ein paar führen aber auch Schmuck.

Avec plus de 30 marchands vendant tout, de la timbale au candélabre ouvragé, c'est le paradis de l'argenterie. C'est ici que les ambassades viennent remplacer les théières disparues et que les décorateurs dénichent des pièces rares pour leurs clients célèbres. L'accent est sur les arts ménagers mais certains vendent également des bijoux.

Interior: Around 1876 the vaults of the Chancery House were rented out to wealthy Londoners as strong rooms. Gradually they became the Silver Vaults, which have existed in their current form since 1953.
Open: Mon–Fri 9am–5.30pm, Sat till 1pm.
X-Factor: English silver is said to be the finest in the world – items from all epochs are available in more than 30 shops.

Interieur: Die Gewölbe des Chancery House wurden 1876 als Tresorräume an wohlhabende Londoner vermietet und wandelten sich allmählich in die Silver Vaults, die in ihrer heutigen Form seit 1953 bestehen.
Öffnungszeiten: Mo–Fr 9–17.30, Sa bis 13 Uhr.
X-Faktor: Englisches Silber gilt als das feinste der Welt – in mehr als 30 Shops wird mit Stücken aller Epochen gehandelt.

Intérieur : Les salles voûtées de la Chancery House ont été louées, en 1876, comme salle de coffre-forts aux riches Londoniens, puis se sont peu à peu modifiées pour devenir les Silver Vaults, inchangés depuis 1953.
Horaires d'ouverture : Lun–Ven 9h–17h30, Sam jusqu'à 13h.
Le « petit plus » : L'argenterie anglaise est réputée comme étant la plus fine au monde. Plus de 30 boutiques vendent des pièces datant de toutes les époques.

16
RCY'S (SILVER) LTD
L BRIAN
MORE SHOPS THIS WAY
AUTRES BOUTIQUES
ALTRI NEGOZI
WEITERE GESCHAFTE
21
NAT LESLIE LTD

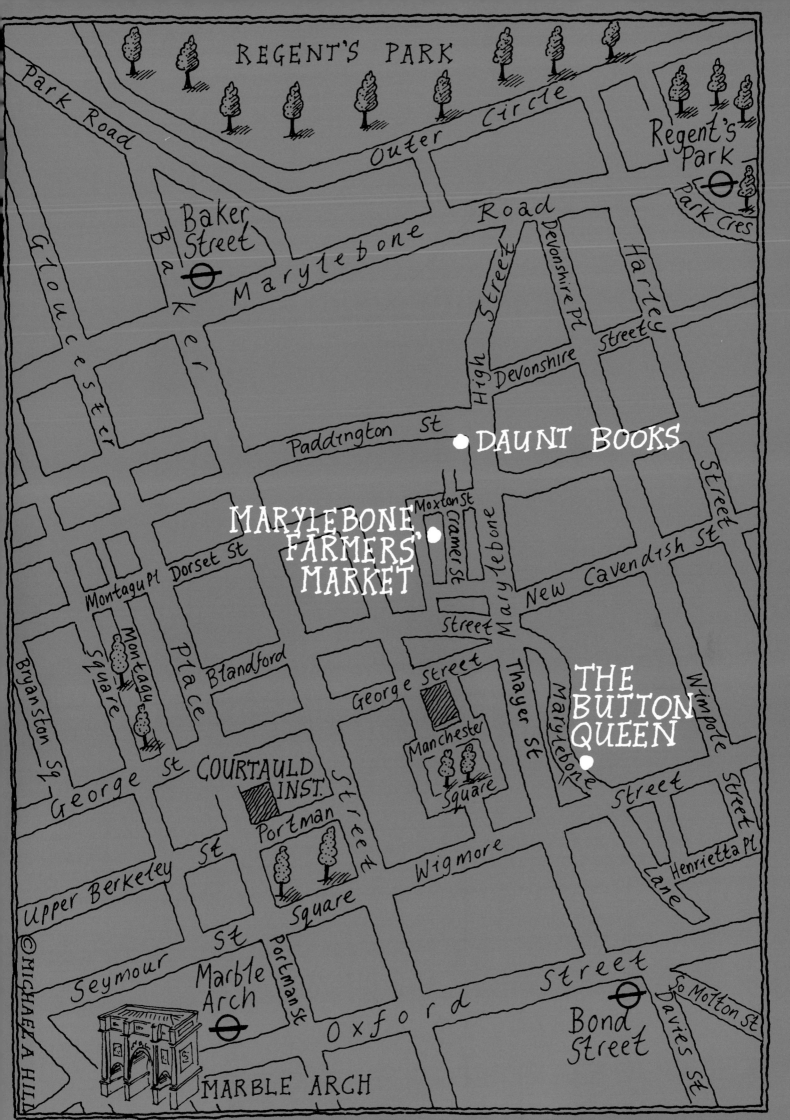

REGENT'S PARK

Park Road

Outer Circle

Regent's Park

Park Cres

Baker Street

Baker

Marylebone Road

Gloucester

High Street

Devonshire Pl

Harley Street

Devonshire Street

Paddington St

● DAUNT BOOKS

Moxton St

Cramer St

Marylebone

Montagu Pl Dorset St

MARYLEBONE FARMERS' MARKET ●

New Cavendish St

Street

Street

Bryanston Sq

Montagu Square

Blandford

Place

George Street

Thayer St

Marylebone

Wimpole Street

THE BUTTON QUEEN ●

George St

COURTAULD INST.

Portman

Street

Manchester Square

Street

Street

Henrietta Pl

Upper Berkeley

St

Portman Square

Wigmore

Lane

Seymour

St

Marble Arch

Portman St

Oxford Street

Bond Street

So Molton St

Davies St

©MICHAELA HILL

MARBLE ARCH

Marylebone Farmers' Market

Cramer Street Car Park (off Marylebone High Street)
London W1U 4EA
☎ +44 20 7833 0338
www.lfm.org.uk
Tube: Baker Street/Bond Street

Thanks to Marylebone Farmers' Market, the area has become foodie central. At this rain-or-shine Sunday market, fresh produce, English cheeses and free-range meat and eggs come from 100 miles around and are sold by the producers directly. Artisanal breads and delicious cakes are on sale, too. Get there early: the farmers pack up around 2pm. Shop for a picnic at St James's Park for a perfect afternoon.

Dank dem Marylebone Farmers' Market ist dieses Viertel zu einem Food-Mekka geworden. Sonntags wird bei jedem Wetter frische Ware, wie Käse aus England, Freiland-Fleisch und -Eier, feilgeboten. Alle Lieferanten kommen aus einem Umkreis von 160 Kilometern, die Waren werden direkt von den Produzenten verkauft. So finden sich hier auch selbst gemachtes Brot und leckere Kuchen. Zeitig vorbeikommen: Die Bauern packen um zwei Uhr nachmittags zusammen. Ideal, um sich für ein Picknick im St James's Park einzudecken.

Ce marché dominical est devenu le repaire des amateurs de bonne chère. Le dimanche, par tous les temps, des producteurs habitant à 160 km à la ronde viennent ici vendre leurs produits frais, des fromages anglais, des œufs et de la viande d'animaux élevés en plein air. On y trouve aussi du pain et des gâteaux artisanaux. Allez-y tôt, ils replient leurs étals dès 14h. Idéal pour s'approvisionner avant un pique-nique à St James's Park.

Interior: The city's largest and best-stocked Farmers Market.
Open: Sun 10am–2pm.
X-Factor: There are numerous cafes and restaurants in the neighbourhood where you can end your stroll around the market with a cup of coffee.

Interieur: Der größte und am besten sortierte Bauernmarkt der Stadt.
Öffnungszeiten: So 10–14 Uhr.
X-Faktor: Ringsum liegen zahlreiche Cafés und Restaurants, in denen man den Marktbummel bei einem Kaffee ausklingen lassen kann.

Intérieur : Le plus grand marché fermier de la ville et le mieux pourvu en marchandises.
Horaires d'ouverture : Dim 10h–14h.
Le « petit plus » : On pourra terminer la visite du marché dans l'un des nombreux cafés et restaurants qui l'entourent.

Daunt Books

83–84 Marylebone High Street, London W1U 4QW
☎ +44 20 7224 2295
www.dauntbooks.co.uk
Tube: Baker Street/Bond Street

This is easily one of the most beautiful bookshops in London, housed in an original Edwardian building with oak galleries and skylights that fill the store with natural light. It has a fabulous selection of children's books, fiction, non-fiction as well as an extensive travel section that has little competition in this city. Staff are friendly, knowledgeable and helpful. Get a novel by Jane Austen and read it in the beautiful garden on Manchester Square in front of the Wallace Collection.

Ein Gebäude aus der Zeit Eduards VII., Eichengalerien, Oberlichter, die den Raum mit Licht durchfluten: Dies ist die schönste Buchhandlung ganz Londons. Kinderbücher, Romane, Sachbücher, die Auswahl ist fantastisch; das Angebot an Reisebüchern so groß wie nirgends. Das Personal steht mit großem Wissen hilfreich zur Seite. Tipp: einen Roman von Jane Austen erstehen und ihn im lauschigen Manchester Square, gleich vor der Wallace Collection, lesen.

Située dans un bâtiment édouardien, avec des galeries en chêne et une verrière qui l'inonde de lumière naturelle, c'est de loin la plus belle librairie de Londres. On y trouve un merveilleux choix de livres d'enfants, de romans, d'essais ainsi qu'un large rayon de livres de voyage comme on en trouve peu en ville. Le personnel est charmant, érudit et serviable. Achetez-y un roman de Jane Austen à lire dans le beau square Manchester devant la Wallace Collection.

Interior: London's most beautiful bookshop is housed in a building dating from the time of Edward VII.
Open: Mon–Sat 9am–7.30pm, Sun 11am–6pm.
X-Factor: Among the travel books you can also find second-hand titles put together with a lot of expertise.

Interieur: Die schönste Buchhandlung Londons ist in einem Gebäude aus der Zeit Eduards VII. untergebracht.
Öffnungszeiten: Mo–Sa 9–19.30, So 11–18 Uhr.
X-Faktor: Unter den Reisebüchern findet man auch Secondhand-Titel, die mit viel Fachwissen zusammengestellt sind.

Intérieur : La plus belle librairie de Londres se trouve dans un bâtiment datant de l'époque d'Édouard VII.
Horaires d'ouverture : Lun–Sam 9h–19h30, Dim 11h–18h.
Le « petit plus » : Parmi les livres de voyages on trouve aussi des exemplaires d'occasion choisis avec beaucoup d'intelligence.

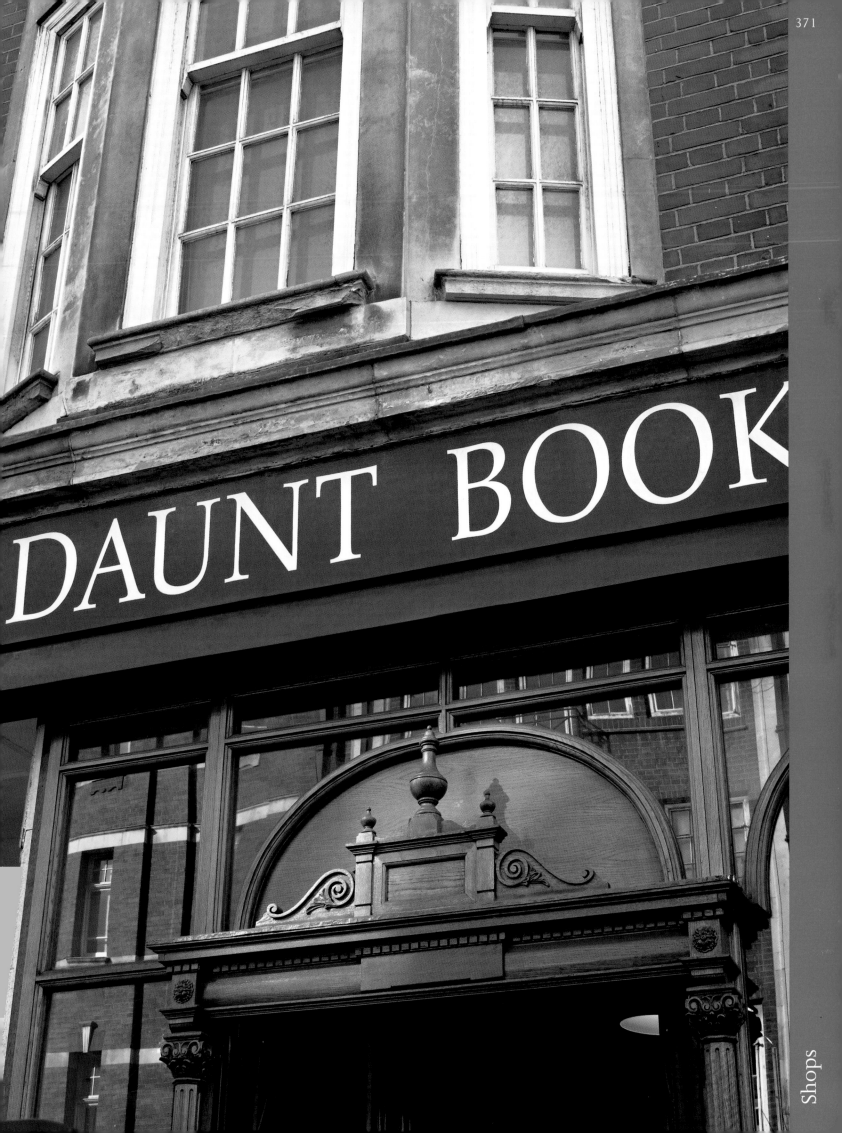

The Button Queen

76 Marylebone Lane, London W1U 2NF
☎ +44 20 7935 1505
www.thebuttonqueen.co.uk
Tube: Bond Street

Rows and rows of browning cardboard boxes hold thousands and thousands of buttons (new and antique) at The Button Queen. It started as a market stall in south London by Mrs. Frith, who was nicknamed The Button Queen. Her son, Martyn, now runs the shop and counts American button collectors, fashion designers and costume designers amongst his loyal clientele.

In diesem Geschäft reihen sich zahlreiche braune, mit Tausenden historischen und neuen Knöpfen gefüllte Pappschachteln. The Button Queen war ursprünglich ein Marktstand in Südlondon und gehörte einer Mrs. Frith, die als „Button Queen" (Knopfkönigin) bekannt war. Heute führt ihr Sohn Martyn das Geschäft. Zur treuen Kundschaft zählen amerikanische Knopfsammler genauso wie Mode- und Kostümdesigner.

Après avoir commencé avec un étal sur un marché du sud de Londres, Mme Frith, « la reine du bouton », a ouvert sa boutique, tenue aujourd'hui par son fils Martyn. Collectionneurs américains, créateurs de mode et costumiers hantent régulièrement ses rayons croulant sous les boîtes en papier jauni qui renferment des milliers et des milliers de boutons, nouveaux et anciens.

Interior: Not one square-inch is left unused; the countless button boxes and holders take up all the space available.
Open: Mon–Fri 10am–5pm, Sat 10am–2pm.
X-Factor: A 1960s legend. You can find wonderful historical buttons here, for example, from the Art Nouveau or Victorian eras.

Interieur: Hier bleibt kein Quadratzentimeter ungenutzt, die ungezählten Knopfschachteln und -schalen belegen jede verfügbare Fläche.
Öffnungszeiten: Mo–Fr 10–17, Sa 10–14 Uhr.
X-Faktor: Eine Legende seit den 1960ern. Hier findet man wunderschöne historische Knöpfe – zum Beispiel aus der Zeit des Jugendstils oder der viktorianischen Ära.

Intérieur : Il n'y a plus un centimètre carré de libre. Les innombrables boîtes à boutons occupent tout l'espace disponible.
Horaires d'ouverture : Lun–Ven 10h–17h, Sam 10h–14h.
Le « petit plus » : Légendaire depuis les années 1960. On y trouve de magnifiques boutons historiques, datant par exemple de l'époque victorienne ou de celle de l'Art nouveau.

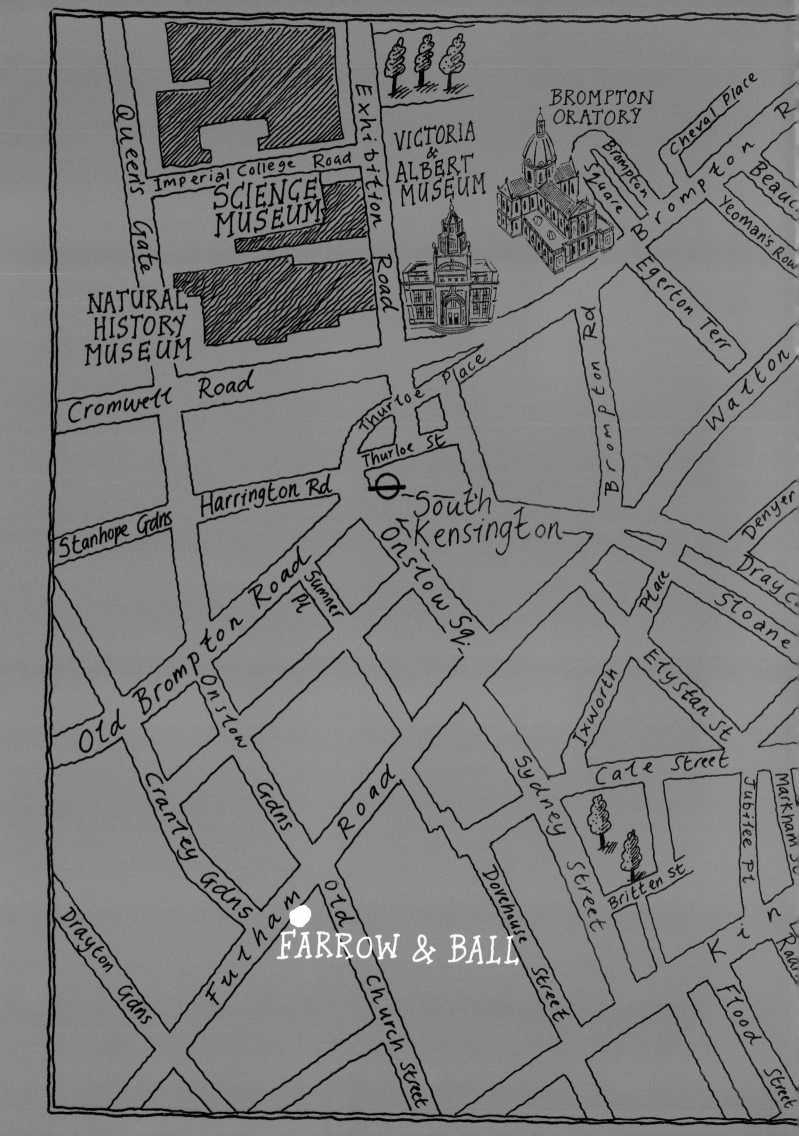

JIMMY CHOO

Hans Crescent

Basil St

Hans Rd

Pont Street

Pont street

Hans Place

Hans

Sloane Street

Pavilion Road

Lowndes St

Cadogan Place

Cadogan Lane

Cadogan Street

Draycott Place

Avenue

Avenue

Road

Sloane Square

Lower Sloane Street

JO MALONE

DAVID MELLOR

PHILIP TREACY

Chesham St

Lyall St

Eaton Place

Belgrave Pl

Belgrave Square

Upp Belgrave St

King's Road

Eaton Sq

Eaton Square

Elizabeth Street

Eaton Terr

Eaton

Chester Row

Pimlico Rd

Ebury

Ronelagh Gr

Bloomfield Terrace

Pimlico Rd

Cheltenham Terrace

Franklin's Row

St Leonard's Terr

Smith Street

Tedworth Sq

Hospital Road

Royal Road

Chelsea Bridge Road

Ebury Bridge Road

ROYAL HOSPITAL CHELSEA

© MICHAEL A HILL

Shops

Farrow & Ball

---

249 Fulham Road, London SW3 6HY
☎ +44 20 7351 0273
www.farrow-ball.com
Tube: South Kensington

Farrow & Ball is a testimony to the British talent for creating exquisite products for the home. The paint company was founded in the 1930s by chemists John Farrow and Richard Ball and all products are still made in Dorset. Farrow & Ball still provide paints for National Trust properties, but new, contemporary colours have been added to suit modern tastes. Get the most subtle shades you will not find elsewhere to paint your home.

Die Briten sind bekannt für die Herstellung bester Haushaltsprodukte. Dazu gehören auch die Farbwaren von Farrow & Ball. Das Unternehmen wurde in den 1930ern von den Chemikern John Farrow und Richard Ball in Dorset gegründet, wo bis heute alle Produkte hergestellt werden. Es liefert die Farben für die Gebäude des National Trust. Doch man findet auch aktuelle, zeitgemäße Farben: Subtilere Farbtöne bekommt man sonst nirgends, da macht es Spaß, einen neuen Farbanstrich für das eigene Heim zu planen.

Les Britanniques n'ont pas leur pareil pour créer des produits exquis pour la maison. Cette entreprise fondée dans les années 1930 par John Farrow et Richard Ball fabrique encore toutes ses peintures dans le Dorset et fournit le National Trust, la fondation qui restaure les demeures historiques. De nouvelles couleurs modernes ont été ajoutées à son nuancier. Vous y trouverez les tons les plus subtils pour redécorer votre intérieur.

Interior: This shop calls itself a showroom – which is what it looks like. In the rectangular interior the graphic design of the paint cans and the range of colours really come into their own.
Open: Mon–Fri 8.30am–5.30pm, Sat 10am–5pm.
X-Factor: Farrow & Ball also print wallpapers using traditional techniques.

Interieur: Das Geschäft bezeichnet sich nicht als Shop, sondern als Showroom – und so wirkt es auch: Das geradlinige Interieur lässt das Grafikdesign der Farbdosen und die Farbpaletten toll zur Geltung kommen.
Öffnungszeiten: Mo–Fr 8.30–17.30, Sa 10–17 Uhr.
X-Faktor: Farrow & Ball bedruckt auch Tapeten nach traditionellen Techniken.

Intérieur : Le magasin ne se conçoit pas comme une boutique mais comme un showroom, et c'est ainsi qu'il se présente : l'intérieur aux lignes droites fait valoir le design des pots de couleur et les nuances de tons.
Horaires d'ouverture : Lun–Ven 8h30–17h30, Sam 10h–17h.
Le « petit plus » : Farrow & Ball imprime aussi ses papiers peints selon des techniques traditionnelles.

FARROW&BALL

FARROW&BALL
Manufacturers of Traditional Papers and Paint
OLD WHITE No.4
FARROW & BALL
F&B
PAINTS
ESTATE® EMULSION
FINEST QUALITY PAINT
MADE IN ENGLAND

Jimmy Choo

32 Sloane Street, London SW1X 9NR
☏ +44 20 7823 1051
www.jimmychoo.com
Tube: Knightsbridge/Sloane Square

Jimmy Choo has come to define everything glamorous about footwear. The
flagship store on Sloane Street is also
the place to find a matching bag or
the right sunglasses. Whether it's a
strappy stiletto or a sky-high boot,
Tamara Mellon, a former accessories
editor, society girl and head of the
company, knows what her chic clientele – which includes Kate Hudson,
Jennifer Aniston and Heidi Klum – are
looking for. She started the company
in 1996 with East End shoemaker
Jimmy Choo, and her empire just
keeps growing.

Jimmy Choo ist die Verkörperung
glamourösen Schuhwerks schlechthin. In dem Flagship-Store auf der
Sloane Street findet man aber auch die
passende Tasche und die richtige Son-
nenbrille. Tamara Mellon, Society-
Girl, ehemalige Modejournalistin für
Accessoires und Besitzerin des Schuh-
imperiums, weiß mit Riemchen-
Stilettos und endlos langen Stiefeln
ihre todschicke Klientel, zu der u. a.
Kate Hudson, Jennifer Aniston und
Heidi Klum gehören, glücklich zu
machen. Den Grundstein für das
erfolgreiche Unternehmen setzte sie
1996 zusammen mit dem East-End-
Schuhmacher Jimmy Choo.

Jimmy Choo incarne le glamour de
la chaussure. La filiale principale de
Sloane Street propose aussi le sac à
main assorti ou les lunettes de soleil
adéquates. Qu'il s'agisse de talons
aiguilles à lacets ou de cuissardes,
Tamara Mellon, ancienne directrice
des accessoires et grande mondaine,
sait ce que veut sa clientèle ultra chic
dont font partie, entre autres, Kate
Hudson, Jennifer Aniston et Heidi
Klum. Depuis qu'elle a créé la société
en 1996 avec Jimmy Choo, chausseur
issu du East End, son empire ne cesse
de grandir.

Interior: Altogether feminine – a creamy
rosé and perfect lighting. The most beautiful
shoes and bags are in mirrored display cases.
Open: Mon–Sat 10am–6pm (Wed till 7pm),
Sun midday–5pm.
X-Factor: Ex-Vogue editor Tamara Mellon
challenges the competition.

Interieur: Sehr feminin in cremigem Rosé
und perfekt beleuchtet. Die schönsten
Schuhe und Taschen stehen in verspiegel-
ten Vitrinen.
Öffnungszeiten: Mo–Sa 10–18 (Mi bis 19),
So 12–17 Uhr.
X-Faktor: Ex-Vogue-Redakteurin Tamara
Mellon läuft der Konkurrenz den Rang ab.

Intérieur : Très féminin dans un rose
crémeux et parfaitement éclairé. Les plus
beaux sacs et chaussures se trouvent dans
les vitrines réfléchissantes.
Horaires d'ouverture : Lun–Sam 10h–18h
(Mer jusqu'à 19h), Dim 12h–17h.
Le « petit plus » : Ancienne rédactrice de
Vogue, Tamara Mellon laisse la concurrence
derrière elle.

Jo Malone

---

150 Sloane Street, London SW1X 9BX
☎ +44 20 7730 2100
www.jomalone.co.uk
Tube: Sloane Square

Jo Malone launched her business out of her flat in the 1980s and her facials quickly became cult treatments with models such as Yasmin Le Bon and her friends. She opened her shop in 1994 and expanded to include fragrances – the grapefruit is delicious – and wonderfully light make-up. Products come in many price ranges and it's hard to resist the cream-and-black packaging.

Jo Malone legte den Grundstein für ihr Geschäft in den 1980ern – in ihrer Wohnung. Ihre Gesichtsbehandlungen begeisterten Kundinnen wie Model Yasmin Le Bon und wurden so Kult. 1994 eröffnete Malone den ersten Laden; gleichzeitig erweiterte sie ihr Angebot mit Düften (der Grapefruit-Duft ist himmlisch) und traumhaft leichten Make-ups. Beim Anblick der cremeweiß-schwarzen Verpackungen fällt es schwer, dem Angebot zu widerstehen.

Jo Malone a commencé dans son appartement dans les années 1980 et ses masques sont vite devenus culte auprès de mannequins comme Yasmin Le Bon et ses amies. Elle a ouvert sa boutique en 1994, élargissant sa gamme aux parfums (le pamplemousse est divin) et au maquillage léger et sublime. Il y en a pour toutes les bourses. Son packaging crème et noir est irrésistible.

Interior: This highly elegant interior focuses on white and black.
Open: Mon, Tue, Sat 9.30am–6pm, Wed–Fri 9.30am–7pm, Sun midday–5pm.
X-Factor: The ten-minute hand and arm massage is a hot tip among London's power-shoppers – and it works wonders.

Interieur: Das hoch elegante Interieur ist in Weiß und Schwarz gehalten.
Öffnungszeiten: Mo, Di, Sa 9.30–18, Mi–Fr 9.30–19, So 12–17 Uhr.
X-Faktor: Die zehnminütige Hand- und Arm-massage ist ein Geheimtipp unter Londons Powershoppern – sie wirkt Wunder.

Intérieur : L'intérieur très élégant est tout en noir et blanc.
Horaires d'ouverture : Lun, Mar, Sam 9h30–18h, Mer–Ven 9h30–19h, Dim 12h–17h.
Le « petit plus » : Les accros du shopping raffolent du massage des mains et des bras de dix minutes. Tout simplement miraculeux.

David Mellor

4 Sloane Square, London SW1W 8EE
☎ +44 20 7730 4259
www.davidmellordesign.com
Tube: Sloane Square

This shop is pure hedonism for those obsessed with cooking and anything to do with kitchens. David Mellor's career was kicked off when his Pride cutlery (now a modern classic) went into production in 1953, when he was still a student at the Royal College of Art. The Sloane Square shop has been keeping Chelsea kitchens looking gorgeous since it opened in 1969.

Wer gern kocht und viel Zeit in der Küche verbringt, wird in diesem Geschäft schwelgen. David Mellor machte sich 1953 einen Namen mit der Lancierung des Pride-Bestecks, das er noch als Student am Royal College of Art entwarf. Heute ist das Besteck ein Klassiker. Und seit 1969 sorgt sein Geschäft am Sloane Square dafür, dass Küchen in Chelsea gut aussehen.

Une boutique qui fera fondre tous les mordus de cuisine. La carrière de David Mellor a démarré en flèche en 1953 quand ses couverts Pride (désormais un classique) ont été produits en série alors qu'il était encore étudiant au Royal College of Art. Depuis son ouverture en 1969, les plus belles cuisines de Chelsea s'équipent dans sa boutique de Sloane Square.

Interior: The large and fine selection of tableware and kitchen utensils is presented over two floors.
Open: Mon–Sat 9.30am–6pm, Sun 11am–5pm.
X-Factor: Should you need horn spoons, a fruit press or earthenware, you are sure to find the best items here.

Interieur: Die große und perfekt sortierte Auswahl an Besteck und Küchenutensilien wird auf zwei Etagen präsentiert.
Öffnungszeiten: Mo–Sa 9.30–18, So 11–17 Uhr.
X-Faktor: Ob man Löffel aus Horn, eine Saftpresse oder Töpferware braucht – hier findet man garantiert die schönsten Stücke.

Intérieur : Le grand choix de couverts et d'ustensiles de cuisine est présenté sur deux étages.
Horaires d'ouverture : Lun–Sam 9h30–18h, Dim 11h–17h.
Le « petit plus » : Que vous ayez besoin d'une cuillère en corne, d'un presse-fruits ou de casseroles, c'est ici que vous trouverez les plus belles pièces.

COOKING POTS
TABLEWARE
MINCERS
SCALES MEASURES
TINS
SIEVES STRAINERS
WOODWARE
KITCHEN GLASS
SPOONS SERVERS
COFFEE MAKERS
CORKSCREWS
KITCHEN LINEN

Philip Treacy

69 Elizabeth Street, London SW1W 9PJ
☎ +44 20 7730 3992
www.philiptreacy.co.uk
Tube: Sloane Square/Victoria

Irish-born Philip Treacy is not just a milliner, he is an artist. This is the view taken by his many fans who rely on his creations to make them look fabulous at Ascot. He started his business in the basement of the eccentric stylist Isabella Blow. This shop opened in 1994 and nobody can resist going in to admire or – if they are feeling brave – to try on one of his splendid creations.

Der Ire Philip Treacy ist nicht nur Hutmacher, sondern auch Künstler. So sehen das die Kunden, die sich für einen effektvollen Auftritt in Ascot hundertprozentig auf ihn verlassen. Seine Karriere startete er in dem Keller der exzentrischen Stylistin Isabella Blow, seit 1994 hat er ein eigenes Geschäft. Es ist unmöglich, dort vorbeizulaufen, ohne die prachtvollen Kreationen bewundert oder anprobiert zu haben.

L'Irlandais Philip Treacy n'est pas un simple modiste, c'est un artiste. Croyez-en ses nombreux clients qui comptent sur lui pour briller à Ascot. Son premier atelier était situé dans le sous-sol de la styliste excentrique Isabella Blow. On ne peut s'empêcher d'entrer dans sa boutique, ouverte en 1994, pour admirer ses splendides créations et, si on s'en sent le courage, en essayer une.

Interior: The glamorous and elegant interior was designed by Tom Dixon.
Open: By appointment.
X-Factor: Models by this award-winning designer are also ordered by Karl Lagerfeld and Alexander McQueen.

Interieur: Das glamouröse und elegante Interieur stammt von Tom Dixon.
Öffnungszeiten: Nach Vereinbarung.
X-Faktor: Die Modelle des mehrfach preisgekrönten Designers ordern auch Karl Lagerfeld und Alexander McQueen.

Intérieur : L'aménagement glamoureux et élégant est de Tom Dixon.
Horaires d'ouverture : Sur rendez-vous.
Le « petit plus » : Karl Lagerfeld et Alexander McQueen commandent aussi des modèles au styliste plusieurs fois primé.

PHILIP TREACY

Chubb

69

OPEN
MON-FRI 10. 0am-6.00pm
SAT   11.00am-5.00pm

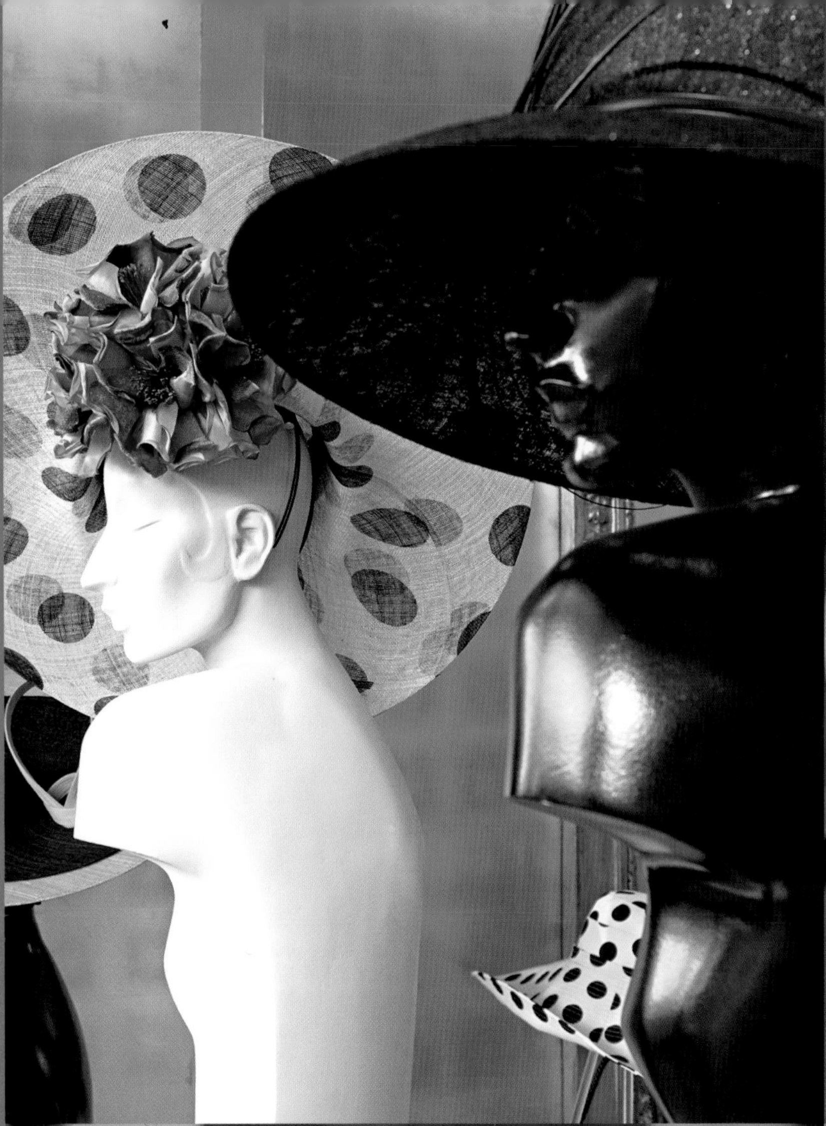

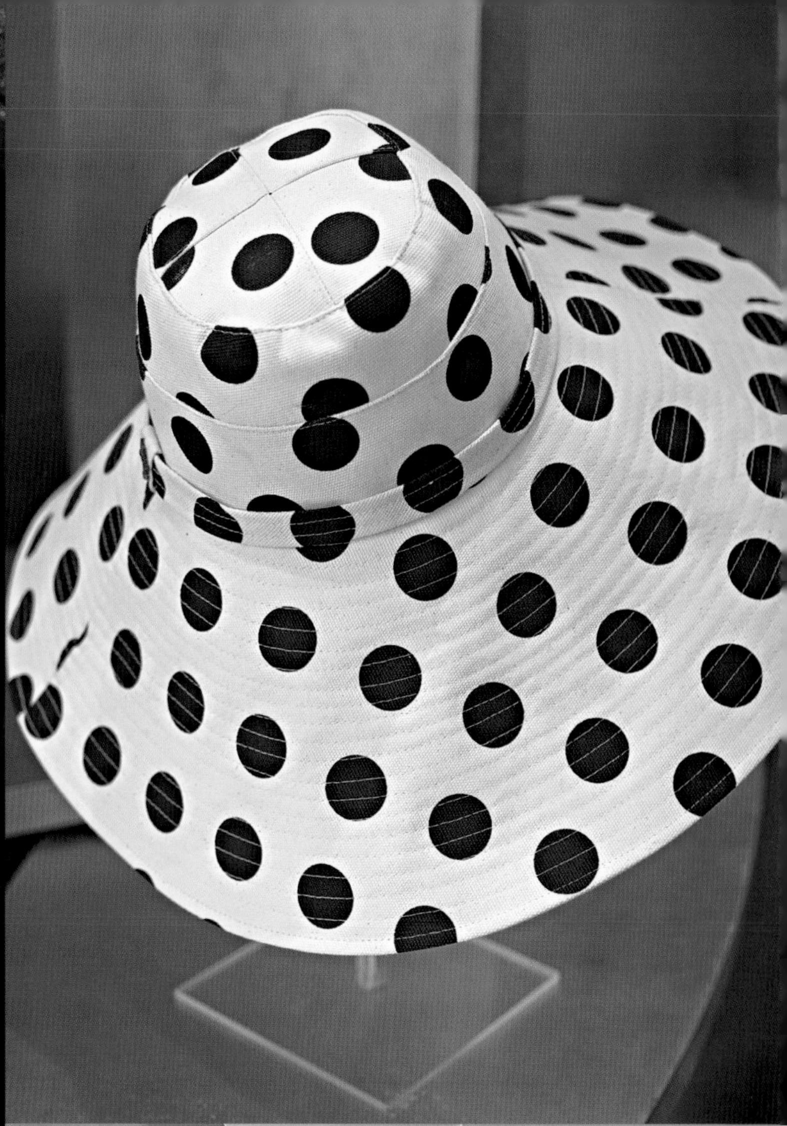

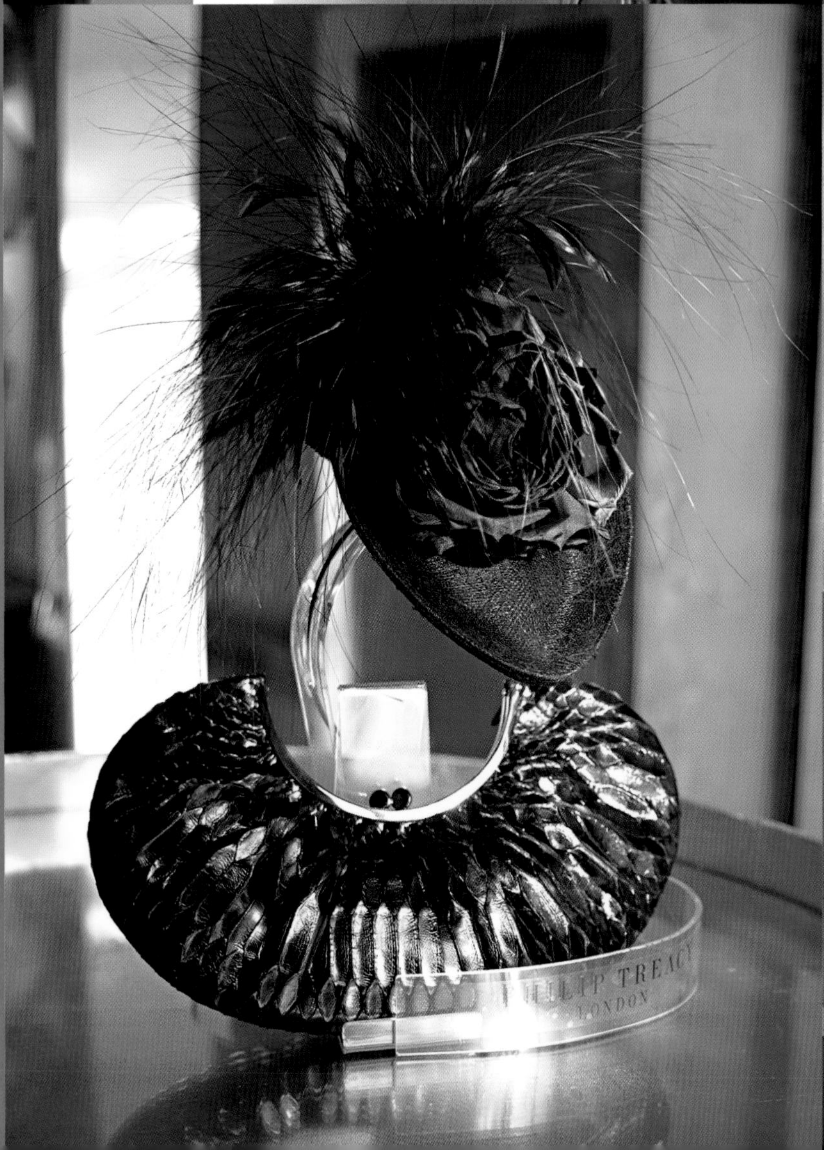
LONDON

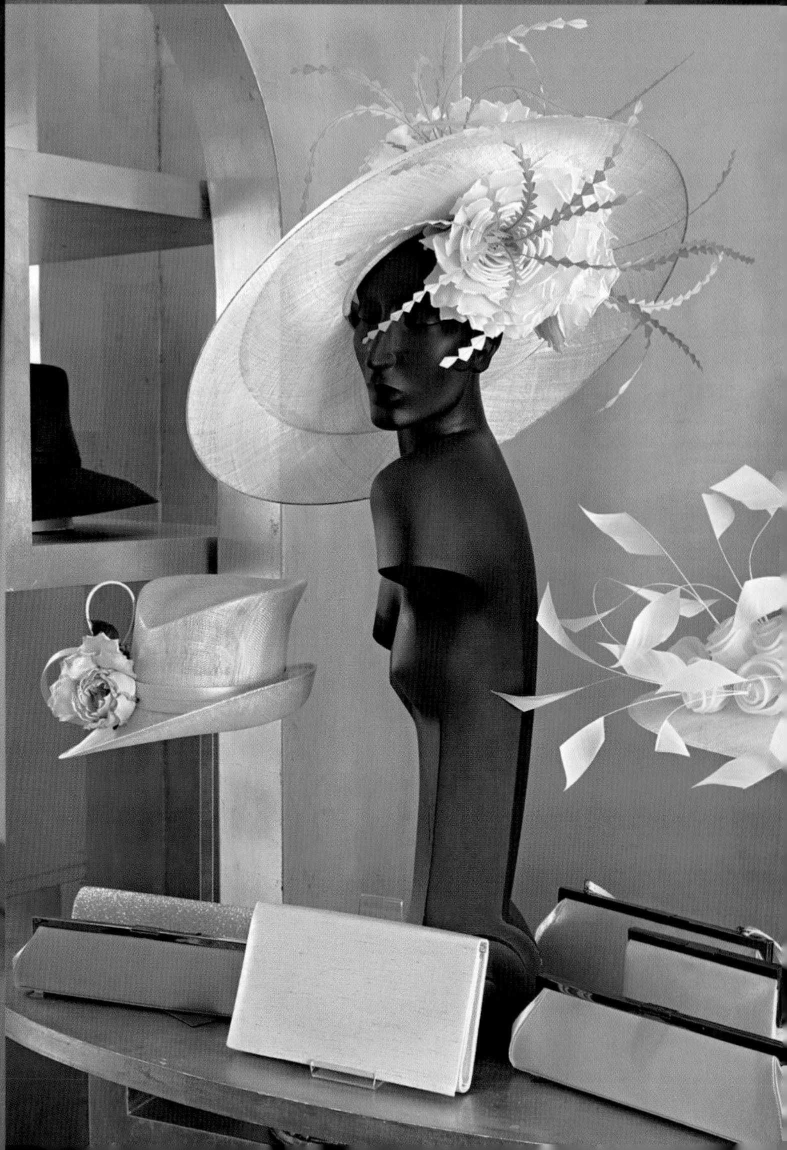

PHILIP TREACY
LONDON

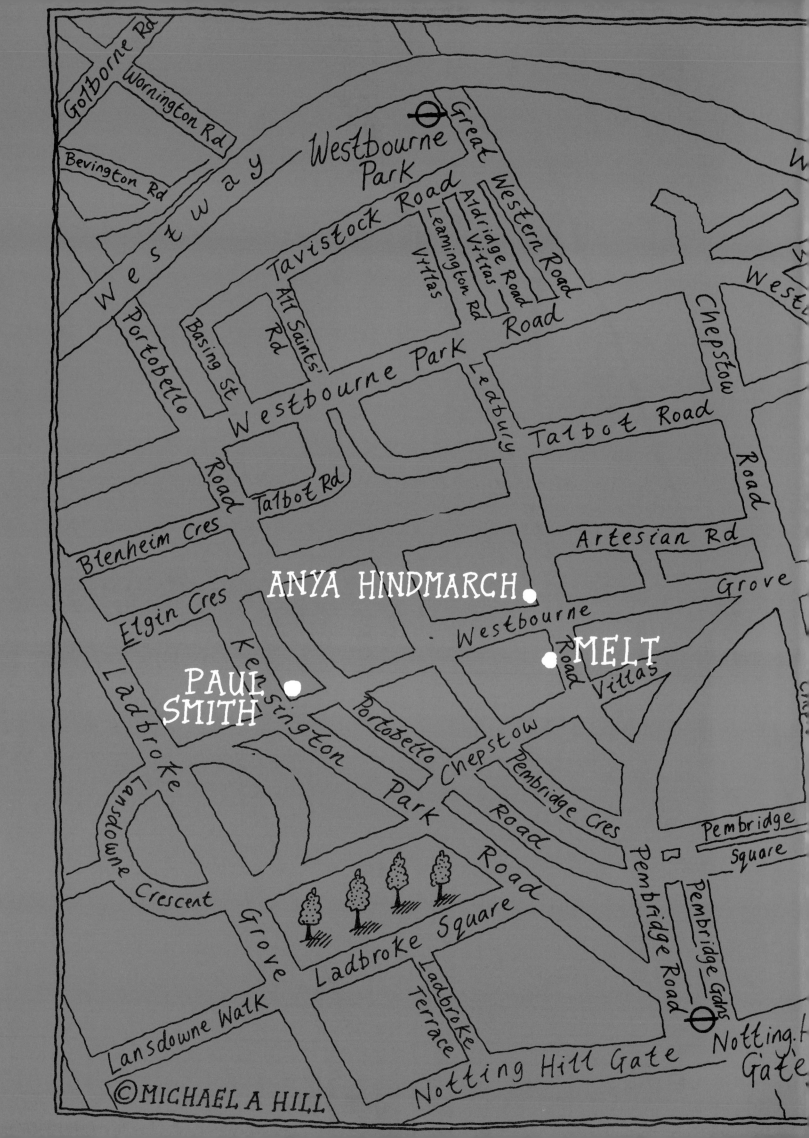

©MICHAEL A HILL

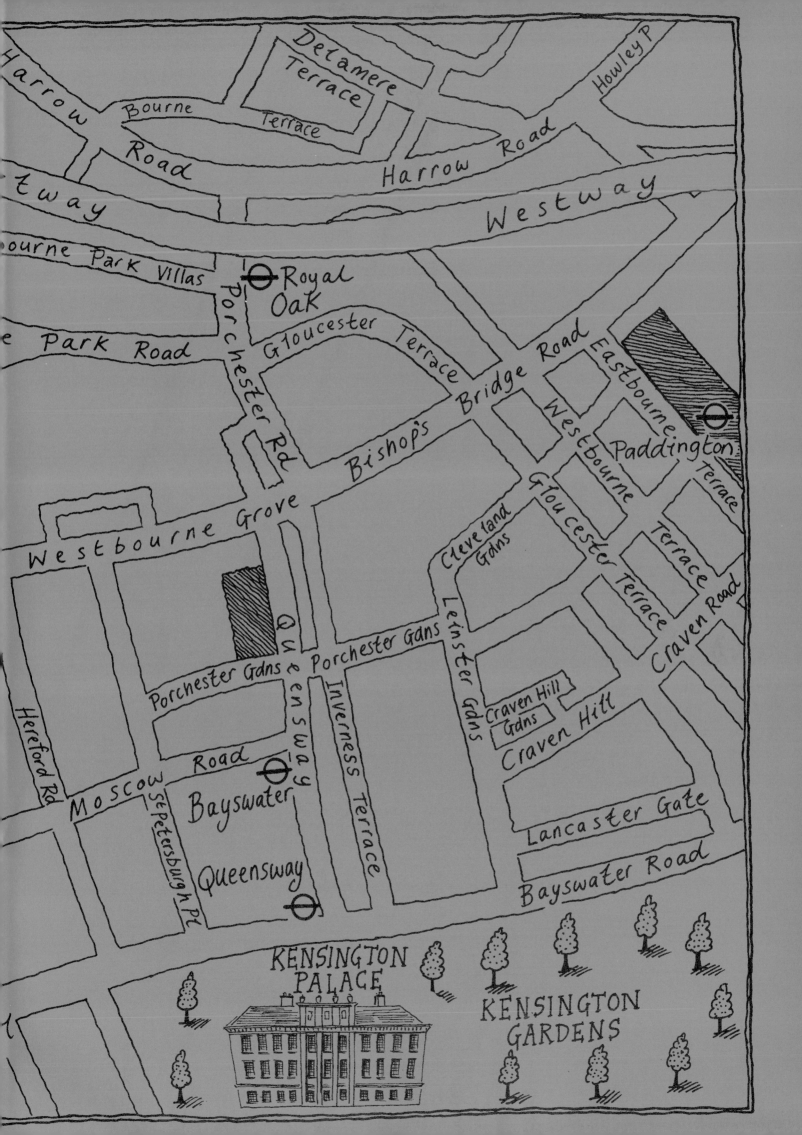

Paul Smith

Westbourne House
122 Kensington Park Road, London W11 2EP
☎ +44 20 7727 3553
www.paulsmith.co.uk
Tube: Notting Hill Gate

This enormous villa, which was converted into a shop in the late 1990s, provides one of the most incredible retail experiences in London. In fact, it was Sir Paul Smith's shop that was instrumental in the gentrification of this area in the past decade. Over three floors, choose from Smith's finely tailored suits, feminine dresses, accessories, vintage toys and books — all quirky and very English, like Smith himself.

Aus einer riesigen Villa wird eine Boutique: In den späten 1990ern eröffnete hier Sir Paul Smith sein Geschäft und löste damit im Viertel einen Boom aus. Über drei Stockwerke verteilt, findet man seine fantastisch geschnittenen Anzüge, feminine Kleider, Accessoires, Vintage-Spielzeug und Bücher. Alles sehr eigenwillig gemischt und englisch, genau wie Smith. Eines der spannendsten Einkaufserlebnisse in London.

Cet hôtel particulier converti en boutique à la fin des années 1990 offre une expérience unique à Londres. De fait, il a sérieusement contribué à l'embourgeoisement du quartier. Sur trois étages, vous pouvez flâner entre les costumes superbement taillés, les robes féminines, les jouets anciens et les livres, tous excentriques et très british, à l'image de Sir Paul Smith lui-même.

Interior: The classical rooms of this town house, with stucco and fireplaces, have been decorated with a bit of a wink, and have become a lifestyle address. You feel as if you were in someone's home.
Open: Mon–Fri 10am–6pm, Sat till 6.30pm.
X-Factor: The accessories and the Home Collection, as well as the bespoke tailoring service on the top floor.

Interieur: Die klassischen Räume des Stadthauses mit Stuck und Kaminen wurden mit einem Augenzwinkern eingerichtet und zur Lifestyle-Adresse. Man fühlt sich wie in einem Privathaus.
Öffnungszeiten: Mo–Fr 10–18, Sa bis 18.30 Uhr.
X-Faktor: Die Accessoires und die Home Collection, sowie der Service für maßgeschneiderte Kleidung auf der obersten Etage.

Intérieur : Les pièces classiques avec leurs stucs et leurs cheminées ont été aménagées avec un clin d'oeil ironique est sont devenues une adresse lifestyle. On se sent ici comme dans un intérieur privé.
Horaires d'ouverture : Lun–Ven 10h–18h, Sam jusqu'à 18h30.
Le « petit plus » : Les accessoires et la home collection, ainsi que le service de la mode sur-mesure au dernier étage.

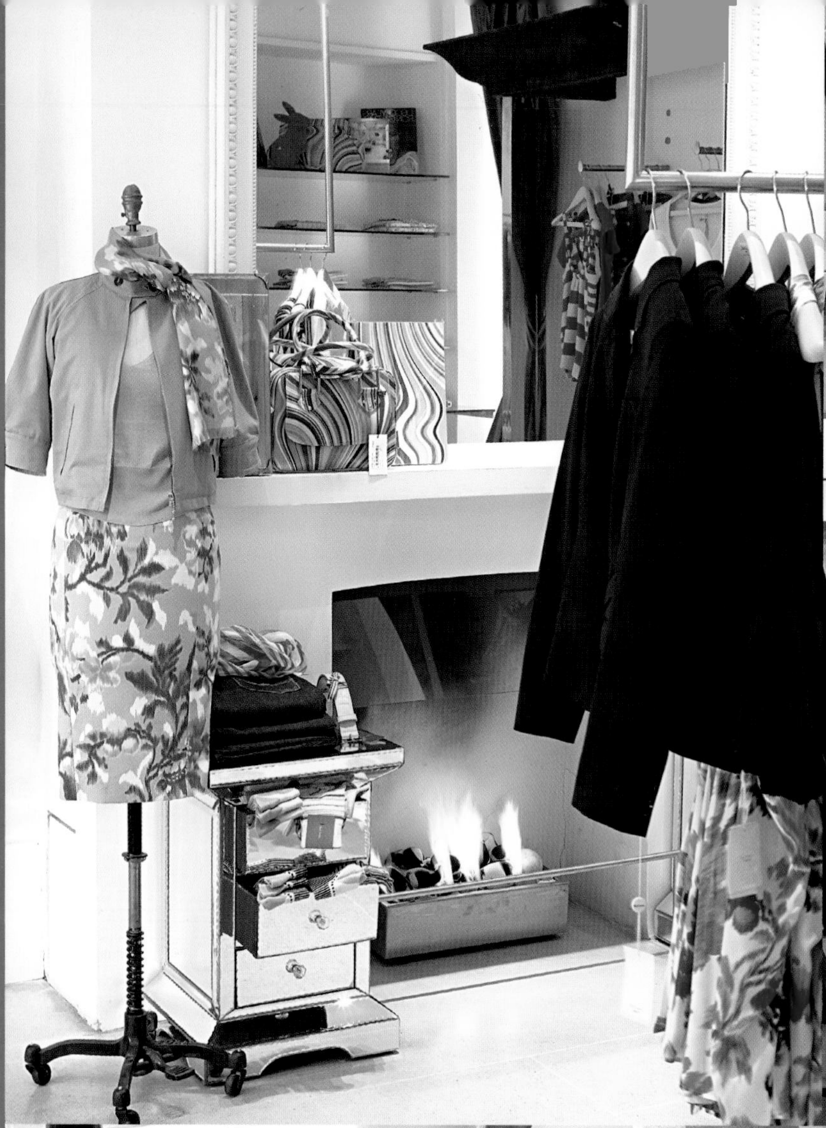

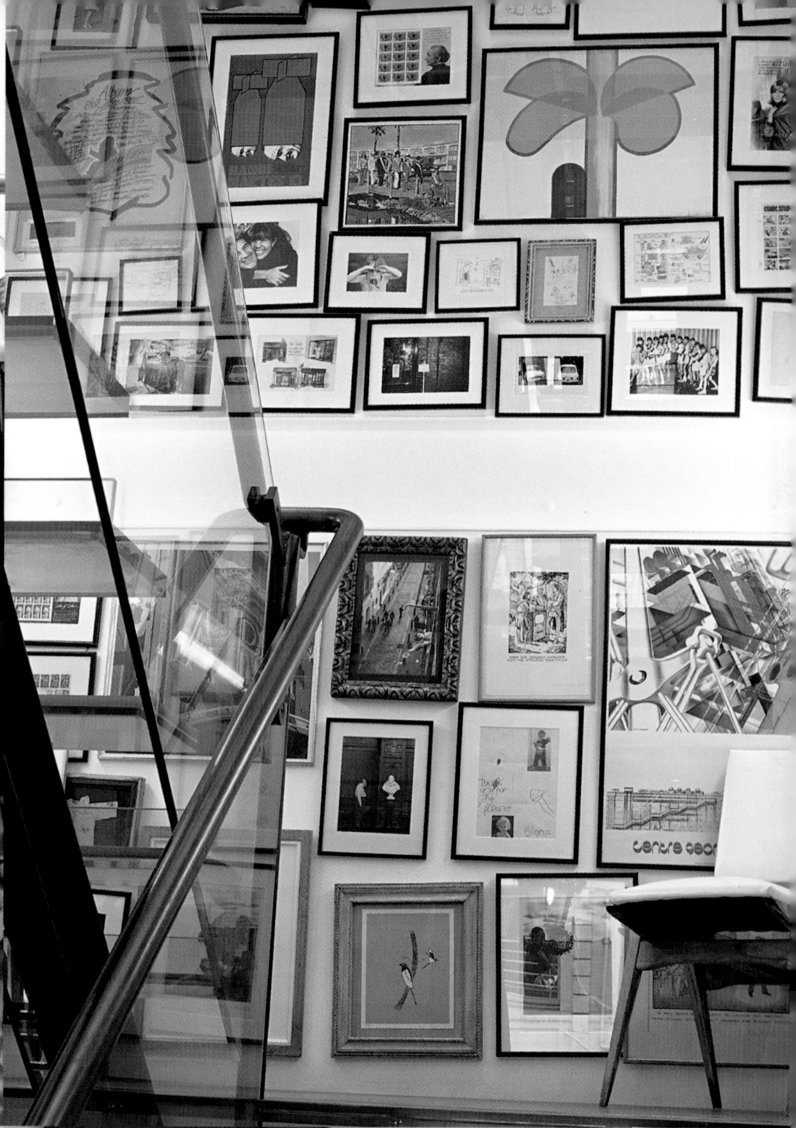

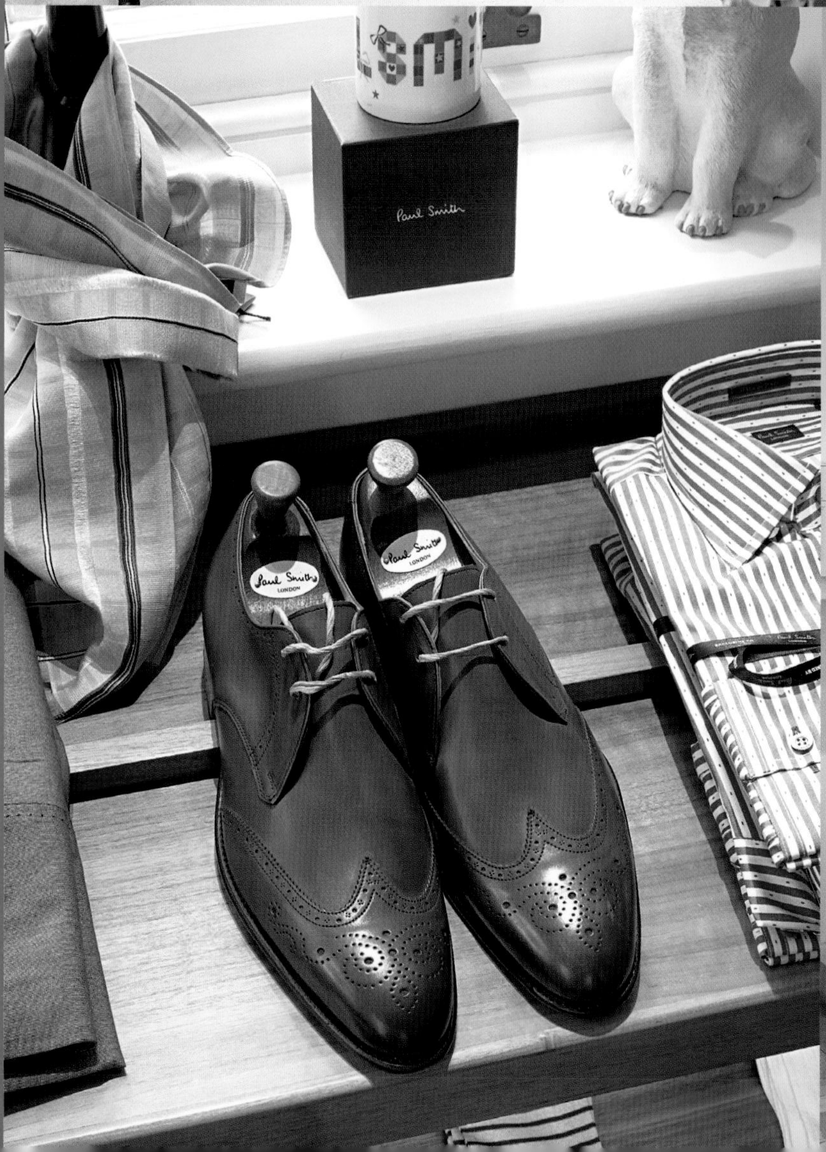
Paul Smith
Paul Smith
LONDON
Paul Smith
LONDON

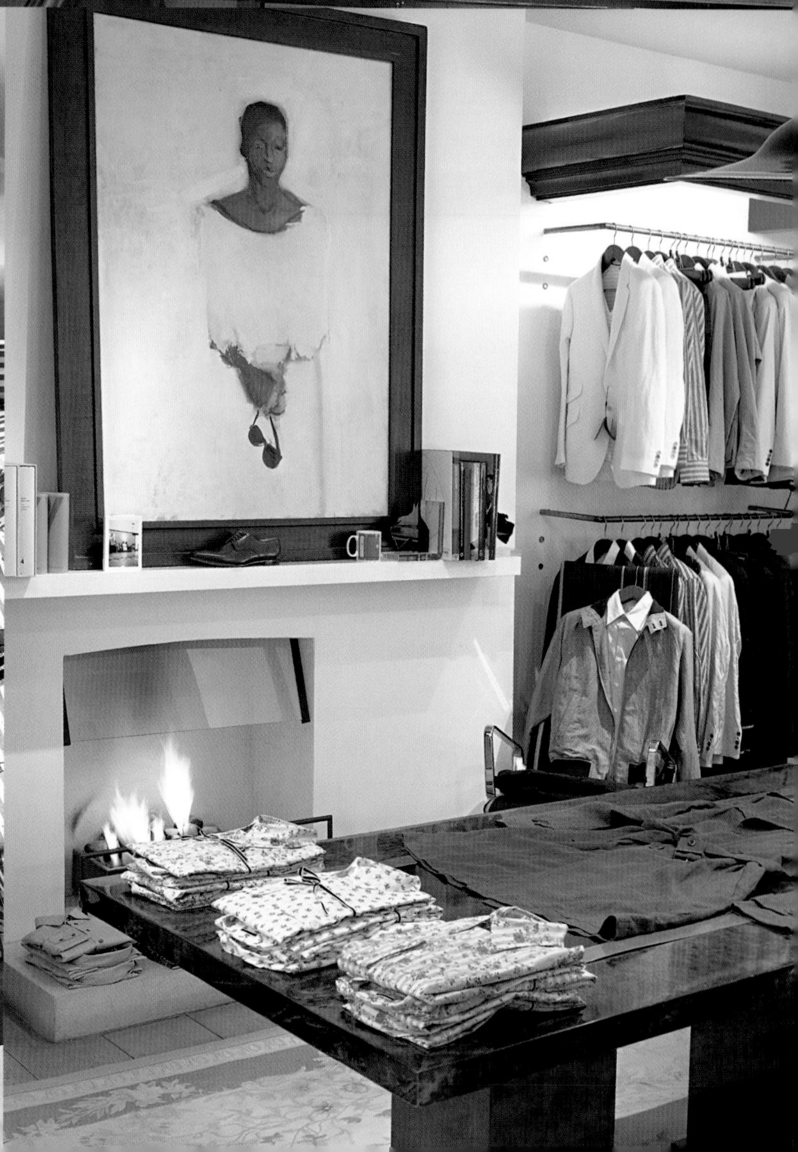

Melt

59 Ledbury Road, London W11 2AA
☎ +44 20 7727 5030
www.meltchocolates.com
Tube: Notting Hill Gate

Notting Hill ladies may be famously trim but even they can't resist Melt, a shop that gives chocolate addicts no hope for reform. Started in 2006 by Louise Nason, Melt's chocolates are made on site and displayed in pristine white surroundings that only emphasise the beauty of the craft of chocolate-making by hand. Jasmine tea truffles are particularly irresistible, but then so is everything else.

Selbst die notorisch figurbewussten Damen in Notting Hill können Melt nicht widerstehen. Schokoladensüchtige kann man hier schon gar nicht mehr retten. In der minimalistischen milchweißen Schokoladen-Boutique, die Louise Nason 2006 gegründet hat, kommen die haus- und handgemachten Kreationen besonders gut zur Geltung. Die Trüffeln mit Jasmintee sind ganz unwiderstehlich, alles andere jedoch auch.

Les dames de Notting Hill sont réputées pour leur minceur mais même elles ne résistent pas à Melt, la boutique où les accros au chocolat n'ont aucun espoir de rémission. Ouvert en 2006 par Louise Nason, tous les produits sont faits sur place et présentés dans un décor à la blancheur immaculée qui met en valeur leur beauté. Les truffes au thé au jasmin sont à se damner, comme tout le reste.

Interior: Here the designers are not behind the minimalist interior but the new chocolate flavours: Sophie Conran, for example, invented a variation with Earl Grey tea, ginger and cranberry.
Open: Mon–Sat 9am–6pm, Sun 11am–4pm.
X-Factor: Chocolate addicts can track down that great secret here in professional tastings.

Interieur: Hier stehen Designer nicht hinter dem minimalistischen Interieur, sondern hinter neuen Schokoladensorten: Sophie Conran zum Beispiel entwarf eine Variante mit Earl Grey, Ingwer und Cranberry.
Öffnungszeiten: Mo–Sa 9–18, So 11–16 Uhr.
X-Faktor: Schokoladensüchtige können dem süßen Geheimnis hier auch bei professionellen Verkostungen auf die Spur kommen.

Intérieur : Ici, les créateurs ne sont pas ceux qui ont fait l'intérieur minimaliste, mais les nouvelles variétés de chocolat : Sophie Conran par exemple a imaginé un chocolat à l'earl grey, gingembre et cranberry.
Horaires d'ouverture : Lun–Sam 9h–18h, Dim 11h–16h.
Le « petit plus » : Les accros au chocolat peuvent déceler les secrets qui se cachent dans les succulentes friandises au cours d'une dégustation avec un professionnel.

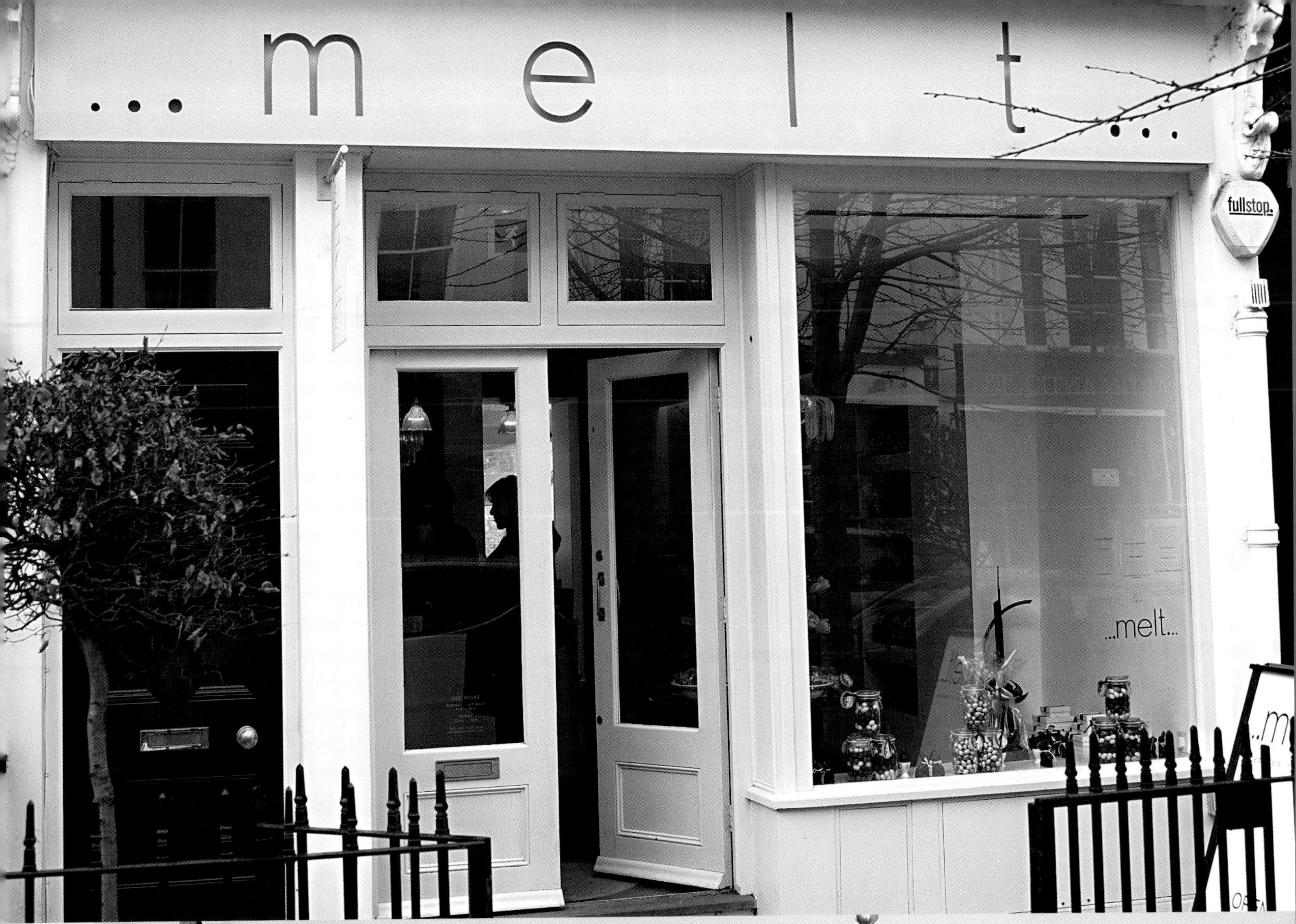
...m e l t...
fullstop.
...melt...

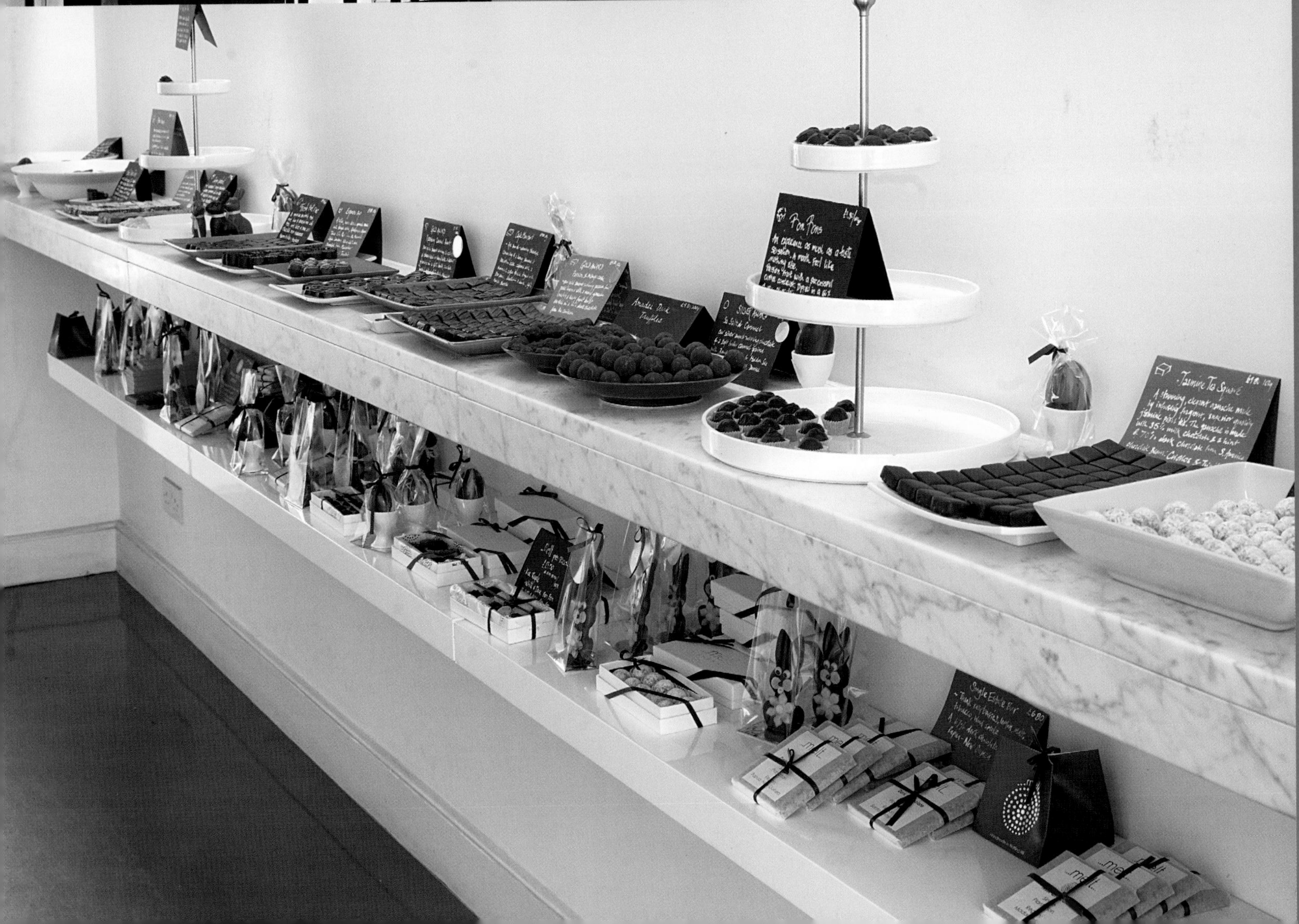

Anya Hindmarch

63a Ledbury Road, London W11 2AD
☎ +44 20 7792 4427
www.anyahindmarch.com
Tube: Notting Hill Gate

You may well tell yourself you don't need any more handbags but wait until you enter Anya Hindmarch's shop and then try and resist. From washbags to tote bags, there is something luxurious in here for everyone. London society girls wouldn't be caught dead going to work without one of her leather day bags.

Mit dem Vorsatz, nicht schon wieder eine Tasche zu kaufen, kommt man bei Anya Hindmarch nicht sehr weit. Ihre luxuriöse Taschenkollektion, die vom Kulturbeutel bis zur Einkaufstasche reicht, ist einfach zu verführerisch. Das wissen bereits die Society-Töchter Londons: Ohne eine der soliden Lederhandtaschen von Hindmarch verlassen sie schon gar nicht erst das Haus.

Vous croyiez ne pas avoir besoin d'un sac à main de plus ? Attendez d'être entrée dans la boutique d'Anya Hindmarch. De la trousse au fourre-tout, il y en a pour tous les goûts. Les mondaines londoniennes préféreraient mourir plutôt que d'être vues sans un de ses solides sacs du jour en cuir.

Interior: Small and luxurious but … almost as cosy as inside a handbag.
Open: Mon–Sat 10.30am–6pm, Tue till 7pm.
X-Factor: The handbags carried by Kate Moss, Claudia Schiffer, Reese Witherspoon and Angelina Jolie are to be found here.

Interieur: Klein, aber luxuriös – man fühlt sich fast wie im Bauch einer Handtasche.
Öffnungszeiten: Mo–Sa 10.30–18, Di bis 19 Uhr.
X-Faktor: Hier findet man die Handtaschen, die Kate Moss, Claudia Schiffer, Reese Witherspoon und Angelina Jolie tragen.

Intérieur : Petit mais luxeux, on se croirait dans un sac à main.
Horaires d'ouverture : Lun–Sam 10h30–18h, Mar jusqu'à 19h.
Le « petit plus » : On trouvera ici les sacs à main que portent Kate Moss, Claudia Schiffer, Reese Witherspoon et Angelina Jolie.

Index | Index | Index

Imprint | Impressum | Imprint

© 2009 TASCHEN GmbH
Hohenzollernring 53, D-50672 Köln
www.taschen.com

Compiled, Edited & Layout by
Angelika Taschen, Berlin

General Project Manager
Stephanie Paas, Cologne

Illustrations
Olaf Hajek, www.olafhajek.com

Maps
Michael A Hill, www.michaelahill.com

Graphic Design
Eggers + Diaper, Berlin

German Text Editing
Christiane Reiter, Hamburg
Nazire Ergün, Cologne

English Translation
Pauline Cumbers, Frankfurt am Main

French Translation
Thérèse Chatelain-Südkamp, Cologne
Philippe Safavi, Paris

German Translation
Simone Ott Caduff, California

Lithograph Manager
Thomas Grell, Cologne

Printed in China
ISBN 978-3-8365-1118-6

To stay informed about upcoming TASCHEN titles, please request our magazine at www.taschen.com/magazine or write to TASCHEN, Hohenzollernring 53, D-50672 Cologne, Germany; contact@taschen.com; Fax: +49-221-254919. We will be happy to send you a free copy of our magazine, which is filled with information about all of our books.